TRANSPERSONAL

Errol Weiner was born and educated in South Africa but came to live at the Findhorn Foundation in Scotland in 1978 where he lived for two years. He has been a student of the Arcane Teachings of Alice Bailey for the last fifteen years and has studied and taught transpersonal astrology and psychology in South Africa, the UK and Europe. He is a full-time networker and in 1990 helped to set up the East Meets West Network which he co-ordinates with his partner. The Network links-up East and West Europeans and organizes workshops, courses and gatherings on transpersonal themes in West and East Europe. Errol now works half the year in East Europe and the USSR.

Errol Weiner

Transpersonal Astrology

FINDING THE
SOUL'S PURPOSE

Foreword by Alan Oken

Series Editor
STEVE EDDY

ELEMENT
Shaftesbury, Dorset • Rockport, Massachusetts

© Errol Weiner 1991
Published in Great Britain in 1991 by
Element Books Limited
Longmead, Shaftesbury, Dorset

Published in the USA in 1991 by
Element, Inc
42 Broadway, Rockport, MA 01966

Designed by Roger Lightfoot
Cover design by Max Fairbrother and Barbara McGavin
Typeset by Colset Pte Ltd, Singapore
Printed and bound in Great Britain by
Dotesios Ltd, Trowbridge, Wiltshire.

British Library Cataloguing in Publication Data

A catalogue record for this book is available from the British Library

Library of Congress data available

ISBN 1-85230-161-9

Contents

Dedication

I dedicate this book to:

SK, Master DK and my higher self, my teachers and guides.

Imogen – partner, friend and co-server. Her unconditional love, patience and selfless service are a continual inspiration to me and this book could not have been completed without her continual support.

My parents, who have had the love and courage to accept and love Imogen and myself for who we are and for what we do.

Derek, Dav, Peter, Merete, Steve, Jan, Felicity and Shedack – soul friends who have supported me through the trials and tribulations of writing this book.

All those human beings who serve the Christ, their higher selves and their fellow human beings – by giving, sharing and supporting.

Special thanks to Derek Williams, Peter Lakos and Jonathan Eveleigh for all their help with 'Coma Berenice', my faithful computer.

Merete Byrial Jakobsen for her lovely illustrations. Merete's Saturn and my Sun are conjunct in Aquarius.

Felicity Keefe for the wonderful zodiacal drawings in Chapter 7. Felicity did these drawings with Neptune trining her Venus.

Imogen and Jan Amery for help with the editing.

Imogen and Shedack for cooking the many meals (I also cooked some) that kept me alive while writing the book.

Brian Lee for his research into past Uranus–Neptune conjunctions.

And last but certainly not least Steve Eddy, my publishing editor, whose patience and continual support I truly appreciated.

Foreword

It is intuitional astrology which must eventually supersede what is today called astrology, thus bringing about a return to the know-ledge of that ancient science which . . . informed humanity as to the basic inter-relations which govern and control the phenomenal and subjective worlds.

I am hoping that some astrologers may be found who will be sensi-tive to that which is new. I am believing that there are investigators along astrological lines who will be open-minded enough to recognize possible hypotheses and then to make fair experiment with them . . . I am looking for these fair-minded astrologers to make experiment with the factors and suggestions which I may indicate.

The Tibetan,
Esoteric Astrology, pp. 3–4 and 27.

The evolution of human consciousness is making a quantum leap in its focus and orientation. A spiral movement is occurring, gradually leading humanity from a totally personality-centred, materially attached awareness, to one of alignment with collective needs. On an individual level, this means that many of us are consciously directing our outer lives, career goals, personal relation-ships, mental activities and creative efforts – in short, our entire egoic enterprise, towards those forms of expression which trans-cend purely self-centred motives. At the same time, we are directing our inner goals towards a focus of receptivity allowing us to per-ceive an intelligent, inclusive Plan for our planet, its natural king-doms and its billions of lives. As our participation in this process unfolds, so does the simultaneous realization of ourselves as souls in action.

There is an international group of men and women of goodwill actively at work today on the planet. We have a name, although many are at work at their various humanitarian enterprises without knowing either that name or the Teachings it represents. We are called 'The New Group of World Servers'. The only qualifications for membership are: a desire to serve, a willingness to create a personal framework through which this desire can expressed in action, and a vision of one's life-work as part of the greater purpose of conscious human evolution.

Such servers are found in every field of human endeavour. Some, like Errol Weiner and myself, are astrologers. Part of our particular mandate is to help unfold an astrological system for the New Age and its humanity. This has had to be done in loving accordance with the teachings of the Tibetan Master, Djwhal Khul. In this respect, and in the eyes of this fellow student and brother, Errol Weiner is accomplishing his part in our collective effort most successfully. *Transpersonal Astrology* is a splendid contribution.

The great challenge in writing such a work as this is to present the arcane wisdom inherent in the Teachings in a form which the seeker can readily understand and use, whilst still retaining the potency of the original revelations. In addition the author has to systematize his presentation in such a way as to make it acceptable to the Western mind. Such a mind tends towards linear and logical expressions of thought, no matter how spiritually aspirational the heart. In both of these processes, Errol Weiner has made a significant achievement. The author relates the spiritual truths of the Ancient Wisdom Teachings in very clear, direct and loving ways without compromising the power of the consciousness contained within the Teachings themselves. This is not a simple task as metaphysical, arcane esoteric astrology has been known to have its complications! As one would say in contemporary computer jargon, *Transpersonal Astrology* is very user friendly.

The purpose of any given incarnation is to awaken the lower self to the presence of the soul. At first this is done through the art of living. This is a process of trial and error often utilizing (at least at this stage of human evolution) the experience of suffering as the illusion leading to the eventual revelation of immanent truth. This is gradually accomplished through the reorientation of desires and in later stages by the personal identification with the higher self as oneself.

Traditional, exoteric astrology reveals much about an individual's biological, instinctual and psychological matrix. It shows us much about the physical, emotional, and lower mental (rational) functions of the personality but fails to take us into the realm of the soul. Such a perspective requires another lens, another tool of perception. So many of us are conscious of our orientation to a larger life purpose; so many of us are actively preparing and/or working for the fulfilment of this purpose; so many of us are becoming increasingly attuned to the work of the soul and increasingly detached from the personal egoic life. Therefore a new astrological road map is required for this journey. This is the road map of the Path of Discipleship. This is 'Transpersonal Astrology' at work.

In addition to sharing the nature of esoteric astrology, the meaning of the Seven Rays and their applications to our lives, some wonderful insights relative to the twelve signs of the zodiac, the significance of the Full and New Moon cycles, and even some openings that allow us to peer through the awe-inspiring portals of Monadic astrology, Errol Weiner shares himself. Perhaps this is what appeals to me the most about his book. While reading this work, I experienced the author not just as an extremely devoted and erudite esoteric scholar (which indeed he is) but also as a fellow Companion on the Way, a co-worker and a friend. It is this humanization of the Ancient Wisdom Teachings that makes *Transpersonal Astrology* so in tune with the New Era and so supportively in touch with each of us.

Alan Oken
Santa Fe, New Mexico

CHAPTER ONE

Transpersonal Astrology: An Introduction

TOWARDS A NEW ASTROLOGY

Soon after the Czechoslovakian revolution of 1989 a journalist asked Vaclav Havel if he would be writing a play on the events of that momentous revolution. Havel replied: 'Even Shakespeare couldn't have written this. This was written from above. We're only assistant directors.'

In 1989 the Neptune–Saturn triple conjunction in Capricorn took place. Astrologically this would be interpreted as the dissolution and collapse (Neptune) of crystallized, authoritarian and centralized power structures (Saturn). These 'revolutions' would come about through the uprising of the masses (Neptune) and would be relatively peaceful and constructive (Neptune). The old leaders, governments and systems (Saturn) would largely disappear (Neptune) to be replaced by a far more idealistic, humanistic, democratic and people-empowered leadership and socio-political system (Neptune). This in fact provides us with a perfect description of the revolutionary changes that actually did occur throughout Eastern Europe in 1989.

What is the relationship between the spiritual factors which influences such changes and the 'assistant directors' (human beings) who co-create them? How are these spiritual and human factors related to the science of astrology – that is to the constellations, signs and planets, and to the Seven Rays, those great sources of cosmic energy in our universe (see Chapters 4 and 5). How can and do these 'energy' systems interact with and influence our small planet and its inhabitants? If astrology is to become a valid science it is necessary to answer all these questions.

In order to understand the deeper significance of the constellations, the signs, the Rays, the planets, humanity itself and each individual human being it is necessary to approach astrology from a very new perspective. Astrologers are apt to forget that astrology is also subject to revolutionary changes, and if new thinking is required in politics, economics, ecology and so on it is also required in the science of astrology.

The aim of this book is to explore and communicate a 'middle path' between the traditional and humanistic fields of astrology, and the more abstract esoteric branches. The former has tended to personalize and humanize astrology to such a degree that it has lost touch with its true purpose and roots, while the latter has tended to ignore the practical day-to-day needs of the individual.

PLANETARY INITIATION

The years 1988–90 were profound in terms of human evolution, for they were three years of planetary initiation. In 1988 the Uranus–Saturn triple conjunction took place, to be followed in 1989 by the Neptune–Saturn triple conjunction. These two years produced the most radical social, political, ecological and spiritual revolutions of the twentieth century. Mikhail Gorbachev, the pioneering architect behind many of these changes, wisely stated that 'Humanity is like a group of mountain climbers; either we support one another on the way up or we all fall down together.' This was the first time in human history that world leaders and the masses began to realize that life is indeed 'one interconnected whole'.

Since 1988 the USSR, all of Eastern Europe, many South American countries, South Africa and a number of other African countries, Japan, Western Europe, the Nato and Warsaw Pact Alliances, the EEC, and the planet as a whole have begun that long-awaited transformation towards a new world order. The years 1988–89, with their two triple conjunctions, together with the Pluto transit through its own sign Scorpio (Pluto reached its midway 15 degrees point in 1989 too), represented a momentous turning-point in human thought and history. They planted the seeds for the final decade of the twentieth century, a decade which would also see the near-completion of the 2,000-year cycle of the Piscean Age and the beginning of the 2,500-year Era of Aquarius as humanity entered the twenty-first century. I will be dealing more comprehensively with these and other collective cycles in Chapter 8.

From a personal perspective I also went through profound and extremely difficult, painful and enlightening changes during the 1988–89 cycle. Literally every aspect of my life had to be redefined and reorganized, for the 1988 conjunction also coincided with my

Uranus opposition, the 39–40-year 'midlife crisis' point, when the planet Uranus reaches its 180 degree opposition to its position in the birth chart. It might be of interest to note that this same 'midlife' opposition occurred in the East European countries in 1989, for their Communist regimes had taken power in 1948–9. This midlife revolution (revolution = the turning of the wheel) is a psychological and spiritual turning-point for individuals and nations alike.

PURPOSE AND MEANING

I have subtitled this book 'Finding the Soul's Purpose' because 'purpose' lies at the centre of all life, and at the centre of all questions pertaining to life. The psychological chaos underlying modern-day society is a direct manifestation of a loss of meaning and purpose, and the conflict between orthodox religion and science has compounded rather than clarified this issue. It is the role of spiritual science, of which astrology and psychology are the 'royal' sciences, to realign humanity to its unique collective purpose, and to the unique purpose of each individual human being. In order to accomplish this, astrologers have to pierce behind personality-based astrology and discover the secret of soul-based astrology, for it is the soul of any life-form that embodies its purpose.

Two questions are vital in this regard:

1. What are the transpersonal dimensions of astrology and psychology?
2. How can this transpersonal dimension be employed to suit the needs of twenty-first-century humanity?

In astrological chart interpretation the Rising sign and the Sun sign are considered the two most important factors in the chart. The vast majority of astrologers still persist in claiming that the Rising sign is the 'mask' one shows to the world, whilst the Sun sign is the true individual identity of the individual (or group, nation and so on). One might thus ask how that which comes first, namely the Rising sign, can be regarded as the 'mask', while that which comes second, namely the Sun sign (for its placement in the birth chart is dependent upon the Rising sign), is regarded as the central reality? How can the persona ('mask') or personality come before the soul, the Light lying behind the personality?

The soul is the higher self, and it is this self which embodies the energy which allows the personality (or lower self) to exist. The soul embodies that very purpose, consciousness and intelligence (the threefold nature of the higher self) which lies behind the persona. If the Rising sign, which is related to the essential energy of one of the zodiacal signs, comes first, and the soul comes before the personality, then obviously the soul and the Rising sign are directly connected, and the Sun sign must therefore be the 'personalized' channel through which the energy of the Rising sign need manifest. The Sun sign is therefore the 'mask of God' and *not the Rising sign*. So why do exoteric astrologers persist in stating the opposite?

The Rising sign is directly connected to the life-purpose or 'dharma' of the individual, and as such is related to the higher self and its specific purpose. The correct understanding and interpretation of the Rising sign clarifies this purpose, and it could well be said that this is the greatest revelation of the astrological birth chart. Every factor in the chart, that is in the life of the individual (or group or nation or event), falls under the overall influence of the energy of the Rising sign, the spirit overlighting the whole chart (life). By misinterpreting the Rising sign one misinterprets the very life-purpose. This to me is the major reason why so few people, including astrologers, are aware of their soul or life dharma.

'Without vision all perishes' and the vision of one's life dharma is embodied in the Rising sign. Astrologers need remember that Aries, the first sign of the zodiac or the natural Ascendant, is connected to the 'original Idea' (purpose) of incarnation, and although the Sun sign plays a major role in its rulership of the fifth sign Leo, it is a secondary role after the Ascendant.

We must now consider the second question, concerning the practical application of this transpersonal dimension. Chart interpretation tends to form the major part of modern-day astrology, but this in itself is a very limited dimension of astrological science. From a practical point of view the time given to chart interpretation is necessarily limited, for the attention of both astrologer and client is limited to a maximum time-frame of two to three hours. One's mental energy and intuitive perception are bound to be drained after such a time. Astrologers can read, study and write books on astrological interpretation, but this is a full-time occupation. What about the millions of people who would like to use astrological knowledge in their daily lives but do not have the time for traditional astrological study? The psychology of living is far more important than the purely personal and complex dimensions of astrology, and a new type of astrology needs to emerge that can transform itself into a new science of life.

THE ANNUAL ASTROLOGICAL CYCLE

How can astrology be transformed to suit the needs of twenty-first-century humanity? The secret lies in the integration of transpersonal astrological knowledge with the annual astrological cycle. This will enable astrology to become a *living* science, applicable to everyone's life, and connecting the life of the individual with the greater life of the group, humanity and the planet.

The annual astrological cycle is the yearly transit of the Sun through the planetary zodiac, which starts from the spring equinox when the Sun enters Aries, the first sign of the zodiac, and evolves with the movement of the Sun through the other eleven signs of the zodiac. The annual cycle completes itself when the Sun moves through Pisces, the last sign of the zodiac, and the final month of the winter solstice. Because the actual energies of the signs and their ruling Rays and planets are manifesting over the twelve-monthly cycles of the year, one can consciously attune to these cycles and learn to co-operate and co-create with them. Astrology therefore becomes a living experience, and not simply a complex intellectual science.

This new science applies not only to the individual, but also to the particular group within which he or she is working, for the individual and the group cannot be separated in the New Era, and the individual and the group are in turn connected to the collective. The integration between individual, group and collective (humanity and the planet), forms the sacred triangle of life, and astrology and psychology must adapt themselves to this triangle. Human beings should study, experience and manifest the energies of Aries and its Rays (1 and 7), planetary rulers Mercury (transpersonal) and Mars (personal), its objective sphere of manifestation (the 1st house), and its two major sub-cycles of influence (the New and Full Sun–Moon cycles) during the monthly cycle of Aries (21 March to 20 April). The same goes for Taurus, Gemini and the other nine signs. The individual and the group will thus consciously, lovingly and purposefully evolve in attunement with the universe 'in which they live and move and have their being'. This is one of the greatest gifts that the ageless science of astrology offers humanity. It is this gift which has been lost and which must be reinstated by those astrologers able to move beyond their personal attachments to astrology.

ASTROLOGY AND TRIANGLES

There is another vitally important aspect of transpersonal astrology and psychology that I will deal with in this book, and that is the fact that all creation, be it an atom, human being, planet, zodiacal sign, solar system or constellation, has a triune nature. In other words each sign and planet, individual human being, group and nation has three dimensions, and thus three interpretations, namely: spirit, or a greater self; soul, or a higher self; and personality, or a lower self. In the past, orthodox astrology and psychology, and for that matter politics, economics, science, education, art, music, work, marriage, sexuality and living itself, have only dealt with the third and most material dimension, namely the persona(lity).

Astrologers will now have to consider the fact that just as human beings are beginning to discover, explore and actualize the second dimension, namely the soul (the 'quality' of consciousness behind form), so one has to discover, explore and interpret the soul of each sign, planet, house, aspect and the chart itself. This adds a whole new dimension to astrology and psychology, and it is this dimension which this book aims to explore.

Although astrology, the new psychology and the new spirituality are still seen as peripheral to the major changes at present occurring in the world, the transits of Uranus through the sign Aquarius (1995 to 2002) and Pluto through Sagittarius (beginning 1995) will bring these three interconnected sciences to the fore. Uranus is the ruling planet of Aquarius, and Aquarius channels the 5th Ray of 'knowledge', so this transit will revolutionize spiritual and material science and knowledge. I will be dealing with the Seven Rays in Chapters 4 and 5, but suffice it to say that these Rays have an overall influence on all that occurs in our solar system, for they lie behind the constellations themselves and originate in the cosmic zodiac. The 5th Ray of 'knowledge' rules all forms of science, both spiritual and material, and it is the only Ray that moves through the constellation of Aquarius. For this reason knowledge is replacing belief, for belief is a characteristic of the 6th Ray which ruled the outgoing Piscean Age and its religious, philosophical and educational belief systems.

Sagittarius is the sign ruling religion itself, for it is related to the search for spiritual meaning and purpose, and it is this journey that subsequently leads to knowledge and understanding and the deeper realities underlying religion and the spiritual nature of things. Pluto will thus bring about the death throes of the old world religions, and the rebirth of a new and inclusive world religion, in which the age-old religious ideal of 'One God, One Planet and One Humanity' will be rediscovered. This is already occurring and will accelerate as we approach the beginning of the twenty-first century. The new astrology and psychology has a vital role to play in the birth of this' new world religion.

ASTROLOGY AND THE COLLECTIVE

The focal points of this new world religion and spirituality will be the global celebration of the Full Moon cycles of the twelve signs of the zodiac. These are called the twelve New Age festivals. Groups of people in every country, city and town will gather together at the time of each Full Sun–Moon (which always occurs at the same Greenwich Mean Time everywhere) to celebrate their common home, the Earth, and their common family, humanity. For this reason it is vital that the new astrologers gain a deep understanding of the New and Full Moon cycles and their meaning, and link this with the deeper significance of the signs of the zodiac, and their Ray and planetary rulers, their 'Herculean Labour' (see *The Labours of Hercules* by Alice Bailey), plus their corresponding sounds/ music, colours, aroma essences (the use of aromatherapy oils), minerals and crystals, flowers, poetry, drama, dances and so on. These twelve festivals, plus the four seasonal festivals, will thus become, and are already becoming, the sixteen annual focal points of 'gathering and celebration' of the new humanity and world religion. This is a vital dimension of group and collective astrology, and the new astrology must integrate this new science and art of living accordingly.

CHAPTER TWO

The Science of Triangles

The word 'transpersonal' is indicative of 'that which is beyond (trans) the personal'. In order to come to a deeper understanding of this word and its implications for astrology, psychology and life in general, it is necessary to clarify the personal and transpersonal dimensions of life and what they stand for.

'Personal' refers to that which we call the personality, the 'persona' or mask of existence; other names given to this side of creation are the lower self, the lower ego, the dweller on the threshold (the esoteric term), the shadow (the Jungian term), the earth self, the outer self, the material self and the mask of God. The Jungian term, 'the shadow' refers to that part of the lower ego that is repressed. The personality is composed of the etheric–physical, emotional and lower mental bodies (diagram 1). Together these bodies or 'vehicles' form what is known as the personality, that aspect of creation which both hides and manifests the transpersonal or higher self, otherwise referred to as the soul or Christ self. Material energy is not simply a facet of the physical material world, symbolized by all forms of physical creation, but is also a facet of the emotional and concrete mental worlds. This applies equally to the individual human personality as it does to a group, a nation, a planet, a solar system or a galaxy for that matter.

It is our attachments to the threefold lower self/ego that makes us 'materialistic', and not simply our attachment to money and material objects. Herein lies the fundamental cause of all human ignorance, for what we are attached to we identify with, and wrong identification lies at the heart of all illusion. Astrologers and psychologists (and politicians, educators, scientists, artists and so on) who identify solely with this aspect of life perpetuate and personify its natural limitations, for the personality is the effect and not the cause of any life-factor. This accounts for the dismal failure of the orthodox sciences in revealing any deeper meaning behind

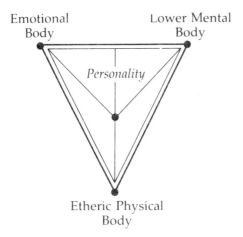

Diagram 1

life, for the lower rational mind in itself does not have the capacity to comprehend such meaning.

The triangle of the lower self has its apex pointing towards the Earth, for it is the energies emanating from the core of Mother Earth, known esoterically as the Sleeping Serpent or Kundalini Fire (fire by friction), which enliven and stimulate the physical body of the personality (diagram 2). In astrology this energy is represented by the base chakra, the lowest energy centre, which faces downwards towards the Earth, and by Pluto, the planetary energy related to 'the Lord of the Underworld' and to atomic fission.

Kundalini Fire is generated by spirit meeting and fusing with matter, and is the gross manifestation of cosmic or spiritual energy, namely 'electric fire'. The planet associated with this energy is Vulcan, and the crown chakra is its energy centre. Vulcan and Pluto both channel the 1st Ray of will or power. Vulcan is related to atomic fusion, for it lies in between the Sun and Mercury, and it is the first planet which receives and distributes the energies of atomic fusion generated at the core of the Sun. Vulcan has not been officially discovered, although there are various myths associated with its purpose and activities. It is known as 'the forger of metals' and Vulcan is often seen as the god who forges the weapons of war. 'Metal' is the symbol of physical form and it requires 'forging by fire' to create a fit body to house the spirit of life; hence Vulcan's inner rulership of Taurus, the sign associated with the creation of beautiful and refined physical forms.

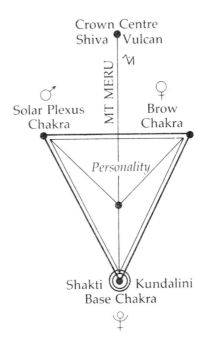

Diagram 2

My feeling is that Vulcan will only be physically discovered when humanity is ready to use atomic fusion, and this can only occur when humanity has adequately transformed darkness into light, ignorance into wisdom and fear into love. In other words it is only when the destructive energy of Plutonic fission has been adequately transformed into the constructive energy of Vulcanian fusion that Vulcan will be discovered. Fusion will provide humanity with safe, clean and infinite energy resources. Buddha is said to have had Taurus Rising and the festival of the Buddha (Wesak) is celebrated at the Taurus Full Sun–Moon. Vulcan also sub-influences Virgo Rising, and this will be dealt with later in this book.

In Hindu cosmology these two principles are referred to as Shiva (Father Spirit) and Shakti (Mother Earth), and it is the circulation of these two fires through the inner spinal chord of the individual, a planet, solar system and galaxy that gives life to existence (diagram 3). Hindu cosmology refers to this chord and its inner fire as Mount Meru, the sacred mountain which dwells at the centre of all life. This mountain exists at the centre of all creation, including of course the human being.

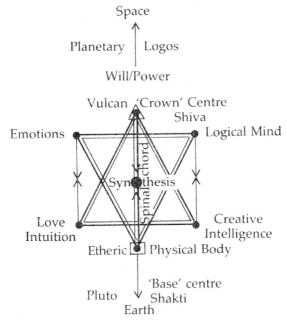

Diagram 3

From the point of view of the Earth these two energy centres exist at the spiritual apex of the Earth and the spiritual core within the Earth. The apex centre is referred to in the ancient wisdom as Shambhala, 'the Centre where the will of God is known'. The Logos of the Earth, Sanat Kumara, who might be associated with Vulcan, dwells within this apex, and Pluto, the Lord of the Underworld, dwells within the core.

THE SOLAR TRIANGLE

One of the most important triangles is that of the Sun itself, for the Sun is the heart centre of our solar system. One could say that the heart of our solar logos, the 'Lord' of our solar system, lies in the heart of the Sun. All life in our solar system is sustained by the Sun, for its light and heat and vital force streams through its system enlivening all its planets and their systems. The Sun's heart beats at eleven-year intervals, and with this 'beat' it sends out its life-force into its entire system, just as the human heart sends out this same vital force, via the bloodstream. It is surprising how we tend to forget that this life-giving force comes to us from the heart of the Sun (via our breathing). Man tends to forget this fact, and presumes in his gross ignorance that he is life and the Sun is merely an unintelligent gaseous form in space. It is the Sun that is a great living consciousness, a great pulsating solar heart, and it is we who are the small insignificant parts within its macrocosmic aura.

Strangely enough it is only when we realize and acknowledge our insignificance that we are allowed to begin to realize our importance. How often do we humans look up to the Sun and give thanks for its life and its grace? The Sun is a star, and every star is, in truth, a vast spiritual life, a god of its own particular system. The ancients knew this and referred to the Sun and the planets as gods. The science of astrology has the capacity to explain the deeper reality lying behind the planets because it is a cosmology of knowledge and not belief.

What we tend to forget is that the energy of the Sun is generated and produced at its core. It is at the core of the Sun that nuclear fusion occurs, and this fusion creates the life of the Sun. From the core this energy streams into the heart of the Sun, and from the heart it travels into the corona and out into its solar system. This is the triangle of the Sun (diagram 4). The triangle of core, heart and corona is applicable to every aspect of creation, from the atom with its nucleus, protons and electrons (diagram 5), to the human being with his/her spirit, soul and personality (diagram 6), to the planet Earth with its three centres of Shambhala, the spiritual hierarchy and humanity (diagram 7). These three centres are governed by Rays 1, 2 and 3, the three major Rays. (See Chapters 4 and 5 for detailed information on this subject.)

There are also the better-known Cardinal, Fixed and Mutable astrological triangles of Aries, Taurus and Gemini; Cancer, Leo and Virgo; Libra, Scorpio and Sagittarius and Capricorn, Aquarius and Pisces. These are referred to as the triplicities (diagram 8a), and these triangles are also governed by the three major Rays whose essential qualities are power or will, love–wisdom and creative intelligence. These three Ray qualities govern their respective sector of the Cardinal (will), Fixed (love) and Mutable (intelligence) triangles.

The triangular decanates of each sign are also ruled by the above three qualities. The first decanate of 0–10 degrees is governed by will, the second decanate of 10–20 degrees by love–wisdom and the third decanate of 20–30 degrees by creative intelligence (diagram 8b; see the end of Chapter 7 for the sub-decanates and their rulers

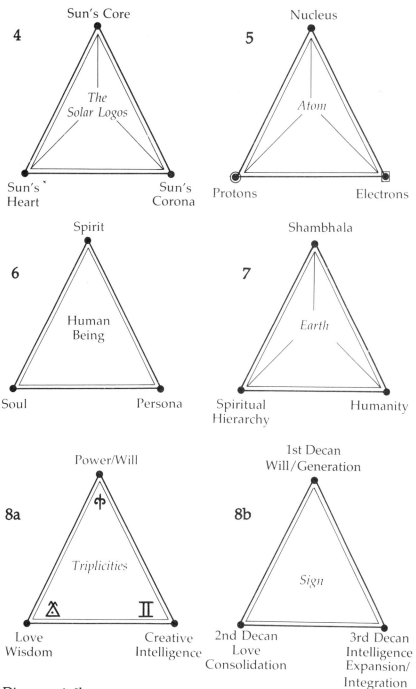

Diagrams 4–8b

and Rays). Cardinal signs generate and initiate energy (power), Fixed signs consolidate and stabilize energy (love-wisdom) and Mutable signs expand, adapt and integrate energy (intelligent activity).

All personality life, be it a planet, a human, an animal, vegetable or mineral or an atom, is sustained by the Sun's rays. The Sun is therefore the causal or apex body of the personality, and this causal body is the first aspect of the soul (diagram 9). In astrology the Sun therefore represents the integrated personality or personal self, and it holds the key to the integration and creative expression of the mind, emotions and etheric–physical body. The position of the Sun is therefore the central, conscious and personal channel through which the soul or Rising sign need manifest. The third aspect or quality of the soul is creative intelligence, and this is the essential quality of the integrated personality (the Sun sign).

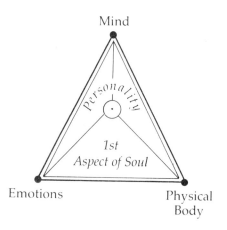

Diagram 9

The Sun sign represents the 'Son of Man', the personality or 'Holy Ghost', whereas the Rising sign represents the 'Son of God', the soul or Christ self. The majority of astrologers interpret the Sun sign and the Rising sign the opposite way around, and this needs to be corrected. The Sun rules the heart centre, but the heart has three aspects to itself: the invisible core or 'flame' situated at its core, the invisible heart which is the actual heart chakra, and the physical heart itself. This is why the heart of the Sun is the transpersonal ruler of Leo and not the corona of the Sun.

THE LIFE TRIANGLE

'Life' itself is triune in nature, for it manifests through spirit or the Monad (cosmos), the soul or the higher self (solar system) and the personality or lower self, which is connected to non-sacred planetary systems, like the Earth (diagram 10). These three correspond

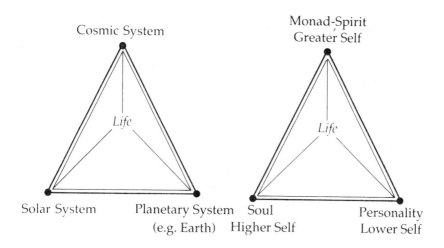

Diagram 10

Diagram 11

to the energies of will/power, love–wisdom and creative intelligence. This triangle is vitally important because it explains the threefold activity of every aspect of life. It also explains the reason why in transpersonal astrology there are three aspects to every Ray, constellation, sign, planet, nation and individual human being (diagram 11).

Every Ray, sign and planet is a spiritual life in itself, and human beings compose just one other aspect of this great cosmic life. Every sign and planet has a triune nature, for it too has a monad, soul and personality. The traditional planetary ruler of each sign rules its personality, but it has other planets ruling its soul and monad (diagram 12). Most of the planets have triplicity rulership too; for example Uranus rules the monad of Aries, Mercury its soul and Mars its personality.

Very few astrologers realize this fact and this is the reason why the majority of astrology books misinterpret the Rising sign, the Sun sign and the Moon sign. Leo Rising should have a soul interpretation, Sun in Leo should have a personality interpretation in relationship to present life factors, and Moon in Leo should have a personality interpretation in terms of past-life factors. All three placements might be in Leo, but each has a very different interpretation in relationship to the soul and personality of Leo.

The planets themselves have three dimensions, and each requires a different interpretation too. For example Venus rules the personality of Taurus and Libra, and thus it has a more personal, lower mental, sensual and financial interpretation in these signs. Venus is the higher soul ruler of Gemini, and the soul dimension of Venus, which is *qualified* by 'intelligent love' (pure reason) needs to be interpreted in this case. Venus is also the greater spiritual or monadic ruler of Capricorn, and the will or purpose of Venus is revealed through this sign. This is why the unicorn is the highest symbol of Capricorn, for the unicorn is the symbol of the initiate who has attained union with the soul. The pure nature of Venus is the soul itself and the highest goal of the personality (the Midheaven of the chart, ruled by Capricorn) is to become the soul (diagram 13).

In the same fashion Jupiter rules the personality of Sagittarius and Pisces; hence its connection to orthodox religion and philosophy and law and to long-distance travel. Jupiter is the soul ruler of Aquarius, and here its qualities of love, intuitive wisdom, subjective spirituality, inclusivity and unity with the group and collective soul are at its highest. Jupiter also rules the monadic side of Virgo, and here the factor of Christ love manifesting through the fully purified personality (the 'Mother Mary' principle) comes into play. In this book we will be concentrating on the personal and

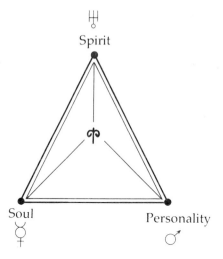

Diagram 12

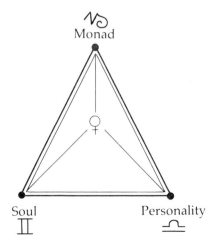

Diagram 13

transpersonal planetary rulers only, for the monadic ruler is only
contacted at the third initiation (see Chapter 3).

Personalities exist as living intelligences within the collective
physical, emotional and mental bodies or atmospheres of the Earth.
Personalities exist on/in all the non-sacred planets, such as the
Earth, Mars and Pluto. The essential quality of the personality is
active intelligence, for the personality is essentially a mind imbued
with creative intelligence. It is only when a person begins to think

dynamically and creatively, and in some way for the good of the whole, that they begin the conscious journey of evolution. Creative intelligence is therefore the first aspect of the soul, for the soul triangle is composed of this quality, plus the qualities of love–intuition and higher will/purpose.

The majority of people identify solely with one or other aspect of their personalities, and are largely unconscious of their higher selves, but large numbers are beginning this new and expanded identification as humanity approaches the dawn of a New Era. As this new identification takes place energy begins to be transferred from the personal self, focused in the base, sacral and solar plexus centres, to the higher self, focused in the *alter ego* centres of the brow, heart and throat.

THE SOUL TRIANGLE

The transpersonal self is also referred to as the soul, the higher self, the higher ego, the Angel of the Presence (its esoteric term), the Christ self, the Buddhic self, the Solar Lord (as in 'solar, sun, soul, solar system'), higher consciousness, the Venusian self (Venus is the *alter ego* or 'twin soul' of the Earth), and the *Atman* in Hindu terminology. The higher self is essentially an entity of consciousness, just as the personality is essentially an entity of form.

Consciousness is often referred to in the singular but it should be remembered that consciousness has a triune nature just as form has a triune nature. There is a tendency amongst many spiritually minded people to relate to consciousness as love and intuition (Ray 2) alone; this quality is indeed the central facet of consciousness but it is not its sole facet. Creative intelligence (Ray 3) and will or purpose (Ray 1) are its other two facets which compose its triangle (diagram 14). The true fulfilment of one's soul purpose can only take place when these three facets have become relatively integrated.

Every individual has a preponderance of one or other of these qualities, but this particular quality has to be relatively balanced with the other two qualities. For example if one is a very wilful individual (1st Ray of power) one will need to develop and integrate love and intuitive understanding (2nd Ray) and creative thought and activity (3rd Ray) if one wishes to fulfil one's life-purpose. The understanding, development and integration of the above soul triangle forms one of the major foundations of the new astrology and psychology and the new patterns of living.

From the point of view of the Earth the higher self is a conscious-

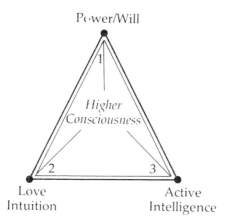

Diagram 14

ness from the planet Venus, Earth's twin or *alter ego* planet. In other words, every human personality has a higher God self, which acts as an inner partner and guide. It is the solar karma of this self to guide his/her human counterpart from 'darkness to light, from ignorance to truth and from death to immortality'. This self is not one of the guides on the emotional or mental planes, but one's highest guide, one's true inner master. It is this soul who is the custodian of one's spiritual purpose, and this purpose is embodied and revealed through the Rising sign of the birth chart.

According to the Master DK (see *Esoteric Astrology* by Alice Bailey) the Ascendant remains in the same sign for seven lifetimes. In other words the higher self unfolds its purpose over twelve seven-year life-cycles, that is eighty-four lifetimes (12 signs times 7 life-cycles each). Eighty-four is the number of perfection, for 12 and 7 are the sacred numbers of our evolutionary system and $12 \times 7 = 84$. In the yoga (yoga = union or wholeness) system there are eighty-four major *asanas* or postures, each representing one facet of incarnation. It is also possible that the degree of the Rising sign can provide some indication of how long we have been evolving under that sign; for example if the Rising sign is 15 degrees then we have reached the midway point of the seven life-cycles, and if the degree is towards the end of the sign then we are completing the seven life-cycles. From all the above it can be seen why a true and deepened understanding of the soul is necessary if we wish to gain a transpersonal perspective of astrology.

THE FOURTH AND FIFTH KINGDOMS

In our planetary system the human personality kingdom is known as the fourth kingdom, and the transhuman soul kingdom composes the fifth kingdom. There are two more kingdoms beyond the soul, namely the monadic and the Divine. The mineral kingdom is the seventh, the vegetable kingdom the sixth and the animal kingdom the fifth (diagram 15). These kingdoms are centres of living energy, and humanity forms the mediating centre between the three lower and the three higher centres (diagram 16). We therefore have two triangles, with humanity forming the mediating centre between the two. When these triangles are interfaced we get the six-pointed star of David (diagram 17), which is not simply a Jewish symbol but the symbol of the synthesis or fusion of the spiritual and material kingdoms. The point at the centre of the star symbolizes this synthesis.

The six-pointed star symbolizes the fusion of the triangles of the lower and higher selves. The evolutionary process of integrating these two selves is directly related to the purpose of human existence, and underlies the science of initiation. Astrology and psychology, the science of triangles and the science of initiation are therefore interconnected. From a collective perspective 'The Great Invocation' (see page 238) is the finest example of how triangular energy functions. There are four stanzas in this invocation. The first three invoke the Light, Love and Will of God. These three qualities form the collective spiritual triangle of our planetary system and are related to the three major planetary chakras called Shambhala (crown), the spiritual hierarchy (heart) and mind of humanity (brow). The fourth stanza invokes 'the race of men/humanity' who are responsible for manifesting the plan of Love and Light on Earth (diagram 18).

Another important triangle helps us to understand the deeper significance of the constellations/signs and their overall functioning. Each constellation is a spiritual life or archetype, as already explained. It has its monad (purpose), its soul (consciousness) and its personality (form) which focus through its three planetary rulers. The sign's corresponding house (11th house for the eleventh sign Aquarius and so on) is the material 'grounding and actualization' point of each sign's threefold nature (diagram 19). This is how one can interpret the triangular and the fourfold square significance of each sign, a system of interpretation which belongs to future exploration, for the vast majority of astrologers are still focusing on the personality of the signs. A good number are also beginning to

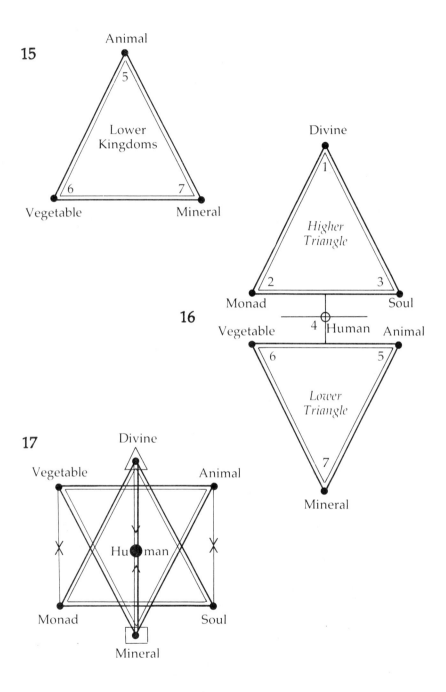

Diagrams 15–17

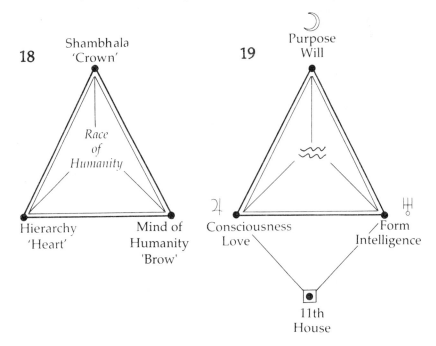

Diagrams 18–19

deal with the soul of the signs and this side of astrology has new and infinite possibilities in itself. In this regard triangular astrology and psychology might well be considered as the science of the future.

All triangular systems work in the same fashion for there are three major centres of energy and a fourth 'manifesting' centre of force. Light, love and purpose have to be integrated and finally manifested through one or other form of creative activity.

Before I complete this chapter I would like to mention one more practical use of triangles. In the New Era, group activity will play a major role in every aspect of life. It will be found that when three people work together in a triangle the work becomes far more effective and fulfilling. This is because each individual will focus one aspect and quality of the triangle. Each will also play a mediating and balancing role between the other two, which is essential for group harmony. There will thus be a far greater balance between the light (mind), love (heart) and will (action) facets of the spiritual–human triangle. The three people can also join up on the inner mental and soul levels if they are so inclined. Energy works in three unfolding levels, and all activity, human or otherwise, manifests in this way. First there is an 'idea' (mind), then there is the 'ideal' (heart) and then there is some corresponding creative action (will). In other words we must first attune to an idea or vision, then desire that this idea be unfolded, and then finally find the channels to manifest this idea objectively. This is the science of triangles in action.

CHAPTER THREE

Astrology and Initiation

The greatest and most important question facing humanity is that of purpose. What is the purpose of humanity and of every human being on Earth? From a rational philosophical, religious and scientific perspective there is no clear answer to this question, with the result that we live in a world seemingly devoid of purpose and meaning. The repercussions of meaningless living are all too evident in every facet of human society, and 'disastrous' would be the appropriate term to describe life in our modern era.

'Disaster' is defined as 'being separated from the stars', and 'stars' are the light-filled heavenly symbols of God or Truth. The ancient wisdom teachings refer to the stars as the outer visible bodies of vast spiritual Lives. Astrology is the science of the stars, the living science of the divine whole, for *logy* refers to *Logos*, meaning 'Lord', and *astro* refers to the stars or star system of the constellations. In esoteric astrology every constellation and planet is said to have its Logos or 'Lord', a great spiritual Life who is the Godhead of the system. Behind every microcosmic or macrocosmic form can be found a spiritual Life, which is the life-giving source of that form.

Psychology differs only in that *psycho* refers to the soul or mind. It is obvious that we cannot separate astrology and psychology, for how can one separate spirit, soul, mind and form when they are intrinsically interconnected? Astrology and psychology are therefore spiritual sciences and systems. If one does not start from the core of things one has already lost touch with the underlying reality, and any such system will obviously be a failure from the start.

Sigmund Freud, the father of modern-day psychology, was humble enough to acknowledge the spiritual element of psychology in his later years, and yet the foundation of modern orthodox psychology is still based on his earlier teachings. Even Carl Jung, by far the greatest contributor to twentieth-century psychology, discovered this greater spiritual reality when he had an 'out-of-body'

THE HERO'S QUEST-THE TWELVE-FOLD
JOURNEY OF THE HUMAN SOUL

DOORWAY INTO SPIRIT
MC

TRANS-
FIGURATION
3RD
INITIATION

BAPTISM
2nd
INITIATION

4th
INITIATION
CRUCIFIXION
COMPLETION
NEW BEGINNINGS

1st
INITIATION

SECOND
BIRTH

PRESENT

ASCENDANT

DESCENDANT

THE PAST
IC
DOORWAY INTO MATTER

Initiation

experience during the later years of his life (see *Memories, Dreams and Reflections*). Before this experience Jung maintained that all reality was subjective and related to what he called the 'collective unconscious'. This new experience proved to him that reality was not simply dependent upon personal subjectivity, but existed independently of subjective observation. In other words 'reality' exists of its own accord, and it related to the 'collective superconscious' and not simply to the collective unconscious. One's subjective experience allows one to tap into this reality (at whatever level), but it is independent of man himself.

To put it simply; there is an underlying (or overlighting) spiritual reality behind all microcosmic and macrocosmic creation, and this reality embodies the meaning and purpose of this creation, which of course includes the individual human being, humanity and the planet itself. The human being is free to tap into and discover this purpose; but if he or she does not take the responsibility to discover and unfold this purpose, reality is in no way disturbed – although, without doubt, man will be disturbed. Reality is therefore subjective or hidden behind form (esoteric simply means 'that which is subjective') and every human being has the choice of exploring or rejecting this reality. In astrological science the Rising sign of the birth chart and its transpersonal planetary ruler and Ray embody this hidden purpose and meaning, and this is why the Rising sign plays such a vital role in astrological interpretation.

THE MONAD – OUR COSMIC CONNECTION

In the science of triangles we dealt with the life triangle of the Monad, the soul and the personality. The Monad, the core of life, originates and exists in the cosmos. It is a cosmic being whose work it is to serve its cosmic system. We should remember that our solar system and Earth are but a minute part of this cosmic system, for they form a tiny part of our Milky Way galaxy.

Aeons ago a part of this Monad incarnated into matter at its densest level, namely the mineral kingdom. It is this Monad which carries the life-force and which therefore gives life to matter. *Matter evolves but it is the Monad, the greater cosmic self, which enables material forms to evolve.* It is the Monad which is evolving through matter. For aeons of time this Monad evolved through the mineral kingdom, then into and through the vegetable kingdom, then into and through the animal kingdom, and finally it evolved into and through the primitive human kingdom. The Monad is anchored in the centre or core of the heart of all matter, including the human heart, for it is the heart that receives and distributes life-force (or *chi*) to the rest of its system. It is the Monad at the core of the Sun, the heart centre of our solar system, that generates and distributes vital force to its entire system, including individual men and women. We breath in this *prana* and our heart distributes it to our micro solar system and thus we live.

VENUS AND THE SOUL KINGDOM

Around 18 million years ago a new evolutionary process began to take place on our planet. The Monad had incarnated and evolved through the three lower kingdoms, the mineral, vegetable, animal and primitive human kingdoms. Spirit (Ray 1) and matter (Ray 3) had interacted. Now the second aspect of the life triangle, namely consciousness (Ray 2) was about to play its part. Humans had reached the stage where they were deemed ready for the initial movement into 'self' ('I Am') consciousness. This required the activation of thought, for consciousness is related to the thinking principle, 'mind'. The planet directly associated with this second aspect of consciousness is Venus, for Venus is a 5th Ray (knowledge) planet and within our solar system Venus is the *alter ego* or twin soul of the Earth.

Three million years before this time (21 million years ago) there had been the first direct contact between Earth as a non-human inhabited planet, and Venus, Earth's *alter ego* planet, a superhuman inhabited planet. The cosmology of Venus being Earth's twin sister originates from this contact. According to the ancient wisdom forty-nine Venusians descended to the Earth and began to assume responsibility for the Earth's evolution. These forty-nine Venusians were the original spiritual hierarchy or 'inner' government of the Earth. One of these great beings was Sanat Kumara, the Lord of the World (depicted by William Blake in his painting by the same name), who is the etheric incarnation of the planetary logos of our Earth. In other words Sanat Kumara is the lord of the Earth, the overall being responsible for our planet's evolution. It should be noted that every planet has its lord and its spiritual hierarchy, who are the custodians and guides of that planet's evolution.

Sanat Kumara resides in Shambhala, the crown or highest chakra of our planet. Shambhala exists in the Gobi Desert in very subtle etheric matter, and it is therefore invisible to human sight. It does not exist in Glastonbury, as some people think. The true significance of every planet therefore lies in its spiritual hierarchy or inner government, for it is the agencies of this government who receive, transform and transmit the energies related to the planet's evolution. In fact planetary astrology has no scientific foundation outside of this esoteric understanding, for there is no scientific basis for stating that 'Venus is the planet of love', or 'Mars is the planet of conflict or 'Uranian energy creates revolutionary changes' outside of this understanding. All energy that enters our planetary system is received, stepped-down (transformed) and distributed by the three major planetary centres, namely Shambhala (Ray 1), the spiritual hierarchy (Ray 2) and the angelic hierarchy (Ray 3). Humanity is only the 4th centre (Ray 4) in this energy system. More detailed information on Shambhala and the spiritual hierarchy can be obtained by studying *Initiation – Human and Solar* and other books by Alice Bailey (see Bibliography).

Venus is called 'the morning star' and 'the evening star' because it is the first 'light' that appears in the morning and evening. What we 'see' with our two eyes holds a deeper symbolical meaning when we 'see' with the eye of intuition. What is the deeper significance of Venus being the first light in the heavens? It is the revelation that Venus is the light of the Earth, that Venus is the higher self or twin partner of our planet. It is beings from Venus who form the central composition of Shambhala, the 'Centre where the will of God is known', and it is the perfected human consciousnesses of Venus who compose the higher angelic selves of every imperfected human personality on Earth. This is the great secret of Venus. The above information might seem esoteric and impractical, but it is one of the most important revelations of transpersonal astrology, for the higher self is the true inner master and partner that leads us from darkness to light, from ignorance to truth and from death to immortality. It is obvious that Venus in the birth chart needs to be seen in a new light, for the Ray that rules the sign Venus is in plays a major role in Ray psychology interpretation.

VENUS AND TWIN PARTNERSHIPS

Venus is a sacred planet and, as such, is inhabited by perfected souls. One might say that these souls are masters of the solar system, and are also the perfect archetypes of human personalities on Earth. An 'archetype' can be described as 'the perfect idea or consciousness' lying behind every form. In other words the soul or higher self of every human personality on Earth is the perfect archetype of that personality, and it is this self that every individual has to journey towards and 'become' in order to achieve perfection and freedom. It is this self that is the true inner partner, one's pure self, and it is this 'Angel of the Shining Presence' (the esoteric term given to the soul) that is the higher God self of every person on Earth.

It was these souls who now began to play their part in Earth's evolution, for just as the solar system is the mediating principle between the cosmos and our planet, so are the 5th kingdom of souls the mediating principle between the monadic (cosmos) and the personality (Earth) kingdoms. This is the key to Christ's statement that 'Only through Me [the Christ or soul principle] can you reach the Father [the Monad or Spirit].'

Many people have had personal contact with their higher selves. This contact can be audio and/or audio-visual. Once the soul establishes audio communication with its personality (ourselves) it begins to guide us on a regular basis through this telepathic communication. Very few people are fortunate enough to receive detailed guidance from their souls (as for example Eileen Caddy, co-founder of the Findhorn Foundation; see Bibliography), but everyone is capable of receiving basic and adequate audio contact. Visual contact is extremely rare for the simple reason that one visual experience of the soul, the perfect archetype of 'who we truly are', is enough to change one's life for evermore. Meditation is the major activity that enables us to build the bridge between the lower self and the higher self. A physical communications system requires a two-way connection and a spiritual–mental communication system requires a similar two-way connecting bridge.

Shirley Maclaine in her book *Dancing in the Light* (see Bibliography) describes the audio-visual communication she experienced with her higher self. Her visual experience was very much the same as that of my partner Imogen and myself, an experience which certainly changed our lives for ever. It should be emphasized that every human personality is destined to experience the reality of their higher self, for this experience is integral to spiritual evolution.

If one can imagine that there is a plane where the perfect archetypes of human entities exist then one can imagine the plane or world of the soul and the 5th kingdom of souls. My visual experience of the soul was one of seeing a perfected human being, a being of pure light. The contact was with my own masculine polarized higher self and its feminine polarized twin partner self, who introduced herself to me (telepathically) as 'Imogen'. Both souls could only be described as physically beauty-full (in the 'perfect' sense of the word) and embodying the qualities of pure unconditional love and unlimited all-knowingness. To put it simply they were 'pure': pure light, pure love, pure will. There were a number of fascinating aspects to this contact which I feel I need to share because the contact was 'real' (one learns to distinguish the difference between real, symbolical and illusionary contacts) and, as such, has vitally important implications for every human being.

Firstly I became aware through these contacts that I was soon to meet my twin partner in her physical body. I had been invoking this connection for many years, and when my soul introduced me to his twin partner 'Imogen' I knew intuitively that the physical connection was soon to follow. Two weeks before I met my life partner physically Imogen appeared to me in a dream. In this dream she was still in her pure light body. The contact was quite exquisite because her light body was completely transparent and she was in a state of complete tranquillity. In the dream I was made aware of certain aspects of our past (lives) and our future life and work together. When we met (physically) two weeks later we immediately connected. Her name was not Imogen but Jane when we met and we both knew that this was not her real name. I had not been able to remember the name Imogen when I awoke from the initial soul contact dream and I told Jane that she had told me her real (soul) name but I could not remember it. One year later we were with a very special spiritual friend discussing this 'name' dilemma when this woman suddenly turned to Jane and said, 'Your real name is Imogen.' As she said this I instantly remembered that this was the name I had been given in the dream. Since that day Jane has been Imogen.

Secondly my higher self and 'Imogen' had a soul child, a beautiful boy-child with pure white Egyptian-shaped hair (our souls also had pure white hair). We have had a number of contacts with this child and at a later stage he made contact with Imogen and told her his name.

Thirdly in the original contact dream 'Imogen' and the child were both sitting on white unicorns. My feeling was that these unicorns were real and not simply symbols. My intuitive feeling at the time and today is that unicorns are not purely symbolical creatures but are real. They are the soul creatures (if one might put it in this way) of the animal kingdom because they are pure; they sit on top of the mountain of animal evolution (the unicorn is the soul symbol of Capricorn). In mythology the unicorn only comes to the disciple when he or she has attained purity. The visionary archetypal contact I had of these unicorns was nevertheless not symbolical, and my sense is that unicorns actually exist on the soul levels of consciousness. In other words the unicorn myths are attempts to describe the actual reality of these creatures. Over the past fifteen or so years unicorn cards and posters have become an integral part of

Western society, and this is a direct indication that the consciousness of the soul has entered the consciousness of the West.

The experience (and experiences since then) enabled me to understand that every human personality has a perfect archetypal soul, and these souls themselves have 'twin' partner souls and families. In other words not only is there a perfect archetype of every male-female human individual, but there is also a soul archetype of the human partnership and the human family. One could go as far as to say that there is already a soul archetype of human society and humanity itself.

Last but not least there is a direct interconnection between twin souls on their own level of soul consciousness and twin personalities on their level of Earth consciousness and form. Twin souls are perfect, twin personalities are very imperfect, and this is an extremely important distinction. The twin personalities (lower selves) of twin souls (higher selves) connect as personalities with all their physical, emotional, sexual and mental imperfections. If this connection is conscious they will obviously be working in 'partnership' with their higher selves, but they will also be working on transforming their lower selves. This brings the dualities into extreme and dynamic conflict. Ecstasy and pain, joy and sadness, peace and battle, meditation and action, beauty and ugliness, honesty and deception, success and failure and all the polarities clash with one another. The vast majority of people who know of the existence of twin souls are under the misconception that if they meet and enter into partnership with their twin soul all will be harmony and beauty. They fail to understand that they are also partnering their twin personality, and this guarantees a great deal of conflict, pain, trial, testing, error, disillusionment and intensified transformation and transmutation. This is the deeper significance lying behind sacred marriage in the subjective and objective sense of the term.

The most important factor underlying twin partnerships is that they are automatically committed to serving God, the Christ, the kingdom of souls and humanity. True partnership is service-orientated because souls are 'Lords of Sacrificial Service'. This is why Venus, the planet directly related to the higher self, is exalted in Pisces, the sign of selfless service, and has higher rulership in Gemini, the sign ruling human evolution. While astrologers delve into asteroids, planetoids and other 'oids' they still fail to understand the deeper meaning of the major planets and the signs, because this meaning and interpretation has a triune foundation, and the second transpersonal dimension is only now coming into awareness.

VENUS AND THE SOUL THREAD

The Venusian Souls established their link with primitive humanity by extending a thread of their consciousness into the brain area. This thread was anchored in the area of the pineal gland, and since that time this gland has been the point of 'consciousness' within the human endocrine gland and chakric system. This gland is largely dormant and it is only activated when higher consciousness and higher purpose become an integral part of one's life. The 'life-thread' of the Monad is anchored in the core of the heart; 'life-force' therefore exists in the heart and flows through the bloodstream. 'Consciousness' exists in the pineal gland centre; consciousness enters the crown centre at physical birth, and leaves through this centre at physical death.

Through this thread of consciousness the Venusian angels gradually stimulated the brain of primitive man. The result was the very first stages of 'thought' or 'I Am' (individual) consciousness. The age-long evolutionary journey from primitive, unconscious man to modern, conscious man thus began. Although this was a very drawn out process it was nevertheless a quantum leap in evolution. It has taken 18 million years of evolution to reach our present stage of human individualization. One might say that the next great leap, that of moving from intellect to intuition, from lower to higher thought/mind, is now taking place, and this will be another quantum leap for humanity. This leap is occurring at a much faster rate, not least because Uranus, the planet of accelerated evolution, is the ruling planet of Aquarius, the constellation our Sun is now entering.

After this initial stimulation the Venusian angels withdrew their energy. Their work is concerned with serving the whole solar system, not just the Earth. All of human history, including the civilizations of Lemuria, Atlantis and so on, up to our modern era, are manifestations of this personality evolution. History is but the screen on which the interrelationship and conflict between our 'earth-inherited' lower self (body, instincts and emotions) and our 'solar-inherited' human self (lower and higher thought, love-intuition, purpose) has been displayed.

Fear dominates the instinctive lower self and love and intelligence govern the human self; fear blocks us off from love, intuitive knowing and true creative living, and intelligent love opens us up to the natural ordered harmony of the soul. This sounds quite simple, but intelligent simplicity has always been the hallmark of truth. This duality underlies evolution itself and lays the foundation for the new astrology and psychology. Lower selves are by their very nature 'separate' entities, and separation breeds conflict. Higher selves are individualized but are intrinsically part of one inter-connected, inclusive and co-operative whole, and co-operation breeds love, harmony, beauty and the art of right living.

In transpersonal astrology the non-sacred planets, the Earth, Moon, Mars and Pluto, together with the IC and the South Moon Node, are connected to the past, to the unconscious self and to the instinctive, emotional, desire-ridden and fearful self. These forces require self-consciousness and self-transformation in order to become channels for the energies of the higher self, represented by the seven sacred planets. These planets, Vulcan, Mercury, Venus, Jupiter, Saturn, Uranus and Neptune, together with the Rising sign, Midheaven and the North Node, are connected to the present and future, the conscious and superconscious, the human self and the higher self and to intelligence, love, intuition and higher will.

The Rising sign and the North Node are the two focal points of the higher self and the future need, whereas the Moon and the South Node are the two focal points of the lower self and the past, including past lives. One feels comfortable with the Moon and the South Node because one has 'done it all before', but comfort is not a breeding ground for creative conflict, true harmony, love and purpose.

The Logos of the Moon left the physical body of the Moon during the Lemurian Era, and the Moon's inhabitants were transferred to the Earth. The Moon is thus a 'dead' form and has no life of its own; it is simply a dead satellite of the Earth. Leftover vibrations from its past filter into the Earth's system and create a great deal of nega-tivity because they influence the instinctive (base) and sexual (sacral) centres at an unconscious level. The Moon's position in the chart is therefore a symbolic indication of the experiences and influences from one's immediate 'past life' and from one's present life upbringing and conditioning. Lunar races like the Japanese, Koreans and Chinese embody the influences from this past Moon civilization and this is why they are so 'mass' orientated. The masses in general (ruled by the sign Cancer) are influenced by the Moon's lower, unconscious vibrations, but these symbolic (past-life) literal influences affect everyone at a deep unconscious level.

The South Node is similar to the Moon but symbolizes the experi-ences and unconscious influences from a series of interconnected past lives. One will be 'chained' to this past until one consciously transforms one's attachments to it and 'uses' the positive lessons gained from these lives to fulfil one's present life-purpose. The focal point for the present life-purpose is the North Node, which is found directly opposite the South Node. The North Node has to be developed, expanded and given time, energy and attention for it is a new factor in the individual's life. The North Node, together with the Rising sign and its transpersonal ruler (and the Ray of this ruler), forms a focal point for contact with the soul and for the unfoldment of the energies of the soul and its purpose.

The Sun is the planet of mediatorship for it stands in between the higher and lower selves. The Sun is a non-sacred planet in the sense that it is related to the integrated personality, which is the first aspect of the soul, namely 'active intelligence'. All energies that enter our solar system from the solar zodiac (the zodiacal constellations of Aries, Taurus and so on) and the cosmos (the greater zodiac like the Great Bear) first enter the Sun, where they are transformed and then distributed into the rest of the solar system. The Lords of the Sun are the agencies who do this work. The Sun in the birth chart is therefore the mediating agency or personality (causal personal self) that receives, transforms and distributes the energies of the Rising sign (zodiacal energy) into its greater system. One has to develop one's Sun sign because individuality is an ongoing maturation process. The Sun sign is who one potentially is as an integrated and mature individual; it is not 'who one truly is' for the Sun sign is not representative of the higher self.

The Rising sign and the North Node sign (and house) represent the present-future, the Moon and the South Node signs (and houses) represent the past, while the Sun sign and its house represents the stage one has reached in the present life. If one wishes to mature and be an individual in one's own right (the Sun sign) and fulfil one's greater life-purpose (the Rising sign), one needs to cut and transform the chains of one's past, and use the forces of this past to benefit the needs of the future.

THE INITIATION PROCESS

A human being has to undergo five major initiations to achieve Mastery over nature. This was the deeper significance of the life and teachings of Jesus, for the birth, baptism, transfiguration, crucifixion and resurrection represented these five initiations. With the advent of the Aquarian Era, individual initiation is being integrated with, and expanded into group initiation, for the Spirit of Aquarius works through group energy. This is why small and decentralized groups are so important in this new era. Not only do individuals and groups fall under the law of initiation, but nations, humanity, planets, solar systems, galaxies and the universe itself fall under this law. Initiation is infinite and underlies every aspect of creation, and it is therefore imperative that astrologers, psychologists and human beings in general learn as much about this law as possible.

Astrology, psychology and initiation are intrinsically connected, for the consciousness of both the astrologer and client largely determine the level of interpretation of the chart. Collective astrological interpretation is also subject to one's level of consciousness. Many astrologers have incorrectly interpreted collective planetary transits, predicting physical catastrophes that have failed to materialize. This is because they have projected their own fears and narrow-minded perceptions, and have failed to see things from a more updated, intuitive and transpersonal perspective. For example in 1981 Saturn and Jupiter had a triple conjunction in Libra, the sign of balancing. The last twenty years of the twentieth century are therefore overlighted by the spirit of Libra, and it is for this transpersonal reason that the spirit of equilibrium will maintain a balance in planetary affairs as this century comes to its close. Catastrophes are already with us (Aids, starvation, pollution, drugs, war and so on) but these are part of the cleansing and balancing process (Saturn, Lord of Karma, is exalted in Libra), for each major imbalance will, by its very nature, bring about the exact opposite balancing situation. This is the work of the spirit of Libra. Transpersonal factors (such as the above), plus the vital significance of the intuition as the sixth 'synthesizing' sense, are integral to correct astrological interpretation.

Initiation is the stage-by-stage process (governed by evolutionary law) whereby we progress from one level of the evolutionary spiral to the next 'higher' level. From the perspective of initiation, the six-pointed star symbolizes the third transfiguration initiation when the three aspects of the personality (body, emotions and mind), have become fused with their corresponding soul triangle of will, love and intelligence. It is only after this initiation that one has become an initiate in the true sense of the word, for one has freed oneself from karma and from the wheel of death and birth. According to the Ancient Wisdom Jesus was a third degree initiate when he incarnated in Palestine. He took the fourth initiation at the crucifixion, and in a later incarnation as Apollonius of Tyana, (a spiritual mentor to a number of Roman emperors) he took his fifth 'Master' initiation.

It is quite impossible to interpret a birth chart without knowing (to whatever degree) the state of consciousness of the individual, group, nation or event one is dealing with. The very fact that millions of people, thousands of groups, humanity and the planet itself are undergoing major initiations at this time requires astrology to take this subject into serious consideration. The vast majority of intelligent (deep thinking) humanity are at present taking the first and/or second initiations. Two-thirds of humanity will take one or both of these initiations as we enter the New Era.

THE FIRST AND SECOND INITIATIONS

The first and second initiations are the initial movement from personality to soul consciousness. The changes inherent in this initiatory process led the Master DK (otherwise known as 'the Tibetan') to reveal the 'Ray' and 'transpersonal' planetary rulers of the signs (see *Esoteric Astrology* by Alice Bailey), for the true purpose of the soul can only be deciphered by using these rulers and Rays. This does not mean that if one does not understand the signs, planets and Rays one cannot decipher and fulfil one's higher purpose; it simply means that such an understanding greatly helps in clarifying this purpose and its unfoldment.

The first initiation is ruled by the planets Pluto and Vulcan (both 1st Ray 'power' planets) which is why this first step on the spiritual path entails a painful break from one's blood family, friends, past beliefs and often one's work patterns too. One might say that this initiation (and the second) allows one to better understand the Christ's statement that 'He who loves mother, father, brother or sister more than Me is not worthy of My Name.' This initiation blends the physical body and the higher will, both ruled by the 1st Ray, which is why healthy food, bodily exercise and the transformation of avaricious material habit patterns play such a vital part in it.

The collective movement towards individualization, ruled by the sign Leo, and health and personal wholeness, ruled by the sign Virgo, is evidence of the millions taking this initiation, for these signs rule this initiation. Individuals, groups and spiritual organizations taking this initiation tend to be separative in outlook (although they profess 'unity') and bodily focused, with a figurehead/guru at the head. Each regards their guru as a great Master (forgetting that professors are not required to teach primary school children), and other gurus as false or of lesser status. Rules and discipline are often imposed by the guru or by the particular system or school of thought. 'God' is talked about as 'within' but is not experienced as such, for 'God' is still being projected onto the outer teacher and/or teaching.

Many people involved with Eastern systems, such as yoga,

macrobiotics and Buddhism are integral to this initiation, for the break with these Piscean Age systems has yet been achieved. These systems are more connected with people's past lives than with the direct needs of their present life. This is not to relegate these systems but rather to put them into a right perspective. The quality of 'soul' love, which is related to group consciousness and to the service of the group and humanity, and the greater understanding of the laws of initiation, is not directly connected to the experiences of this initiation. This is the first stage of direct development of the higher will, physical body purification and the humiliation of the ego. By 'humiliation' is meant the giving up of the ego to some greater force, for in this initiation the ego submits itself to the will of the guru and school of thought (a fact worth pondering upon).

The second initiation is ruled by the planets Venus, Jupiter and Neptune (all 2nd Ray love–wisdom planets), which is why 'soul love' and contact with the inner teacher, the higher self, become the major qualitative characteristics of this initiation. Group consciousness and 'guidance' from within begin to replace the outer attachments of the first initiation. The emotional–desire body and the 'love' quality of the soul blend here, which is why the sexual and emotional dimensions of personal and group relationships play such a pivotal role in this initiation. It is in many senses the most difficult of the three initiations because the transformation of sex (sacral centre) and emotions (solar plexus centre) into creative action (throat centre) and love (heart centre) is, to say the least, not the easiest of exercises. The heart chakra (love) is the *alter ego* of the solar plexus (emotions) centre, and unconditional love is very different from the fear-ridden, possessive nature of the emotions. Scorpio rules this initiation.

Large-scale movements (ruled by Neptune) such as the Rajneesh and Rebirthing organizations are linked to this initiation, although these movements have still not broken free of the first initiation, which is why the guru often has to pass on for this to occur. Even when these guru figures do pass on, their disciples and followers still persist in worshipping (another Neptunian characteristic) their outer form, forgetting that the true teacher is not concerned with form but with the reality within the form. The Findhorn Foundation and other decentralized New Age communities and groups, plus the millions of other people under a different Ray (the 'New Age' movement is ruled by the 2nd and 7th Rays) undergoing this intensive transformation are descriptive of this initiation.

Astral (emotional) glamour and a good degree of illusion, self-delusion and escapism (Neptune's shadow) are well-known phenomena in many of these movements, especially those with a 6th

Ray influence. This Ray has a strong link to India, with its devotional or *bhakti* yoga, and to the USA with its strong 6th Ray personality. For example the physical body 'immortality' movement has its origin in both these counties. This movement claims that it is possible for ordinary people to achieve physical immortality. Little do these people realize that it takes four major initiations to achieve this aim. The aim of initiation is to attain union with the soul and thereby to become immortal because the soul is immortal. This entails a greater and greater detachment from physical body identity rather than an attachment to it. This form of self-delusion is typical 6th Ray (Neptune) escapism, but 6th Ray ego types become so glued to their illusions that it takes a great deal of 'fire' (the physical death of the guru; death is related to Pluto and the burning ground) to break such patterns. The 6th Ray (emotions) is the lower counterpart of the 2nd Ray (love), and 2nd Ray soul types often have a typical 6th Ray emotional 'shadow'. Attachment to outer gurus is a manifestation of emotion and not love.

Many partnerships and groups are undergoing the 2nd initiation and out of this turmoil and experimentation will gradually emerge the new soul-based individuals, partnerships, groups, communities and networks. The 1991 Gulf crisis is a planetary (not an individual) manifestation of this initiation because the Middle East, with Jerusalem as its centre, is the solar plexus centre of the planet. Emotional turmoil, which manifests as fear, insecurity, isolation, distrust, hate, revenge, bitterness, jealousy and war must be transformed into love, forgiveness, unity-in-diversity, understanding and co-operation. Jews and Arabs must learn to live as brothers and sisters (in the real sense of the words) if they wish to join the New World Order. These two cultures are mirrors to one another for they represent two sides of the same coin. They cannot attain wholeness unless they meet on equal terms and live together in peace.

In a paradoxical sense it is modern-day weapons (like the Scud missile and chemical and biological agents) that are forcing this transformation, for no longer is any nation safe from the nightmare of such weapons. Israel must join the world community and realize that 'she is part of the whole' and the whole is not part of her. The Jewish priesthood were 'chosen' as custodians of the ancient wisdom during the Arien Era (2000 BC to 0 AD) and the Ram's horn thus became their symbol. This custodianship was transferred to the Christian priesthood (Christ's disciples) when the Age of Pisces set in 2,000 years ago. By rejecting the Christ and His new teachings the Jewish race failed to recognize this change and rejected the planetary initiation into Pisces. This was catastrophic for their evolution and they have suffered terribly since that time. The law of karma takes no sides; cause and effect operate outside of human belief. 'That which goes against the tide of planetary evolution will suffer the consequences of such separation' and in this sense God and the planet are one. Israel is thus a vacuum nation within the planetary body. The Gulf War was the beginning of a new phase in this nation's evolution. According to the Master DK the Jewish race will be offered a second opportunity to take the Piscean initiation in the near future; this will come about through the reappearance of the Master Jesus to the Jews (in Israel). This time they will accept Him because His appearance will occur at their darkest moment, and their racial ego will have to submit to divine will if they wish to enter the New Era. I share this not in antagonism to the Jews (I was born into the Jewish race) but in compassion for their plight and the fulfilment of their greater planetary destiny.

THE THIRD INITIATION

The third initiation is ruled by Mars and the Moon plus Saturn, although Saturn, Lord of Karma and initiation, has overall ruler-ship of all three initiations. Mars provides the one-pointed, coura-geous, progressive and warrior-like 'will' to pioneer ahead, bring spirit into matter and achieve one's highest goals.. Mars is thus exalted in Capricorn, the sign ruling this initiation. The Moon, ruling Cancer, Capricorn's opposite sign, embodies the regressive powers of the past, and Mars and the Moon therefore enter into direct battle in this initiation. The higher and lower minds conflict and merge in this initiation, for the lower mind is the third aspect of the personality and the higher abstract mind is the third aspect of the soul. Fusion thus occurs on the mental planes and the mind comes under the control of the individual.

The symbol of this initiation is the goat of Capricorn, the human personality with its mental focus, climbing the mountain of achievement. On reaching the top the goat is transfigured into the unicorn, the symbol of the soul (see the section on 'Venus and Twin Partnerships', page 28, for more on the unicorn and its symbology). At the third initiation all one's past karma (symbolized by the Moon) is transmuted and integrated, for the human goat has now become the unicorn soul. Union is achieved and future physical incarnations are no longer necessary. This does not mean that one does not incarnate again physically, for the majority of souls do incarnate to serve in Aquarius and later in Pisces. What it does mean is that there is no more Earthbound karma to work out. The 'fused' six-pointed star in the symbol (see 'Triangles' page 20). This is not to say that if one is born into Capricorn (Rising or sun) that one is taking this initiation. Third degree initiates are not self-conscious from a selfish perspective. The late Anwar Sadat, Vaclav Havel and Nelson Mandela might be considered such types; all three it might be noticed spent time in gaol (Saturn) and achieved freedom at a very high cost to themselves. All three became leaders of their nations and are respected worldwide. The lives of these three leaders shed a great deal of light on some of the experiences related to this initiation. Third degree initiates often work in the political field (Capricorn and Saturn rule politics and international relations) because this is where spirit enters matter at its deepest level. Capricorn is the natural Midheaven (MC) and the MC and the 10th house are related to authority, power, politics, economics and one's vocation in society. Such initiates often choose to be unconscious of their spiritual status because they can work more constructively without this awareness. They are embodiments of Christ consciousness and manifest this light, love and power in their vocational activities. Capricorn has no love Rays working through it (see Chapter 7) and needs to integrate the energies of its opposite and complementary sign Cancer in order to receive these Rays (6th and 4th).

The shadow of this initiation is the lower rational mind (the lower side of Saturn) and its characteristics of pride, arrogance, coldness, insensitivity, negative manipulation and separative competitive thinking. Capricorn rules the Jewish race, and Israel embodies this principle for humanity. The Jews have a 1st Ray soul (thus their pioneering activity) and a 3rd Ray personality (thus their business sense). From a positive perspective this race has also produced some of the world's greatest pioneers and leaders (Ray 1 and Saturn). This is the dual face of Saturn. The stern, authoritarian and ambitious father (Saturn) and the emotionally attached mother (Cancer and the Moon) are archetypes of the shadow of the Jewish race, whereas the one-pointed, dedicated, service-orientated and dynamic male initiator/leader and the all-loving, wise and freedom-giving female represent the 'light' of Capricorn and the Jewish race. It could well be said that when the Jews free themselves from their deadening past and unfold their true inclusive light, love and purpose (which serves the race of humanity and not the Jewish race itself) the time will be ripe for the emergence of a new human race. This provides some hidden clues to the crisis in the Middle East.

When Jesus stated that 'the goats shall be separated from the sheep' he was referring to the initiation process, for the goat is the symbol of Capricorn and the sheep is the symbol of Cancer. Goats symbolize individuals who climb their own mountain and leave behind the chains of the past; sheep symbolize those people who are trapped in the past and in the emotional currents of mass consciousness and past belief systems. This separation is now taking place. Exoterically, Mars rules Aries, the sign which holds the seeds of the future; it also rules Scorpio, the sign in which we go to war with the past; it is exalted in Capricorn, the sign in which we ascend to the highest peaks of the mountain of spiritual achievement. Mars is not a malefic planet but it is the planet of conflict, battle and warriorhood. This is the opposite viewpoint to that of traditional astrology, in which Mars is seen as masculine and malefic and the Moon is seen as feminine and benefic. Both planets are non-sacred and rule the personality, the Moon ruling the physical body and instinctive attachments to the past and Mars ruling the emotional body and the fiery dynamic idealism (6th Ray) that leads us to aspire towards self-transformation and self-actualization. The shadow of Mars is the tendency to act in an aggressive and separative manner. The further one ascends up the mountain the more different the viewpoint (so to speak) from which we see the planets.

Although the first, second and third initiations are focused through the physical, emotional and lower mental bodies, all three bodies are naturally interconnected and all play a part in each initiation. The transformative and transmutative processes of the initiations create a wide diversity of experiences, many irrational and unnatural to normal living. The spiritual path (the path of life) cannot be contained in books or in the limited mind. One-pointedness and great flexibility need to work hand in hand. Initiation requires a purging and pushing to the surface of deep-seated anger, frustration, fears, pain, desires, illusions and so on, plus a great intake and unfoldment of light, love, purpose, understanding, sensitivity, joy, illumination, peace, freedom and expanded creativity. Objective experiences will mirror these inner changes and life becomes the playground or stage upon which these purposeful experiences are played out. Everything has hidden purpose and pain and joy and all the dualities dance together as they seek a higher harmony, beauty and unity.

Study of the ancient wisdom teachings (for the New Age), dynamic meditation, intuition and matured experience rather than logic and simplified spiritual concepts enable one to comprehend the above. The higher self is always in the background, moving and guiding its human personality towards greater light, love, harmony, purpose and service. Initiation in the New Age is interconnected with daily living and is not some separative and glamorous activity. The objective guru–disciple relationship needs to be replaced by the subjective soul–disciple relationship. Spirituality is the magic of life itself and is not related to a formal religion or organization. One gradually learns that life itself is the Master teacher and initiator, for the soul and the Christ weave their magic through every facet of life. Washing dishes, making one's bed, cooking food and serving humanity go hand in hand. Traditional and humanistic astrology and psychology do not have the means to understand initiation and this is why they have failed to accomplish their greater tasks.

The essential keynote of initiation is service, for service implies a greater and greater degree of self-forgetfulness. This should not be an ignorant and unintelligent self-forgetfulness, for it needs to be guided by an intelligent and loving approach to life as a whole. One's personal needs have to be met if one is to serve some greater inclusive goal. Self-forgetfulness does not imply a rejection of self-awareness and transformation but rather an ongoing self-transformative process as one serves the greater whole.

The magical battleground of initiation is wonderfully portrayed in two films. The first is *Perseus and the Clash of the Titans*. The second, of which there is also a book, is *The Dark Crystal* (see Bibliography). The film depicts a battle between two opposing forces, the Skeksis (or 'baddies') and the urRu (or 'goodies'). Jen, a 'Gelfing', symbolizing the individual hero/heroine, has to undertake a mystical journey to restore a crystal to its rightful place in the Dark Crystal in the castle of the Skeksis. The film comes to a climatic end when Jen restores his crystal and this restoration results in the fusion of the Skeksis and urRu. Out of this fusion emerges a third force, a being of light, who is the synthesis of both these forces. Jen the 'hero' has to undertake the journey into the underworld (the dark castle in this case) with his twin partner Kira, whose co-operation he cannot do without. Such mythological stories, whether ancient or modern, are the mainstay of esoteric tradition, and reveal the hidden significance of evolution and initiation.

THE FOURTH AND FIFTH INITIATIONS

The fourth initiation is ruled by Pisces, the sign of death and rebirth, for Pisces is the final sign of the zodiac. This is related to the crucifixion experience of Christianity and the Great Renunciation of Buddhism. Here the personality as a whole is given up to the soul, and one gains control over all nature. After this comes the fifth Masters' initiation. There are Masters and there are Masters; the majority of so-called Masters (as claimed by themselves and/or their followers) are not Masters but false and deluded prophets or disciples and initiates of a certain degree. No first or second degree disciple can recognize who is or is not a Master. It is far better for people to transfer their 'Master' projections onto the Christ Himself, for He is the Master of all (Earth) Masters, and it is His presence and not his physical form which is His reality. From a personal perspective the higher self is the true inner Master, and this self, together with the Christ (Lord Maitreya to the Buddhists, the Iman Mahdi to the Muslims, the Messiah to the Jews), our greater planetary Master, forms the mainstay of our relationship with divinity. In the New Era the reliance upon outer Masters/gurus must go and be replaced by an integrated and communicative relationship with the inner Master, one's true higher Christ self.

There is a Master at the head of each of the seven Rays, and other Masters who work with one or other of these Rays. For example Master Jesus is the head of the 6th Ray of devotional idealism and religion, Master Morya is the head of the 1st Ray of power and politics, Master Hilarion (an incarnation of St Paul) heads the 5th Ray of knowledge and science, and Master Koot Humi (an incarnation of St Francis) heads the 2nd Ray of love and education. Master Racoczi, a Hungarian Master better known as St Germain, heads both the 3rd and 7th Rays.

Each of these Rays forms an Ashram or Light Centre on the inner planes of consciousness. Every angel, soul and human being is ruled by certain Rays and falls under their influences (see Chapters 4 and 5). The New Age will see a number of these ashrams manifesting on the physical plane. Findhorn (7th Ray) is the first of these Light Centres to do so. After the Master's initiation comes the sixth 'Chohan' initiation. Master Morya and Koot Humi are Chohans. The final initiation is the seventh, in which one becomes a 'Lord'. Lord Christ and Lord Buddha are seventh degree initiates. After the fifth initiation one has the choice of continuing to serve the Earth (in Buddhist terms taking the Bodhisattva vow) or moving on to serve some other planetary and solar system.

INTO THE GREATER WHOLE

The seventh initiation, the final planetary and solar initiation, is the first step into the cosmos, because the seventh planetary initiation is but the first cosmic initiation. Sanat Kumara, the Lord of the Earth, has taken the third cosmic initiation. This is why the Earth is referred to as a non-sacred planet, for a sacred planetary Logos (like the Venusian Logos) has taken the fifth 'Master' cosmic initiation. There are Logoi who control whole solar systems and whole galaxies; just try to envision a being whose aura encompasses an entire galaxy. It is the destiny of every human being to become a Logoi of some great system, and the Earth is one of the training grounds for this destiny. Life is eternal and infinite and it is this very infinity that makes it so exquisite and beautiful. It is better to feel the beauty than to fear the reality. When one sees the direct inter-relationship between evolution and initiation, how can one sepa-rate astrology and psychology from these realities? The problem of course is finding a practical way to communicate this complex sub-ject, and the new astrologers and psychologists have the responsi-bility to do just this.

INITIATION IN THE NEW ERA

One important factor should be understood in relationship to initiation in the modern era. Initiation in the past was focused around various forms of ritualistic ceremony, conducted between a priest or priestess, or guru, and their disciple. It usually took place in a temple, ashram or monastic situation. It was a secret ritual, and not connected to the daily process of living. 'Initiation' in many people's minds therefore takes on a secretive, mystical and often glamorous air, in which magical rituals, secret formulae and a priesthood are involved. The vast majority of books on 'Initiation' (whether in Atlantis, Egypt, Tibet, India or wherever) tend to be concerned with this subject in past eras and not with initiation in the New Era.

In the Aquarian Age initiation is fundamentally a subjective and not an objective process. Consciousness and not form takes prece-dence, and the relationship between the personality and the soul, and their subjective step-by-step fusion, is the decisive factor in the initiation process. It is the inner teacher, the higher self, and the Christ Himself as the World Teacher, who guide and direct these initiations, and not some outer guru or figurehead. Life itself becomes the teacher, and it is the experiences of life itself which form an integral aspect of initiation. Each new initiation opens the doorway into greater life, opportunity, love, wisdom, knowledge, power and, most important of all, service. Service, and for that matter 'selfless service' is the key to true freedom, and initiation, in the end result, is nothing other than the acceleration of real free-dom. Integral to initiation in the New Era are spiritual self-reliance, attention to the will of one's soul, intensified self-transformation integrated with greater and greater self-forgetfulness and active service in the world.

Initiation is not some secret ceremony open to the chosen few, but a doorway to freedom open to humanity at large. Anyone who chooses to serve humanity and to work at transforming the lower self is automatically initiated into a more intelligent, loving, wise and purposeful life. This in turn opens the door into greater service, and the work of service can find its path in politics (see Gorbachev, Mandela, Havel and many others), economics, ecology, science, the media, religion, health, psychology, astrology, natural birth, dance, sport, parenthood, education and whatever. God enters one's daily living process and all life becomes sanctified. In the New Era, spirituality is a way of life and is not disconnected from daily living. The various initiates and Masters who will appear towards the end of this century (and into the next) will appear as politicians, financiers, artists, musicians, educators and not simply as conventionally spiritual figures. Mikhail Gorbachev has wisely stated that 'life is the teacher', and Nelson Mandela and Vaclav Havel have shown that years of imprisonment cannot hold back the spirit of love, wisdom and purpose.

The planet itself is approaching a major initiation, for it has a birthday once every 2,100 years, the cycle it takes the Sun to move through one of the constellations. The Earth's Aquarian birthday is on the horizon, but its initiation entails far more than this alone. Humanity, the mediating kingdom between matter and spirit, is taking its own major initiation as it moves from intellect to intuition, and from human to spiritual government. The Christ, as head of our planet's spiritual hierarchy, accompanied by a number of His major disciples, the Masters of the Wisdom, 144,000 third degree initiates, and many millions of first and second degree disciples, will inaugurate this birthday celebration. This does not mean that all will be well or that conflict will disappear. What it does mean is that meaning and purpose are being restored to humanity, and with the seed of meaning comes love, creative intelligence, personal responsibility and the celebration of life. In this sense all is well, for when pain, suffering and all the 'ills' of humanity can be seen in their true light, then, and only then, can healing begin. Transpersonal astrology has a vital and rightful part to play in this great turning-point in human affairs.

CHAPTER FOUR

The Seven Psycho-spiritual Rays

The Seven Rays are of major significance in transpersonal astrology because they underlie the entire functioning of the universe 'in which we live and move and have our being'. The Rays are cosmic in original and, as such, have an overall influence on every aspect of life throughout our cosmic, solar and planetary system. The Rays originate in the Great Bear constellation. The seven stars of this constellation are the visible bodies of these seven great Ray Lives, archangels (the seven 'Candles before the Throne') or cosmic 'Lords', 'Lord' being the title given to any cosmic initiate. These Lives transmit their energies into and through their cosmic systems, including our solar system and the six other solar systems which make up our septenary constellation.

THE 2ND RAY AND OUR SOLAR SYSTEM

The Lord of the 2nd Ray is qualified by love–intuition or Christ consciousness at it is known in the West. This Ray transmits its energies into our solar system via the twelve zodiacal constellations. The 2nd Ray subdivides into its other six sub-Rays as it enters our solar system. The rest of the six major Rays transmit themselves into the other six solar systems. The 2nd Ray and its six sub-Rays each work through three zodiacal constellations, thereby creating seven Ray triangles (see Ray Triangles, page 71).

CONSTELLATION TRIANGLES

The 1st sub-Ray of power/will works through Aries, Leo and Capricorn. The lives of these constellations therefore receive, embody, transform and distribute the energy of spiritual power, will or purpose. The colour of this Ray is flame red. The 2nd major

Ray works through Virgo, Gemini and Pisces, and these constellations work with the energies of love–wisdom/intuition. The colour is deep royal blue to midnight blue. The 3rd Ray works through Cancer, Libra and Capricorn, and these three zodiacal archetypes work with the energies of the higher abstract mind or creative/ active intelligence, the causal energy of the Earth itself, for Earth is a 3rd Ray planet. The colour is nature green.

The 4th Ray works through Taurus, Scorpio and Sagittarius, and these three constellations work with the energy of 'harmony and beauty – through conflict', the Ray which mediates and links the higher and lower mental worlds. The 4th Ray also rules human evolution and initiation, for it is the work of humanity to 'bridge the gap' between spirit and matter. The colour is deep yellow. The 5th Ray works through Leo, Sagittarius and Aquarius, and these three Lives (the constellations are also great Cosmic Lords) work with the energy of concrete knowledge of the lower logical mind. The colour is deep orange. The 6th Ray works through Virgo, Sagittarius and Pisces, and these constellations receive, embody and transmit the energies of devotion and idealism, which are related to the astral or emotional/sentient planes. The colours are rose-red, pink and sky-blue. Finally the Lord of the 7th Ray works through Aries, Cancer and Capricorn, and these constellations bring spirit (1st Ray) into direct fused relationship with matter, thereby producing the forms necessary to manifest 'the will of God'. The colour is violet. The Rays reveal the psycho-spiritual purpose and qualities lying behind the constellations or signs, the planets and all creative life in our solar system.

The Rays are living dynamic beings (see Vera Alder's description of the Rays, page 59). These beings relay their energies from the Great Bear, Sirius and the Pleiades, the major cosmic constellation triangle, into the twelve solar constellations, who are in turn twelve great cosmic lives. If the Logos of our planet is a third degree cosmic initiate whose will and consciousness encompass our entire planetary system, what initiatory status has the Logos of a constellation achieved? The Lord of each constellation receives, embodies, transforms or steps down and finally transmits this Ray energy into the solar system. This threefold movement of energy is of major significance, for it occurs throughout all cosmic, solar, planetary, human and atomic life. All systems, including the human system, receive particular types of Ray, constellation/sign and planetary energies. These energies have to be transformed to suit the system they are entering into. These transformed energies have to be embodied (to whatever relative degree) and finally distributed and transmitted to whatever system the particular being is part of and has responsibility towards. Communication is thus vertically and horizontally based.

THE RAYS, THE SUN AND OUR SOLAR LOGOS

The sun is the heart chakra of our solar system. Our solar system is founded on the 2nd Ray system, the Ray of love and unity, which is why our sky is blue. As the Sun moves through the energy field of the zodiacal belt in its annual cycle, it receives, embodies, steps down and transmits the Ray(s) of each constellation into its solar system. It must be emphasized that the Sun is a living dynamic entity – It is *alive*. It is not only alive from the point of view of physical vitality in that its energy 'enlivens' the entire solar system, including of course human life-forms, but it is also 'alive' as a centre of consciousness (Soul) and life (Monad). It is the heart centre of the solar Logos, the Lord of our solar system. The new astrology demands that we recognize things as they truly are and not as they seem to be. In recognizing who we truly are as human beings, we likewise have to recognize the truth of that greater life 'of which we are but a minute part'. 'As above so below' – and vice versa.

Scientists know that the true life of the Sun exists at its core and not its periphery (corona). Nuclear fusion, or the fusion of atoms, occurs at the core of the Sun. This fusion is the true life (Monad) of the Sun, and this life in turn produces the consciousness (soul) of the Sun which exists and moves in the Sun's heart. This finally produces the objective heat and light (personality) of the Sun's corona. The life of the Sun is transmitted via the core into and through its heart and finally through its body (the corona) into its entire solar system, be it a planet, a human, an atom or a cell. This triune nature of the Sun of course applies to all creation, for the Monad is life, the soul is consciousness and the personality is form.

Pluto, the planet furthest from the Sun, is 4,600 million miles (at its maximum) distance from the Sun. This equals nearly 40 astronomical units, one astronomical unit being the mean distance of the Earth from the Sun – that is 93 million miles. The Sun's corona or outer auric body transmits its energy this distance and more, for Pluto is not the periphery of the solar system. Astronomers say that light, which travels at 186,000 miles per second, takes eleven hours to move from one end of the solar system to the other, and this claim will probably be extended as more discoveries are made. This tells us a little about the 'consciousness' of the solar Logos, a being whose living aura extends throughout its system. To regard this being as a mere physical gaseous star is, to say the least, an insult to life itself. Scientists, astronomers, priests and all 'logically' minded humans should give this serious thought, for it is the Sun who is alive and we humans who are 'the living dead'.

The Lord of the 2nd Ray has its centre in the Sun, just as the Lords of the other six Rays have their centres in the stars of the other six solar systems. The Rays are always transmitted via the constellations to the Sun, for the sun is the centre of the solar system. When the Ray(s) of any particular constellation enter the Sun they automatically synthesize with the Sun's 2nd Ray. These Rays and the 2nd Ray are then transmitted into the planets ruling the constellation in question. In the case of Aquarius, Jupiter (2nd Ray) and Uranus (7th Ray) are the inner and outer rulers. We thus have the 5th Ray (knowledge/science), the 2nd Ray twice (love and intuition), and the 7th Ray (synthesis, organization). We have the brow as the overall ruling chakra (5th Ray), heart (2nd Ray), and sacral (7th Ray) centres activated. Orange, midnight blue and violet are the associated colours. The importance of this information will become evident when we deal with the annual astrological cycle later in the book, for an understanding of the particular energies of each constellation or sign enables one to attune to and manifest these energies accordingly. This is the secret of the future use of astrological science.

THE RAYS AND THE EARTH

The Rays of the constellation/sign, the Sun and the ruling planets finally are transmitted into the energy field of the planetary Logos of the Earth (see Aquarian example and planetary triangle). The three major Chakras of our planet are called Shambhala (crown centre), the spiritual hierarchy or 'inner' government (heart centre) and the soul kingdom of humanity (brow centre). Humanity itself is the 4th 'mediating and manifesting' kingdom, the throat centre. The Rays of the Earth are the 1st (Monad), the 2nd (soul) and the 3rd (personality). Because the Earth is a non-sacred 'personality-focused' planet the 3rd Ray of 'active intelligence' plays a major role in its evolutionary life. This is once again a sub-Ray of the 2nd major Ray, for the solar Ray has overall rulership of all its planetary systems. Love–intuition–wisdom, the energies of the Christ and active intelligence or 'light', the essential energy of the human personality are thus the two major influences on human and planetary evolution.

On entering Shambhala these energies are stepped-down and transmitted to the Hierarchy, who in turn transform and transmit them to the soul kingdom of humanity. The higher self of humanity finally transmits these energies to humanity itself, that is to its lower self or personality. Humanity itself, every continent, nation, race, culture, town, city, group and individual has a soul or 'angelic self'. This soul acts as the personal Godhead or 'mediator' between the Hierarchy and the human personality. This is why the Master DK (*Arcane Teachings*) states that 'for all intents and purposes the will of the Higher Self/Soul is the will of God'. This also provides the key to why the Rising sign, the symbolical soul of the chart, is connected directly to the higher purpose of the individual, group, city or nation. It is the soul, angelic presence or 'Holy Ghost' that embodies the vision, purpose and path of the Godhead within its consciousness. This is also why the Angelic Hierarchy compose the archetypes of all creation, for they are the perfect angelic blueprints lying behind all form. The higher self is the perfect(ed) angelic self of the human personality; the Christ or Messiah is the perfected angelic self of humanity itself.

The initiates and disciples (in their various ranks) of humanity are the first to receive or pick-up these energies. The New Group of World Servers, the Network of Light and Goodwill or the Invisible Church of Christ are the names given to this large grouping of human beings. They are to be found in every country and comprise a living decentralized network of world servers.

This network communicates or gives out these energies to a larger group of humanity called 'men and women of goodwill'. These are people who have goodwill at heart but are not consciously attuned to these energies. They work in every sphere of human activity and, in their own unique fashion, distribute these energies to the system of which they are part.

THE RAYS AND HUMANITY

Humanity, the mediator between the Gods and the material world, has the final responsibility to transmit and distribute the Ray energies (consciously and/or unconsciously, and there are many degrees of consciousness) into the four lower kingdoms, namely the human, animal, vegetable and mineral kingdoms. Any nations, cities, towns, groups or individuals whose ruling Rays are synchronized to the incoming Rays of the sign or planet(s) will be directly affected by these incoming energies. For example the incoming Rays of Aquarius and its ruling planets are directly affecting all Aquarians (Rising or Sun) and Aquarian groupings, nations and activities. The USSR and the USA with their Aquarius Rising and 7th and 2nd Ray souls will be directly influenced over every

Aquarian cycle (19 January to 20 February) and both these countries plus Great Britain (with its Ray 2 soul) will play a major role in manifesting the energies of the New Era.

If an individual, group or nation has a 3rd Ray soul or personality all 3rd Ray sign/planet cycles will affect them. In other words the monthly cycles of Cancer, Libra and Capricorn, and Sagittarius, ruled by the Earth, a 3rd Ray planet, will influence 3rd Ray types. The combination of the birth chart with its ruling signs, Rays and planets and the living experience of the annual astrological cycle work together in the implementation of this new science and art of living.

During the Aquarian cycle humanity is required to receive, embody, use and distribute the Rays of Aquarius (5th), the Sun and Jupiter (2nd), Uranus (7th), and of course the Earth (3rd), plus the Rays of Leo (1st and 5th), with its ruler the Sun (2nd), for Leo is opposite and complementary to Aquarius. We can clearly see why the 2nd Ray of love–wisdom, the Ray of the spiritual hierarchy, and the Christ, who is the Lord of this Ray, and the Ray of the 5th kingdom of souls, is playing and will play such a profound role in the new era now descending upon humanity. In the same way the Rays of the Rising sign and its transpersonal planetary ruler (see next chapter) and the Rays of the Sun sign and its personal planetary ruler play a major role in the life of the individual, group, nation and so on.

The soul of humanity is ruled by the 2nd Ray and Gemini, and its personality by the 4th Ray. Its mind is ruled by the 5th, its emotional body by the 6th and its etheric–physical body by the 3rd, although the 7th Ray is beginning to assume rulership of this body in large numbers of people, especially the younger generations. Domesticated animals, especially the horse, dog and cat, through their relationship with humans are attaining the germ of mind, but the door from animal into human incarnation has been closed and will not be opened for a long period of time. The 6th Ray has rulership over the animal and vegetable kingdoms and the 7th Ray governs the mineral kingdom. The 5th Ray has rulership over the 'thinkers', whereas the 2nd Ray governs the 'intuitives'. The mineral, vegetable and animal kingdoms have 'group' souls, whereas human incarnation (5th Ray) brings in the 'I Am' consciousness and thus an individual soul. It is the purpose of humanity to serve and raise up the lower kingdoms, including of course its own lower self.

THE RAYS AND THE PLANETS

The 2nd Ray and its six sub-Rays are embodied and distributed by the Sun into its seven major or sacred planets and its four minor or non-sacred planets. The Sun itself is a mediator between sacred and non-sacred planets, for in the birth chart it represents the personality in its overall or integrated dimension, and the personality is also the first aspect of the soul (Ray 3). In other words the seven sacred planets represent the seven aspects or qualities of the soul, and the four non-sacred planets represent the four bodies (physical, etheric, emotional and lower mental) and characteristics of the personality, with the Sun being the integrating personality. This is why the Sun sign in the birth chart represents the here-and-now integrating principle between the soul and the future (Rising sign) and the personality and the past (the Moon).

Vera Alder's description of this Ray transmission from the Sun to its planets (see page 53) gives a beautiful understanding of how these living dynamic Ray Lives manifest themselves through the solar system. In other words the solar Logos and its heart centre, the Sun, does not simply distribute heat, light and what are loosely termed solar rays, but it is the central solar transmission centre of the 2nd Ray and its six Sub-Rays.

Each Ray focuses itself through one of the seven major planets and one of the four minor planets. These Rays play an overall influence in that planet's entire life system. Each planet is a living dynamic being, a god in the true sense of the word. The ancients knew this and referred to the planets as gods. If human beings are 'gods in the making' then the planets are, in their own right, 'gods already made'.

What differentiates a sacred and a non-sacred planet? I dealt with this subject in the last chapter, explaining how a sacred planet is one in which its Logos or Lord has taken five cosmic initiations and is therefore a cosmic Master, and a non-sacred planet is one in which its Logos has taken three cosmic initiations and is therefore a cosmic initiate. The Earth's Logos, Sanat Kumara (depicted by William Blake in his painting *The Ancient of Days*), has taken nine initiations for he has evolved through both planetary evolution (the first four initiations) and solar evolution (second three initiations) and has taken three cosmic initiations, namely the 7th, 8th and 9th. He therefore has responsibility for an entire planetary system. Sanat Kumara and those great beings who reside with him in Shambhala are in constant contact with the many systems and Logi that comprise our solar system. The brotherhood of the solar system has existed since the beginning of time and beyond, but one cannot participate consciously in this system until one has reached a certain degree of consciousness. The exploration of space is a subjective process and no amount of material exploration will succeed in finding life on other planets until man's consciousness has expanded accordingly.

A number of evolved human beings have had contact with Sanat Kumara (obviously including William Blake), although it is only after the third initiation that one is allowed true access to Shambhalic energy. Shambhalic energy *is* nevertheless 'destructive' to form, for the will of God (the 1st Ray) often shatters forms in order that higher consciousness may evolve through more appropriate and restructured forms. People ruled by the 1st Ray are not very popular, and this applies even more so to 1st Ray types in spiritual groups, for they carry the sword of will and will destroys that which is crystallized. Love is the central energy of our solar system but will is the central energy of our cosmos. The 3rd initiation gives one initial access to divine will; before this time one has access to intelligence and love.

The non-sacred planets only affect the life of the personality, whereas the sacred planets are related to the life of the soul and its interrelationship to and with the personality.

The 1st Ray works through Vulcan, the planet of one-pointed purpose which forges and shapes the shield of matter through the fire of the will; the 2nd Ray works through Jupiter, the planet of expansion, related to Zeus or the Christ, the Lord of love and wisdom; the 3rd Ray works through Saturn, the planet of concentration and restriction which focuses the mind, blueprints the Plan and tests ones resolve; the 4th Ray works through Mercury, the 'Messenger of the Gods' and the grand mediator and communicator; the 5th Ray works through Venus, planet of beauty, intelligent love, pure reason and all forms of partnership; the 6th Ray works through Neptune, planet of unity, unconditional love, spiritual idealism and devotion to a higher abstract cause and the 7th Ray functions through Uranus, the planet which fuses spirit and matter through magical ritual, ceremony and organization. These are the seven sacred planets and the seven major chakras of our solar system.

The 1st Ray of destruction functions through Pluto, the planet of Kundalini fire and the destroyer and regenerator of forms; the 3rd Ray functions through the Earth, Saturn's lower counterpart, the planet of testing and trial and objective action; the 4th Ray works through the Moon, for this satellite of the Earth acts as a reminder of that which is dead and gone and is the 'mediating veil' for the energies of the Sun as they enter the Earth; the 6th Ray functions through Mars, planet of war, battle and warriorhood, emotional idealism, sexuality and one-pointed action; the 2nd Ray functions through the Sun, linking and integrating the above four Rays and planets. These are the non-sacred planets.

THE RAYS AND THE HOUSES

Mars and the 1st and 8th houses, the Moon and 4th and 6th houses (the Moon is the inner ruler of Virgo), Pluto and the 8th and 12th houses, the Earth and the 9th house (the Earth is the inner ruler of Sagittarius), and the Sun and the 5th house (as the 'integrator') are related to the lower self and its transformation and integration. It will be noticed that all three water houses are included here, for the astral or emotional plane is the major plane of illusion, glamour, fear, envy and attachment, and the majority of humanity's problems are focused on this plane. Scorpio is the only sign ruled by two non-sacred planets, and this is why it is the central 'nine-headed hydra' battleground of personality transformation and transmutation, and the regeneration of the reorientation of the personality.

Mercury and the 1st, 3rd and 6th houses, Vulcan and the 2nd, Venus and the 2nd, 3rd and 7th, Neptune and the 4th and 12th, the heart of the Sun and the 5th, Uranus and the 7th and 11th, Jupiter and the 9th, 11th and 12th and Saturn and the 10th are related to the sacred planets and their influence. When the planet is the transpersonal ruler it rules the 'qualitative' influence of the soul and when it is the personal ruler it influences the manifestation of soul energy through the personality.

When a non-sacred planet rules the soul of a sign (Virgo, Sagittarius, Pisces) it indicates that the transformation and transmutation of the personality is directly related to the soul purpose of that sign. The Moon, veiling Vulcan, ruling Virgo, Pluto and Mars ruling Scorpio, the Earth ruling Sagittarius and Pluto ruling Pisces are the four examples here. This relationship of the ruling planets to their signs is essential to the new astrology.

THE PLANETS AND THE RAYS AND THEIR FUNCTIONING

Vulcan (which lies within a 3 degree orb of Mercury) and Pluto work with the 1st Ray. Vulcan is the most powerful planet in our solar system, and this is exactly why it has yet to be discovered. The Logos of a planet only reveals its body when the time is right. The discoveries of Uranus in 1781 advented the Industrial Revolution and the French and American revolutions; Neptune was discovered in 1846 and advented anaesthetics, hypnotism, spiritualism and a renewed idealism; Pluto was discovered in 1930 and with it came atomic power, economic depression, the mafia and the birth of Western psychology.

Vulcan will be discovered when humanity is ready to use power for the good of the whole and atomic fusion (safe unlimited energy) will probably be discovered around this time too. Whereas Vulcan is associated with 'space power' or the power at the core of the Sun, Pluto is associated with 'earth power' or the power at the core of the Earth. One is light and the other is darkness; Vulcan is the Lord of the Overworld and Pluto the Lord of the Underworld. Both are required to 'redeem the world', for it is the interplay and synthesis of spirit and matter that produces consciousness. Vera Alder witnessed this when she saw how the Rays from the core of the Sun and the core of the Earth met, fused and produced new life. From a human point of view we witness this when the male sperm fuses with the female eggs and produces a new life-form. Vulcan rules the soul of Taurus and Virgo; It has no outer rulerships. Pluto rules the soul of Scorpio and Pisces and also has a sub-influence in Aries.

The 2nd Ray works through Jupiter and the Sun. Jupiter rules the soul of Aquarius and the personalities of Sagittarius and Pisces; the Sun rules both the soul and personality of Leo. Love, unity, service, intuitive knowledge and wisdom and the process of developing and expanding consciousness are 2nd Ray attributes. These two planets therefore focus the quality of love–intuition into our solar system. The Sun is more concerned with self-awareness, individual identity and creative expression in relationship to and with the larger whole, whereas Jupiter is concerned with the expansion of this awareness into the larger whole – that is into group, social, national, international and planetary consciousness. Jupiter is the largest planet in our solar system – it is concerned with the larger things in life and with those higher feelings and thoughts that allow one to penetrate into the greater spiritual whole. This is what we normally term philosophy, but it is not the dry, dead, and copied philosophy of the university professor and student, but the dynamic, living philosophy of the individualized mind perceiving, understanding and manifesting the greater laws and life of the soul.

The 3rd Ray Lord works through the planets Saturn and the Earth. Both planets are therefore related to the green Ray; from space Saturn and the Earth have a green hue. These two planets are karmically connected through the 3rd Ray, Saturn being the soul and the Earth being the personality of this Ray. Both planets are related to the Luciferic principle, for Lucifer is both 'Light Bearer and Fallen Angel' simultaneously and both planets put humanity through test and trial. Humanity (3rd Ray) had to fall to Earth in its capacity as a collective group of 'Light Bearers' in order to redeem the Earth and learn the lessons of Earthly existence. Saturn is the border zone between the personality and the soul and is referred to esoterically as 'the dweller on the threshold', for no one passes into the world of the soul until they have passed the tests and trials of Saturn. The Earth (position) is where these tests have to be experienced.

The Earth, being a non-sacred planet, takes on the objective material focus of the 3rd Ray. Her placement indicates where we have to materialize our solar potential, for the Earth is placed opposite the Sun in the chart. The Sun may be the light of our heroic nature, but the hero has to enter the world of matter to purify, transform and raise it up to the light. As one group soul, humanity has incarnated into the Earth to fulfil this individual and collective work. The placement of the Earth indicates where one's energy is most gross, and the Earth and Pluto are therefore closely connected, although their 3rd (action) and 1st Ray (will) energies determine their difference.

The Lord of the 4th Ray works through Mercury and the Moon. This is the mediating and linking Ray, which is why Mercury is referred to as 'the Messenger of the Gods'. This yellow Ray acts as a link between all the dualities – between spirit and matter, the three higher and three lower kingdoms, the soul and the personality and the higher and lower minds. Mercury is not only related to the rational mind, brain and central nervous system (the system of material inter-communication), but to the higher abstract mind and the higher intuitive mind. It acts as the inter-communicator or 'time traveller' between all these mental realms. The mind (Mercury) can travel wherever it wishes; it can think on many levels and it can connect and link all these levels right through to etheric-physical expression. This is why Mercury rules Aries transpersonally and Gemini and Virgo traditionally, for it works with the higher mind(s) in Aries and lower mind, brain and body in the case of Gemini and Virgo. Mercury's new exaltation is in Aquarius because here it can work with the highest intuitive thought and corresponding communicative activity.

The Moon is a dead planet, for its Logos left its body during the Lemurian Era. The Earth is alive, the Moon is dead. The moons of planets symbolize their past lives, for planets also have past existences. During the Lemurian Era the inhabitants of the Moon were transferred to the Earth. Present-day lunar-type peoples such as the Chinese, Japanese and Koreans (and the 'Moony' sect) are connected to this past Moon civilization and embody lunar characteristics, namely 'look-alike' physical features and powerful emotional reactions and attachments to the past. The masses are also ruled by the Moon because they are trapped in the past and its traditional belief systems. The past is only transformed and harmonized through the conflicting nature of the 4th Ray.

Vera Alder in her book *From the Mundane to the Magnificent* (Rider Books) describes an 'out-of-body' experience in which she saw the Moon in the following way:

> Far away on our left hung the Moon, looking rather rigid and cold. It did not seem to palpitate with life like the Earth did, nor could I discern any etheric web around it. Like a great ball of roughened glass with a mirror surface it threw back the rays of the Sun with blinding brilliance.

If there is no etheric web there is no life, and this confirms the deadness of the Moon. Women astrologers and women in general might well get upset at this definition of the Moon, but Vera Alder's description simply confirms what has been stated in the esoteric teachings. It is the Earth and not the Moon that represents the true feminine mother principle.

The Lord of the 5th Ray works through the planet Venus. Although Venus in traditional and humanistic astrology is related to the attractive principle, to the feeling nature, to partnerships and marriage and to values, beauty and art, there is a deeper and more profound meaning to this planet. The true keynote and quality of Venus is 'intelligent love', for balance, harmony and beauty emerge out of the integration of mind and heart. Venus is the *alter ego* or twin soul of the Earth (see Chapter 3 for more on this subject), and, as such Venus represents the higher self in the chart. The higher self is a consciousness of love and light, and it is the synthesis of these two qualities which brings about intelligent love, right values, true beauty, right relationship and sacred partnership. Intelligent love can also be described as spiritual common sense, pure reason, higher logic, embodied intuition or inner knowing.

The Lord of the 6th Ray works through Neptune and Mars. Emotional desire is more connected to Mars, for Mars carries the impulse, devotional ideal and desire to manifest our ideas, visions and purpose. Mars is the planet of battle and conflict in both a negative and positive sense, for it takes battle, courage and initiative to transform the material world. Neptune is more connected to aspiration because Neptune carries the impulse of devotion to some higher abstract ideal or dream. Neptune and the 6th Ray's human emotional manifestation is often tinged with evasiveness, escapism, glamour, illusion (and self-delusion), but it also embodies the highest qualities of Christ-consciousness such as sacrificial service and unconditional love, for the 2nd and 6th Rays are closely connected. Religion, which is governed by the 6th Ray, has always had this dual Neptune–Mars expression.

The Lord of the 7th Ray works through Uranus, the planet ruling Aquarius and thus the New Era. This Ray therefore has overall rulership (with the 2nd Ray) in the New Era. The 7th Ray is the objective manifestation arm of the 1st Ray of will, for its work is to manifest higher will or purpose through the medium of ordered, rhythmic, ceremonial activity. This is the violet Ray of synthesis, where spirit (will) meets matter (action) and produces synthesis or 'that which is greater than the sum total of its parts'. The 7th Ray unifies all the other six Rays and this is why it is so powerful a creative force. Uranus is the planet of awakening and illumination – its electrical mind-opening force awakens both the individual, the group and the collective to new revolutionary thinking, ideas, visions, possibilities and creative activities. It rules the future, and it attempts to reveal ('reveal' = revelation) this future by breaking through (and breaking down) outmoded and crystallized thinking and physical structures. Uranus embodies the vision (Ray 1) and creative activity (Ray 7) of the soul and its manifestation on Earth. Its 84-year cycle through the zodiac symbolizes the perfected unfoldment of the soul's purpose, for 7 times 12 = 84, and 7 and 12 are the two numbers that govern our septenary system.

The 7th Ray and Uranus need to work through groups and networks; the true New Age group is relatively small, decentralized and inclusive. Individuals and groups compose a network, and all these networks comprise a decentralized global network of light and goodwill. The emergence of such groups and networks around the world, and the activity of human and informational networking, is a direct manifestation of 7th Ray Uranian energy. This Ray began to manifest far more powerfully from 1962 onwards due to the conjunction of seven planets in Aquarius (2–5 February 1962). People born during this time are archetypal 7th Ray types, and will be capable of manifesting the higher will and needs of the future through organized ritualistic activity.

The three books that best describe the Rays in practical terms are Alan Oken's *Soul-Centred Astrology* (Bantam Books), Torkum Saladarian's *The Symphony of the Zodiac* (Aquarian Educational Group) and *Ray Paths and Chakra Gateways* by David Tansley (C. W. Daniel). Vera Alder's book *From the Mundane to the Magnificent* (Rider Books) is the only book that I know of which describes the Rays in their true beauty. In this autobiographical book the author describes how she was contacted by her spiritual Master and guided through a series of out-of-the-body experiences. Her inner sight was opened by her Master and this enabled her to see firsthand the inner reality of the Seven Rays and their manifestation through the solar system, the Earth, and the individual human being. I will be quoting a good deal from this book because I feel it gives a wonderful and living description of the Rays, thereby providing a deeper understanding of the true science of transpersonal astrology. During one out-of-body experience the author was 'taken up' into space, where she saw the following:

> The scene below me gradually took on a strange and beautiful significance. At first I could dimly perceive a fine pulsating web of living electric strands [the etheric body], in which the stars were caught like morning dewdrops on a cobweb. This web clasped them round like a gigantic woman's hairnet enclosing heavenly tresses, thus dividing a few hundred or thousand stars completely off from the rest of the universe. In the middle of this colossal net glowed our little Sun, a globe of rich and gorgeous beauty. The Sun was the heart and centre of the cobweb, the very nucleus of it, for I saw that glowing filaments, tinted in the colours of the rainbow, were spread out from its heart and linked up with the planets. I counted seven of these living Rays, and was thus able to locate the seven major planets. I saw that they gained their different tints from these filament Rays, and that they were nourished and fed with the essence of life by the Sun itself.
>
> Each planet in turn radiated again seven coloured Rays, and these were divided and redivided amongst the smaller stars until they spread into the finest electric cobwebbing. Such a glorious vision it was, impossible fully to describe' (Pages 47–8).

Further on in the book the author goes on to describe another view of the solar system and the Rays.

> 'I began to discern the solar system. I saw it as a huge living moving bubble and discovered that it was completely one – an entity. At its heart was the Sun which now looked like a hollow circle within the greater one. I concentrated upon the Sun and looked for the seven coloured strands of light, flowing from its planets. I saw them but they looked different. They shimmered and pulsated like living serpents. With a shock I realised that I was looking at living beings – marvellous and glorious, vast lives, each of whom held one particular planet within its convolutions.

The author's Master than asked her to observe Him, and this is how she described what she saw:

> Before me was a small solar system around which I could dimly sense the outline of my friend's form. The central Sun was at about the place where his heart would be. From it the seven coloured living strands swirled as serpent-like mermen, and at the core of each one was a fiery planet, every one of a different colouring.

Each one of these planets was observed by the author to be situated at the region of the seven chakras, and thus the law of 'as above so below' was brought to her notice. Both the science of the Rays and astrology are intrinsically linked to this law of correspondence; in fact it could be said that nothing exists outside of this law and its manifestation.

Continuing to observe the larger solar system Vera Alder saw

> . . . the vast luminous cluster below us was teeming with almost invisible living beings. The more I looked the more I saw: living, moving, busy beings, great and small, semi-visible, as if each one were made of the stuff of a glittering soap bubble. The lesser beings were contained within the serpentine bodies of the greater beings.
>
> 'What are those seven great spirit-like beings into which the solar system has divided itself?' I gasped earnestly. 'They are known by many names in many lands' answered Raphael. 'Have you heard of the seven Spirits before the Throne? Or the Seven Archangels? (Pages 87-9)

This description leaves us in no doubt that the Rays play the most fundamental role in true astrology. Every planet, nation, group and individual is ruled by one or other of the Rays. There is a ruling monadic Ray, soul Ray, personality Ray, mental body Ray, emotional or astral body Ray and an etheric–physical body Ray. These Rays ultimately determine the purpose, qualities, characteristics, functioning and activities of each of these bodies. For example the Earth has a 1st Ray monad, a 2nd Ray soul and a 3rd Ray personality. The 3rd Ray is green and this is why the body of the Earth is nature green; from space the Earth looks blue–green because of its blue soul and green personality Rays. From the cosmos itself the Earth would look red because of its red monadic Ray. From an overall point of view human beings must therefore synthesize (to whatever relative degree) spiritual will or purpose, love–intuition and creative intelligence, and these qualities have to be manifested through one or other form of dynamic service-orientated action (Rays 4, 5, 6 and 7) if they wish to be true servers of the planet and fulfil their higher destiny.

The Rays allow us to decipher the underlying purpose and qualities of each nation, and for this reason I include a few national Ray rulerships below. These are taken from *The Destiny of the Nations* by Alice Bailey (Lucis Trust Pub.). It is worth reading this book to gain a deeper understanding of the nations and their ruling Rays and signs. In a few cases sign and Ray rulerships may have changed due to major revolutions in some countries, although the soul Ray will have remained the same.

Table 4.1: National Rays and Rulerships

Country	Rising sign	Ray	Sun sign	Ray
Argentina	Cancer		Libra	
Austria	Libra	4	Capricorn	5
Belgium	Sagittarius		Gemini	
Brazil	Leo	4	Virgo	2
Canada	Taurus		Libra	
China	Taurus	1	Libra	3
Finland	Capricorn		Aries	
France	Pisces	5	Leo	3
Germany	Aries	4	Pisces	1
G. Britain	Gemini	2	Taurus	1
Greece	Virgo		Capricorn	
Holland	Aquarius		Cancer	
India	Aries	1	Capricorn	4
Ireland	Virgo		Pisces	
Italy	Leo	6	Sagittarius	4
Japan	Scorpio		Capricorn	
Poland	Taurus		Gemini	
Romania	Leo		Aries	
Russia/USSR	Aquarius	7	Leo	6
Scandinavia	Libra		Cancer	
South Africa	Aries		Sagittarius	
Spain	Sagittarius	6	Capricorn	7
Switzerland	Aries		Aquarius	
Turkey	Cancer		Scorpio	
USA	Aquarius	2	Gemini	6

Canada and China

In cases where two countries have the same signs, as with Canada and China such countries would have a natural affinity to one another, creating strong political, economic and social ties.

France

Pisces Rising indicates why France has such a strong Catholic orientation, and why its past is littered with religious persecution and bloodshed. The 3rd and 5th Rays give it a powerful mental–intellectual focus, which is both a blessing and a curse. Its 5th Ray soul nevertheless indicates why its scientists are in the forefront of pioneering activity, and it is said that French scientists will be the first to prove the reality of the soul. There is a very strong 'scientific' spiritual/esoteric movement in France too. The Leo Sun sign indicates why France is so concerned with individuality and its own independence.

Germany

I do not know if the two reunited Germanys will create any differences in this composition, but I suspect that Germany now has the opportunity to move into a higher octave of her pioneering Aries soul, although this will come about through the energy of the 4th Ray – 'harmony through conflict'. Her younger generations are very different to her older Second World War generations, and Germany has gone through her crucifixion over the past forty years. Germany's powerful will (Aries and the 1st Ray) will always put her in the forefront of things, but she has to learn to use this power for the good of the whole. Having the most masculine (Aries) and most feminine (Pisces) signs creates a contradiction in the German people, for they tend to be very active and receptive simultaneously.

Great Britain

Certain astrologers use a Libra Rising, Capricorn Sun chart for the UK, but Gemini–Taurus are the true overall rulers. Notice the strong Ray link between Britain and Germany with their 2nd–4th Ray souls and 1st Ray egos. This is a love–hate relationship. Whether Taurus or Capricorn, Britain has her Sun in an earth sign, and this explains her pragmatic and slow approach to everything. Britain has no hope of keeping pace with Germany in the new Europe (economically that is). Her 2nd Ray soul and Gemini Rising, strongly connected to the USA's 2nd Ray soul and Aquarius or Sagittarius Rising, indicate why the New Age (2nd Ray Soul) is being pioneered most strongly by these two nations.

Holland

The New Age is manifesting most strongly in Continental Europe in Holland. This is due to her Aquarius Rising; the soul of Holland, the USA and the USSR all are connected through Aquarius Rising.

India

Here we see the connection between India and Britain through the 1st Ray and Capricorn Sun. Capricornean politics (India, Japan) is well known for its ambitious and corruptive influences. India is now regarded as the most powerful military nation in the Far East.

Ireland

This explains why Ireland is so dominated by religion and the fanatical idealism of the 6th Ray which works through both Virgo and Pisces. These are opposite signs, and Ireland is pulled in the opposite directions of soul order and service (Virgo) and personality chaos (Pisces). Both signs also contain the highest qualities of the Christ force, namely love, wisdom, unity and selfless service. Ireland has a great future ahead when its peoples learn to manifest these qualities. When its troubles have been resolved a major planetary initiation centre will be established in one of its power points, just as Findhorn, a major preparatory initiation centre, has been established in a Scottish power point.

Italy

Both of these fire signs create the 6th Ray idealistic individuality which creates so much political chaos in Italy. The artistic genius of this nation comes through its 6th and 4th Rays.

Japan

Here we have the reason for Japan's Scorpionic warrior *samurai* (Bushido) tradition and its hidden secretive nature, plus its Capricornean economic genius and its 'shadowy' manipulative counterpart. The Japanese control their emotions (Capricorn) but beneath this control ticks a time-bomb of dark emotions that manifest in a hidden self-destructive manner (Scorpio). The 4th and 3rd Rays must play a major part in the Japanese make-up. No wonder the Japanese love Scorpio Rising Margaret Thatcher. The transits of Pluto through Scorpio, and of Neptune and Uranus through Capricorn, are dissolving and decrystallizing Japan's Capricorn ego (evidenced in the erosion of her Stock Exchange and her political scandals), and this will hopefully turn many of her people towards an inner journey of her Scorpio soul.

Poland

Lech Walensa, the leader of Solidarity, is the perfect Taurus Rising type. His steady uncompromising leadership of Solidarity awakened not only the soul of Poland but the soul of Eastern Europe itself. Poland and Britain have very strong links due to their opposite Taurus–Gemini connection.

Romania

Mars, the planet of war, rules Aries Sun, and this is why the Romanian Revolution entailed so much bloodshed. These two fiery signs give this country great pioneering creative potential, but also many problems when it comes to self-centred egotistical expression and dictatorial-type leaders. Romania might well be the dark self of Eastern Europe, but she also has a warrior-like pioneering spirit. More than any country, she needs love, for love is the Ray of the Sun, her ruling planet. 'The power of love' and not 'the love of power' should become the keynote of her government and peoples.

Russia/USSR

The revolutionary 'Aquarian' experiment going on in this great country will produce a new socio-political, economic and spiritual nation that will do vital pioneering work in the New Era. Gorbachev and his close group are guiding this 7th Ray experiment, and the fact that Russia has the sign and Ray of the New Era ruling its soul is indicative of why the Master DK states that 'out of Russia will emerge the New World religion' (*The Destiny of the Nations*; Lucis Trust Pub.).

Scandinavia

Libra Rising is the reason why these countries are the peacekeepers of the world, and also why they are great mediators and wish to balance the spiritual–humanitarian and material aspects of their activities.

South Africa

This fiery energy is typical of this country, but since its change to being a republic it has Pisces Rising and Gemini Sun. The 27-year imprisonment of Nelson Mandela and his love, wisdom and courage in guiding this country into a new era speaks of the sacrificial and unconditional loving nature of its Piscean soul. F. W. de Klerk is also a Piscean; Gemini is indicative of the black–white and white–white dualities seeking resolution. South Africa is the Kundalini point of the Earth and if she can demonstrate unity in diversity it will be a major breakthrough for humanity as a whole.

Switzerland

Thus this country's Arien desire to remain outside of the community of nations (she is neither a member of the EEC or the UN), which is not to her highest good. Some astrologers give her Virgo Sun and Scorpio Rising. She is very closely linked to the USSR and the USA through Aquarius, and the incoming 7th Ray is awakening her spiritual nature. Inclusiveness needs to be her keynote.

Turkey

Joining the EEC would be a good move for Turkey for it would help her to get into a larger family-home framework (Cancer) and thus also help to transform her violent self-destructive Scorpionic tendencies.

USA

Here we clearly see why the USA and the USSR are so closely linked, and are at last co-operating to create a New World Order. They both have Aquarius Rising and 6th Ray personalities, so although their ideologies may be very different, they can still find a common soul ground and transcend these ideals. The New Era has its major triangle focused through the USA, the USSR and Britain, and these three nations hold the key to the new world order. Britain needs a new 2nd Ray Labour government to help this co-operation along, for the Tory government is more aligned to Britain's 1st Ray personality. Many astrologers give the USA Sagittarius Rising and Cancer Sun, and the present transits of Saturn, Uranus and

Neptune through Capricorn, Cancer's opposite sign, are causing the dissolution and demise of the old and corrupt USA political–economic system. As I write this chapter Neptune is opposing her Sun sign (2nd–8th houses) and her economic system is in a state of dissolution.

The capital of a country embodies that country's essential purpose and qualities, and one can read more about this subject in the book *Destiny of the Nations* (Lucis Trust Pub., page 69).

THE RAYS AND THE INDIVIDUAL

Every individual is qualified by six Rays, the Rays of the monad, the soul, the personality, the mental body, the emotional or astral body and the etheric–physical body. The monadic or overall ruling Ray is always the 1st, 2nd or 3rd, and this Ray remains the same throughout one's evolution. The monadic Ray is of practical importance after the 3rd initiation. Up to this time it is the soul Ray which has overall practical rulership.

The soul Ray can be any one of the seven, and this remains the same for a number of incarnations. As the Rising sign remains the same for seven life-cycles it would seem that the soul ray remains the same for seven incarnations. This Ray is determined by the ruling Ray of the transpersonal planetary ruler of the Rising sign. For example I have Sagittarius Rising and the 3rd Ray of 'active intelligence' rules the Earth, transpersonal ruler of Sagittarius. Green is my soul Ray colour, and people have often commented that green is my 'soul' colour. I feel the same way, for green is the true colour of the 3rd Ray; 'Green' politics, economics and living is likewise the true healing and balancing energy of the Earth, a 3rd Ray planet. As we become more and more attuned to our Rising sign, its keynote and its ruling planet, we also become simultaneously attuned to our soul colour. The problem with deciphering the Soul ray is that there is a ruling astrological Ray (as described above) and a ruling psychological Ray. Sometimes these are the same and sometimes they are not.

The four Rays of the personality bodies tend to change with each incarnation, thus allowing for a whole series of diverse experiences, lessons, knowledge and skills. This is how the soul gains a wide diversity of experience through its personality. The overall ruling Ray is that of the personality itself, and this is directly related to the sign the Sun is in. The problem is that this rule is not fixed, for this Ray could be the 5th if the Sun is in Aquarius (a 5th Ray sign) but this is not always the case. The Ray governing the personal planetary ruler of the Sun sign gives a clue to the mental Ray. In the case of Aquarius this would be the 7th (Uranus). Clarification of these Rays needs to come from the soul itself.

It is a very complex matter deciphering the Rays of the lower self. The vast majority of people have 6th Ray emotional bodies. This 6th Ray body transforms gradually into the 2nd Ray as the 2nd initiation is taken, for love begins to replace the normal reactive emotional patterns of this body such as fear, envy, jealousy, attachment and desire. This is nevertheless a slow transformation, for the transference of energy from the solar plexus chakra (emotions/fear) to the heart chakra (sentiency/love) is an arduous and painful process.

The Moon rules the physical body and it would therefore seem to play a role in determining the Ray of the etheric–physical body; for example I have the Moon at 25 degrees of Capricorn and I have a 7th Ray body (one of the three Rays ruling Capricorn), but this is not always the case either. The best way to discover one's Rays is to invoke this information from one's higher self. This might come through in many ways – in meditation through visual and/or audio telepathy, through dreams, or by 'guidance' to read this or that section of a book such as *Discipleship in the New Age* (Lucis Trust Pub.), which deals with information on Ray compositions.

THE RAYS AND THE SEVEN-YEAR CYCLES

Each Ray has a special rulership in its particular seven-year cycle. The physical body Ray governs the first seven-year cycle (birth – 7; the Aries cycle), for this is when consciousness is anchoring itself into physical form. This Ray embodies itself in the child from 4 to 7 years of age, for this is when the Soul appropriates the physical body. From 7 to 14 (the Taurian cycle) the emotional 'desire' Ray governs, and this Ray anchors itself between 11 and 14 at the time of the puberty cycle. This is the time when the soul appropriates the emotional body, which is why it is such a difficult cycle. The mental Ray governs from 14 to 21 (the Gemini cycle) and onwards to 24, for it is only between 21 and 24 that the soul appropriates the lower mental body. Gemini is the sign ruling lower education or the development of the lower rational mind.

From 21 to 28 (the Cancer cycle) these three Rays synthesize and the overall personality Ray begins to emerge. By the time one turns 28 these three Rays/bodies should be relatively integrated. From 28 to 35 (the Leo cycle) the personality Ray becomes the dominating factor. From 32 to 35 is when this Ray anchors itself. This Leo cycle also witnesses the emergence of the soul Ray, and the major conflict in this cycle is the polarity clash between the Ray of the lower self and the higher self. One seeks recognition for self and the other seeks to serve the greater self. The soul Ray does not emerge unless one is intent on individualizing oneself.

The personality and soul Rays begin to integrate between 35 and 42, during the Virgo cycle. This is an extremely difficult and conflict-ridden cycle, for the initial process of integrating these two Rays (especially if they are in conflict) is one of battle and 'the labour of birth'. Both rulers of Virgo, namely the Moon and Mercury, are 4th Ray planets. This seven-year cycle includes:

- the return of the Moon's Nodes (37–38);
- the Uranus opposition to natal Uranus (39–41);
- the Pluto square to natal Pluto (40–42); and
- the Neptune square to natal Neptune (41–43).

It is of course the well-known 'midlife crisis' cycle, 'midlife crisis' meaning 'the time when the lower self/Ray and the higher self/Ray seek integration'. Virgo is known as the sign of 'gestation' when the soul or Sun (Leo) and the personality or Moon (Virgo) begin to integrate, and the labour of spiritual birth reaches its crisis stage. It is of interest to note that in physical labour the gestation or crisis month is also the sixth month (Virgo).

'Crisis' indicates that the battle between the duality of soul and personality Rays reaches an intensity; the individual becomes aware of both sides of his/her nature and both these sides battle for supremacy. This is why Virgo is associated with dis-ease and with health and healing, for this battle increases the stress and tensions of normal living, and dis-ease, both psychological and physical, is the natural result of such tensions. Paradoxically if one is dis-eased one seeks to remedy the problem by becoming healthy, and Virgo governs all the 'holistic' health and healing therapies. True health and healing is impossible without an understanding of the battle between the dualities, for this battle for integration is the key to the cause of dis-ease and to the gift of healing. This is why a deep understanding of the Rays and transpersonal astrology is vital in the holistic therapies of the future.

It might be of interest to note that I wrote the above 'Virgo' section on the final day of the Virgo cycle (1990), and that a long-standing and irritating earache and burning stomach pain was healed overnight as transiting Venus trined my birth Venus (Venus is the higher self). The morning before this healing occurred I had a dream in which I was told to prepare for an inner marriage. Venus is also associated with partnership, and this gives a clue to the subjective side of Venusian 'marriage'.

The Libra cycle (42–49) is a rest and balancing cycle between the battleground of Virgo and that of Scorpio (49–56). This does not make the Libra cycle one of ease and peace, but it does create the opportunity for balance, harmony and peace between the dualities. The Soul and personality Rays 'rest' during this cycle, for they seek to achieve the beauty of harmony and co-operation. This balance is focused between 46 and 49. By 49 one should have attained a relative balance and maturity between these two sides of one's nature.

MASCULINE AND FEMININE RAYS

The Rays are divided into masculine and feminine 'qualitative' energies. The 1st, 3rd, 5th and 7th are masculine, the 2nd, 4th and 6th feminine. The 7th is also the Ray of synthesis between masculine and feminine energies. Depending upon the Ray composition one will have a predominating masculine or feminine make-up. This is the individual's karma and dharma, and very few people will have a perfect balance of masculine and feminine Rays. Each individual (and group or nation) has to learn to utilize their Rays for the highest good and in the most balanced way possible – and this balance will always be relative. The glamour of perfect male-female balance in the New Age movement is due to a lack of understanding of the Rays. Even the Masters and the Angels have a masculine–feminine polarization, depending upon their Ray make-up. The aim of course is to attain a relative balance between the will, heart and mind. Love/feelings, knowledge/thinking and will/action need to be integrated to the greatest degree possible, but the Ray composition will determine which predominates. Each Ray can be regarded as a spiritual path; one's path is therefore ultimately determined by one's Ray make-up.

In order to provide a deeper understanding of the Rays I have included a section on each one in Chapter 5. By studying the Rays in this way one can get a deeper feeling and knowledge of their individual purpose and qualities, both from an overall and individual perspective. By studying the Ray of one's ruling transpersonal planet one can come to understand one's astrological soul Ray and how best to embody and use its energies. The same goes for the personality Ray, and for the Rays of the nations. By learning about the spiritual paths associated with the Rays, we can recognize people, qualities and activities that belong to them. This enables us to respect the diversity of life and to develop tolerance and love for the unique way in which individuals, groups, societies and nations evolve and express themselves.

CHAPTER FIVE

Interpreting the Seven Rays

RAY 1 – THE PATH OF POWER OR PURPOSE

Keynotes	*Colours*	*Signs*	*Planets*	*Centres*
Will, Power, Purpose	Flame red	Aries/Leo	Vulcan	Crown
	Purple	Capricorn	Pluto	base

The 1st Ray is the originating, initiating, pioneering Ray of divine will, power or purpose. This is the central Ray of the cosmos, for its constellation is the Great Bear. It is the Ray of the creator and the destroyer, for its energy initiates new evolutionary activity and destroys old and crystallized forms and structures. These forms can be mental, emotional and/or physical (the personality); they can be personal, national, racial, religious, cultural, planetary or solar.

True will is purpose one-pointedly directed. It is that power which generates, directs, initiates, pioneers and activates energy. From a human point of view people on this Ray have tremendously strong will-power which is directed either towards good or evil purposes. A Gorbachev or Mahatma Ghandi and a Hitler or Stalin are good examples in this regard. Julius Caesar, Alexander the Great and Napoleon were great first Ray types. They were responsible for destroying old structures and helping to bring in new forms of civilization and culture. The Master of this Ray is Master Morya, author of Agni Yoga, the Yoga of Fire. It is necessary to integrate will with love, wisdom (2nd Ray) and intelligent activity (3rd Ray) if the highest potential good is to result from 1st Ray work.

First Ray types are born leaders, pioneers and initiators, who are fearless, courageous, one-pointed and largely indifferent to comment or criticism. Nevertheless they are deeply hurt by negative and destructive criticism, especially when their larger motives are misunderstood, which is frequently the case. The path of power requires these people to 'lead from the front' and without the above

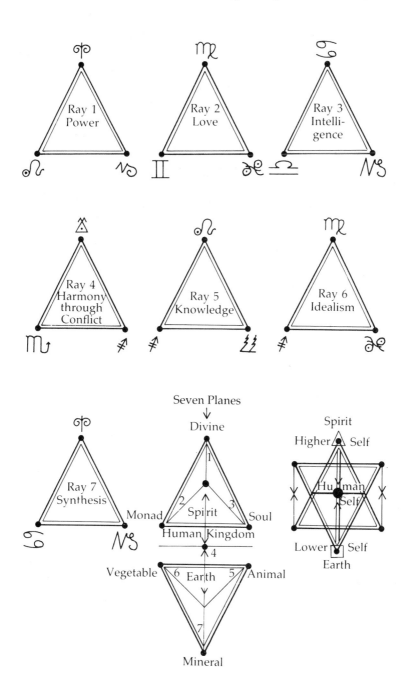

Ray Triangles

qualities they would simply not be able to lead successfully and accomplish their chosen task. They have strong and powerful feelings and contrasting natures and are far more inwardly sensitive than they seem. In fact many 1st Ray types are hypersensitive to the hurts and pains of humanity, and their work is dedicated to the alleviation of this suffering. The spiritual types know that all suffering is due to ignorance, crystallization and stagnation, and their work is to break up and destroy these forms (to whatever appropriate degree), and to set into motion the creation of new and updated structures and activities that best suit the evolution of consciousness. Mikhail Gorbachev, a 1st Ray initiate, has stated that the demolition of the old Soviet system is required before the new system can be built.

They are warriors of the first degree in the material and/or spiritual sense. Their focus is not so much on the 'parts' but rather on the larger whole. They 'take the kingdom of heaven by storm'. They tend to restrict and subjugate their emotions and feelings for they often see these feelings as being obstacles in following their destined path. In one sense they are correct for the emotions create the major fears, insecurities and blocks that turn people back from their path. They nevertheless need to acknowledge and express their feelings and emotions if they wish to demonstrate their common humanity, for the negation of feelings often leads to insensitive actions which blight their path. In the case of the dictatorial type, whether the little dictator in the home or the national dictator, the suppression of feelings often leads to excessive insensitivity and cruelty, and in the case of the Hitlers and Stalins ruthlessness and brutality. These 1st Ray types have the capacity to see the larger picture and the greater need, and their task for this reason is all the more difficult. Power is the most difficult energy to handle and work with, and 1st Ray people should always be aware that 'all power comes from above'.

Outwardly 1st Ray types tend to be cold, detached, hard, one-pointed and insensitive. They are very quick to act, highly intuitive, and have flashes of inspiration. They are extremely impatient, easily irritated, quick to anger, but just as quick to forgive and forget (unless they are deceived or manipulated). They are aggressive psychologically and sometimes physically, love a psychological conflict, speak in quick sharp bursts, have powerful electric auras and penetrating eyes, are often inspiring and are natural leaders. They have a great disdain for 'ordinary' and small-minded people. In fact, many 1st Ray revolutionaries and leaders have little or no respect for the very people for whom they are fighting. They respect and love power, and often disdain love and its qualities, and have to learn the painful lesson that 'without love all else is but the tinkling of bells'.

They have great powers of concentration, and can work for long hours without rest. Napoleon is well known for his capacity to take only a quick sleep before a battle and yet be fully alive on awakening. They can tire quickly and yet regenerate just as quickly too. They are very critical, and expect themselves and those they work with to be perfectionists to the last degree. They tend to project their many imperfections onto others, and hate to be let down by other people. They have great mental pride and arrogance, and those born under the 1st Ray signs Aries, Leo and Capricorn are well known for these negative characteristics. Ambition is often their initial driving force, and part of them seeks recognition while another part gets quite bored with it. The spiritual types can often reach a stage where ambition is transcended and replaced solely with the will to serve.

They need to be 'centre-stage', and the strength and power of their consciousness is an inspiration to others. They can also be great co-operators in important projects, but they do not like to take second place. They despise deception (real or imagined) above all things and it is deception by others that can bring out their worst 'shadowy' aspects – destructive criticism, burning hatred, revenge (history is witness to this), and ultimate self-destruction. Saddam Hussein of Iraq is a good example in this regard. Pluto, a 1st Ray planet and its ruling sign Scorpio, are well known for this dark side of human nature, which is why they are concerned with the purging and transformation of this self.

These types tend towards isolation. They require few companions outside of a dedicated partner and a few dedicated friends and co-workers. This is both their gift and their curse.

It is interesting to note that many male dictators have been dictated to by their partners; perhaps this is what might be called 'rough justice'. First Ray women can often be subjugated power types whose power works beneath the surface; the statement that 'the wife is the real power behind the throne' attests to this. It is far more difficult for a woman to handle 1st Ray energy because it is a masculine Ray, but 1st Ray women are also more capable of integrating the 2nd Ray love principle with power. Eva Peron of Argentina was a remarkable woman in this regard. A peasant with little educational background, she became the leader of her country. She was ever trying to integrate these two Rays and would shift from giving away money to the poor, to imprisoning her best friends. She died of cancer at 33, the age of crucifixion, loved by the many and hated by the few. Leadership is a science in itself and very few people comprehend the huge pressures and contradictions that leaders have to bear.

The 1st Ray type both initiates the new and destroys the old. The builders of the new (2nd Ray) require the 1st Ray type to destroy the old before they can start their work. There can be no true creation (or recreation) and stabilization (2nd Ray) without prior demolition. A delapidated building must first be destroyed before a new one can be built. This is true of the individual as it is true of a group, network, organization, nation, culture, civilization or planet itself.

The 1st Ray type needs to temper their fiery sword with the 'rose' of love and wisdom if they are to make the true leader and serve the highest good. They make the best leaders, and know instinctively and intuitively how to govern, organize and inspire. They are loved and/or hated by the masses. They need to learn the great lessons of 'giving to the least of men what one gives to the greatest of men', and 'loving those nearest to one as much as one loves those furthest from one'.

They love powerful effects, be it in music, art, theatre, sport, politics, action or the spoken or written word. Their major fields of expression are through politics, the military, certain sports, esoteric or occult groups, and organizational projects of a pioneering nature.

The 1st Ray has sub-influence through Mercury and Mars (Aries), the Sun (Leo) and Saturn (Capricorn). It also has a sub-influence in Scorpio through Pluto and in Taurus (Rising) through Vulcan.

Light qualities: Strength, courage, fearlessness, tenacity, dedication, commitment, personal responsibility, directness, self-confidence and assurity, truthfulness, impersonality, indifference, positive manipulation of forces; capacity to see the larger picture and the needs of the future, capacity to transform past limitations with rapidity, sense of humour, ability to guide and lead, intuition, and the ability to respond quickly to its promptings; the use of the will to break the chains of the past, the use of the will to heal – psychologically and physically.

Shadow characteristics: Pride, arrogance, personal ambition, wilfulness, hard-headedness, stubbornness, desire to control others, masculine-type self-centredness, over-centralization of power and policy-making, great anger, psychological violence (and of course physical violence and brutality in the case of the dictator); inability to take criticism, negative manipulation of forces, impatience, intolerance, insensitivity, a tendency to avoid dealing with the small things in life, bonds others to him/herself, gross in mannerisms.

RAY 2 – THE PATH OF LOVE

Keynote	Colours	Signs	Planets	Centre
Love–wisdom	Midnight blue Royal blue	Gemini/Virgo	Jupiter Sun	Heart

The Lord of the 2nd Ray embodies the energy of love–wisdom, the quality which rules, influences and evolves all life in our solar system. This is the energy of 'attractive cohesion', where duality (Ray 2) emerges out of initial unity (Ray 1) and seeks cohesion through attraction. Polarities are attracted to one another in order to create synergy and unity (= love). All life in our solar and planetary system is both polarized and unified by this Ray. Because it governs our solar system it plays an overall influence in the evolution of 'consciousness', where quality and not quantity is the keynote.

It is paradoxically the Ray of least resistance, and the vast majority of human beings respond directly to its influence. This means that while this Ray and its essential quality of love–wisdom stand at the centre of the evolution of consciousness, its shadow characteristics also stand at the centre of human glamour, illusion, stagnation and crystallization. The emotional or astral body (6th Ray; solar plexus centre) is the lower counterpart of the 2nd Ray (heart centre), and fear, attachment, possessiveness, jealousy and envy are therefore the dark or unconscious side of this Ray.

These types are generally good and loving people but are simultaneously attached to the objects of their love. Their major lesson is to learn the difference between true unconditional love and emotional possessiveness and attachment. Traditional security and stability are very important to these people, as are traditional blood family, cultural and religious ties. The past and its laws and regulations, its rights and wrongs, and its crystallized way of living are of great importance to 2nd Ray types, for this safety of tried and trusted ways gives them the emotional security they desire. It is this crystallization of the past that lies at the core of many of society's ills, for this traditional system serves the past and not the future. There are many good and positive aspects of the past that need to be carried forward into the present and future, but much of the past is dead and gone and holds humanity back from its chosen destiny. Jupiter and the Sun represent Ray 2, whereas the Moon (the past) is a Ray 4 planet.

The Spiritual Hierarchy, inner government or heart chakra of our planet is governed by this Ray. At the centre of this chakra is the Christ or Lord Maitreya (the Iman Mahdi or Messiah to Muslims and Jews) who is the Master of Masters and the World Teacher. His counterpart disciple is Master Jesus, who is the Master of the 6th Ray. The Christ overlighted Jesus 2,000 years ago and together they inaugurated the Piscean Era. As promised the Christ will return (physically) towards 'the end of the age', and many predict this appearance towards the end of this century. He will guide humanity into the New Era of Aquarius, a 'New Era' which the politicians themselves now talk about openly.

All the feminine Rays are receptive and sensitive, and people along these Rays are very receptive to imprints from within and outside themselves. They make the best psychics, clairvoyants, clairaudients and sensitives for this reason, but they are also subject to the worst glamours and illusions (with the 6th Ray type) in this area. They are simultaneously subject to 'brainwashing' from outside sources, and the 'guru syndrome' is largely a 2nd and 6th Ray problem. The 2nd, 6th and 4th Ray types are easily led and respond to the mood and opinions of leaders, gurus, society and their peers. In this sense they are both group- and mass-orientated; they are the 'group' conscious in the higher sense and 'mass' conscious in the lower sense. They are both materialistic and avaricious, and altruistic and humanitarian, for their emotional instincts and their loving intuition are naturally active. These 2nd Ray types are very active in all the humanitarian, charitable and service-orientated groupings and organizations. The Red Cross, Oxfam, Help the Aged, the RSPCA and so on are 2nd Ray organizations, as are Greenpeace and Friends of the Earth, although these Green organizations have 3rd and 7th Ray energies too.

This Ray is the ruler of higher consciousness, that is the consciousness of the soul, higher or Christ self. It is the soul Ray of our planet and of humanity. The Master DK, who transmitted the Arcane Teachings through Alice Bailey, and the Master KH, who helped transmit the theosophical teachings through Madame Blavatsky, are two of the Masters of this Ray. The soul is essentially a consciousness of love–wisdom and selfless service, for consciousnesses inhabit the solar system. On the level of pure soul consciousness there are 'twin' souls and 'group' souls. Souls exist in twin partnership and in group formation (soul-mates) simultaneously and these two should not be confused. It is the energy of 'attraction–cohesion' that attracts atoms, human souls and all polarities towards one another to create 'that which is more than the sum total of the parts'; atoms create organs, humans create children and so on.

Ray 2 colours are the midnight and royal blue hues, for these colours are the manifestations of love, unity and wisdom. This Ray rules education and has a strong influence on all the arts. It is *par excellence* the Ray of the teacher, the guide, the healer, the counsellor, the social worker and the humanitarian.

Ray 2 types are easy-going, loving, kind, social, hospitable and serving and the population of the USA and Britain (2nd Ray soul nations) are good examples of this type. They can also be superficial, long-winded, greedy for constant new comforts, indulgent, fearful and suspicious of things that are foreign to them, closet racialists and bigots, inclusive in their consciousness but exclusive in their living patterns. They love to socialize and need to be with people, for they tend to realize themselves through others. They are easily swayed by other people's opinions. Their openness and flexibility is their gift but it also creates great difficulty in the focusing of their consciousness. They have a tendency to talk a great deal about nothing, and this is where the Ray 2 and Ray 1 type differ greatly. In fact this feminine–masculine difference makes for many conflicts in male–female relationships, for the Ray 1 person gets to the point quickly whereas the Ray 2 person is a lot more long-winded.

Ray 2 is the major feminine Ray and women are governed by it. Women are naturally 2nd Ray types, whereas men have to develop its qualities for inner–outer balance, and vice versa for women. The 2nd Ray therefore embodies all the feminine qualities of caring, nurturing, healing, mothering, inner wisdom, tolerance, sensitivity, sharing, group consciousness, intuition and so on. It also hides the shadow of the feminine, which is far more subtle than the masculine 1st Ray shadow. The 2nd Ray type can easily detect the dark side of Ray 1 such as patriarchy, male chauvinism, excessive activity, insensitivity, lack of and escapism from feeling, gross abuse of power, sexual manipulation and so on, but they often fail to detect their own subtle feminine dark side such as overprotection, interference, jealousy and envy, attachment to that which is safe and tried, emotional, financial and subtle sexual manipulation, indecisiveness, and the projection of these conscious/unconscious characteristics on to male-dominated society. The light and dark of these two Rays are in constant interaction, and their cohesion leads to balance and harmony.

The 2nd Ray has sub-influence through Venus and Mercury (Gemini), the Moon and Mercury (Virgo) and Jupiter, Neptune and Pluto (Pisces). It also sub-influences Sagittarius and Pisces (through Jupiter; not only is Pisces a 2nd Ray Sign but three of its rulers are 2nd and 6th Ray planets) and Leo (through the Sun).

Light qualities: Love, intuition, patience, calmness, inner strength and endurance, inner wisdom, faithfulness, inclusiveness, selflessness, service, tolerance, sensitivity, stability, empathy and compassion, openness, flexibility, the gift of healing, group consciousness, caring and nurturing, forgiveness.

Shadow characteristics: Superficiality, insipidity, feminine-type self-centredness, laziness, over-receptivity, lack of discrimination, diffusion of energies, procrastination, lack of self-confidence, over-concern for others, leading to attachment and possessiveness, over-absorption in reading and study, acquiescence, avarice, interfering, indecisive.

RAY 3 – THE PATH OF INTELLIGENT ACTION

Keynotes	Colour	Signs	Planets	Centres
Active intelligence	Green	Cancer, Libra	Saturn	Throat
Adaptability		Capricorn	Earth	Spleen

The 3rd Ray is the Ray of active or creative intelligence, the energy related to the 'mind of God'. This 'intelligence-in-matter' functions from the highest creative level of archetypal intelligence related to the Angelic or Devic Hierarchy, who are the archetypes behind all form, to the instinctive intelligence of the mineral, vegetable and animal kingdoms. The Angelic Hierarchy are called the 'building forces' for they work directly under the will of God or the Seven Rays, serving the divine plan by creating the forms necessary for its fulfilment. Under these Devas work the nature kingdom forces, namely the elementals or nature spirits, such as the fairies, elves, gnomes and the elementals that enliven the etheric–physical human form. The Devas create the inner 'blueprint' structure of the form, whether these be mineral, vegetable, animal, human, or planetary forms, and the nature spirits and elementals animate or enliven these forms. This is the invisible creative intelligence lying behind all form, and without these intelligences there would be no creation as we understand it. The Angelic Hierarchy is a 3rd Ray creative building force whereas the nature spirits and elementals are 7th Ray builders.

Vera Alder (*From the Mundane to the Magnificent*, Rider Books) was allowed to witness this deva, nature spirit and elemental activity directly when her Master guided her through the inner nature and human system. This is the way she describes the nature experience:

> As I gazed and gazed I was aware of a great green spirit-form brooding over the meadow, which lay spread beneath us.

'That is a Deva,' announced Raphael, her Master. 'Each of the seven Spirits or Rays contains many lesser lives to do the work, and they in turn contain still smaller lives to do their bidding. Come closer and you will see.'

As we descended rapidly to the surface of the Earth the great Deva's form was hardly distinguishable, but flowing down from His robes were many little green dancing figures. 'Fairies! Surely!' I burst out. 'But fairies are not real?'

'And why not?' queried Raphael, almost it seemed in exasperation. 'Fairies have been written about, described and painted all over the world and throughout history, and yet people are so woodenly dull that they take it for granted that they do not exist. Of course they exist, in their millions and in every colour – nature could not carry on without them. No flower grows nor a fruit ripens nor a bird sings without the help of some of these lovely little beings. There are many ranks of them and the tiniest are those who look after the atoms.'

Further on the author saw '. . . the birds coming to drink at the water's edge and also a rabbit. It appeared that these birds and animals were all aware of the fairy creatures. In fact they often stopped to play with them' (pages 92–4). The world-famous Findhorn Foundation is renowned for its communication and work with the Deva and nature spirit kingdoms, and the books *The Magic of Findhorn* and *The Findhorn Garden Book* are highly recommended in this regard.

The author, when allowed to enter a human auric field, saw 'a beautiful spirit or fairy of a transparent orange hue. He was swaying back and forth with a careful rhythmic movement.'

'That is the living creature, sometimes called an elemental, who takes care of the stomach – one might say that the stomach is his physical body. He controls within himself many smaller lives who produce the various digestive juices and activate the lesser movements of the stomach. Now let us look at the elemental who dwells in the heart.'

Soon I began to see the form of the heart spirit or Deva hovering or crouching within the sphere of the heart's astral bubble. He was very, very beautiful. His body seemed to be formed of warm golden light which flowed with a wonderful sense of peace, of comradeship and of understanding. 'The wisdom of the heart' I thought. The elemental was sunk in deep concentration as he worked to produce the muscular and etheric activities within his body, the heart. Various small beings could be seen under his control, working busily at the functioning of the different valves.

Her Master goes on to explain that all complex happenings must have an intelligent initiator of some kind, and that the devas and elementals are these intelligences. He further explains that the human being in truth is (or should be) the Master of all these intelligences, with whom he or she should be developing wise control, co-operation and communication. 'If one is sufficiently single-minded they will understand and obey. Their vices are a reflection of our own, that is if we are lazy or fearful or greedy they will follow suit.' Raphael also explained that for true healing to occur, love and intelligence must be combined, for knowledge and co-operation with the devas and elementals of the nature and human kingdoms are integral to healing in the deeper sense of the word.

If we can understand that all creation, right up to the stars and galaxies themselves, is under the guiding and animating hand of these subjective natural forces, we may get an inkling of the nature of intelligence and the 3rd Ray. The Earth has a 3rd Ray personality, and, as such, all human personalities fall under the influence of this Ray (no matter what Ray the individual personality falls under). It is one thing having or sensing purpose (Ray 1), it is another having or feeling love and intuition (Ray 2), but it is quite another thing knowing how to manifest these qualities through intelligent, structured, creative action. The Earth is thus the 'landing dock' for God's will and love, for it is here that we have to use our dynamic intelligence to 'think and plan' how to act creatively. Higher knowledge, love–intuition and will-in-action need to be synthesized if one is to succeed in any task of a greater nature.

Third Ray souls or personalities are the planners and doers of humanity, and this provides the clue as to why business is such an important part of our planet's activity. Business should be the channel through which humanity manifests God's purpose, love and plan, but it cannot play this vital role until human beings desire to know and manifest this plan. The New Age movement, which is a 2nd Ray grouping, often lacks 3rd Ray energy, and this is why it often fails to materialize its visions and ideals. Sagittarius and Capricorn Rising (and Capricorn Sun) are the true agents of the 3rd Ray, because their rulers the Earth and Saturn are the two 3rd Ray planets. For example the vast majority of networkers I have come across have Sagittarius Rising (including the Findhorn Foundation), and these individuals or groups have the gift of 'organizing spirit into matter' (3rd and 7th Rays).

What has become known as 'the Green movement' is a result of the transits of Neptune, Uranus and Saturn through Capricorn, the major 3rd Ray sign. This has produced major changes in the political (1st Ray), social (2nd Ray), economic, business (3rd Ray) and ecological (7th Ray) fields, changes which are in line with the divine plan for humanity. In fact the last twenty years of this century are ruled by the spirit of Libra, and Libra is a 3rd Ray sign through which balance and equilibrium manifest. This is why the Master DK states that there will be no great cataclysmic events as we close down this century, for the green Ray of balance and healing will ensure that each major imbalance (disastrous as these may be) will be counteracted by a balancing of the opposite degree.

This is also the Ray ruling 'the law of economy and the laws of manifestation'. These laws are concerned with the relationship between creative thought and the manifestation of material energy. 'Energy follows thought' is the dictum of this law, and by this we can understand that the power of one's thinking is the determining agent behind what one manifests on the material plane. Concrete energy or money falls under this Ray and its Devas' and that is why money is referred to as 'green' energy. One-pointed, positive and powerful imaginative thought can attract one's needs to oneself, although the difference between one's needs and one's wants is part of the determining factor. David Spangler's book *The Laws of Manifestation* (Findhorn Press, but out of print at the time of writing this book) is the classic text in the above context. One can see why business and industry are ruled by this Ray. The 3rd Ray has overall rulership of the rest of the four manifesting Rays (Rays 5, 6 and 7). In our planetary system the Lord of Civilization and Culture, otherwise known as the Mahachohan, is the Lord and Master of this Ray. In his past incarnation he was known as St Germain, and his exploits at this time are well known in France.

Third Ray types are the manipulators of matter, be this for good or evil purposes. They are the business people, industrialists, financiers, bankers, stock exchange brokers, accountants, architects, builders and organizers of people and situations. Multinationals fall under this Ray. The finances of the world are controlled by people and organizations on this Ray, and for this reason alone it is called the Ray of manipulation. A good number of these financiers are great disciples of the Mahachohan, while a small but powerful grouping are under the power of the dark forces of our planet. This small grouping has been largely responsible for the chaos on our planet, for it is concerned with the manipulative use of finances for destructive and evil ends. The transits of Uranus and Neptune through Capricorn, the 1st, 3rd and 7th Ray sign most related to politics and economics, are breaking up and revolutionizing (Uranus) and dissolving and transmuting (Neptune) these crystallized institutions and structures. Japan has the Sun in Capricorn and the USA has the Sun in Cancer, and these forces are most concentrated in these two countries. Evidence the continuing collapse of the stock exchanges and other financial institutions of these countries.

It should be stated that in the New Era all the Rays will have an equal importance (outside of the 6th, which is being withdrawn), and politicians, financiers, communicators, educators, artists, scientists and 'spiritual' teachers/groupings will work in co-operation as equals. The Gorbachevs, Havels and Mandelas, and the new 'ecological' financial institutions are proof of this new 7th Ray evolutionary movement.

Money is the most concrete form of matter, for it is the medium of exchange on our planet. Third Ray people have the *responsibility* to acquire, manage and use money for the good of the whole. Only they can accomplish this because the vast majority of finances, whether liquid or solid, are in their possession. Up to the present time money has largely been used for selfish and often destructive ends; the saga of the corrupt multinationals, banks and finance institutions are well known to many. Since the late 1980s this has begun to change, largely due to the ecological disasters now facing the planet. It is now possible to invest in ethically and ecologically sound funds ('conscience' funds) and other constructive financial enterprises, and this trend is likely to grow. Money is perhaps the most difficult of energies to manage, for so much fear and anxiety is tied up in this 'green' 3rd Ray energy. It is not surprising therefore that Saturn, a 3rd Ray planet, is related to Lucifer, the 'testing' agency of matter, and also to money, time and organization, all 3rd Ray agencies. Saturn is related to 'the dweller on the threshold' esoterically, and a great deal of this 'dweller' (fear) is connected to money.

Third Ray types tend to be intelligent, mentally alert and creative, extroverted, physically active, enterprising, efficient, and practical. They can be very generous and giving and/or miserly and attached to what they own. 'I made this money and achieved this success through my own hard won efforts – why should I give it away?' is an oft-repeated statement from the 3rd Ray person. I heard this statement repeatedly in my earlier days in Johannesburg, South Africa, a very 3rd Ray city and country. What was never stated was that cheap black labour had largely contributed to this hard won success. The 3rd Ray type tends to forget that his money was made through a whole number of factors, including many other people's labour, the support of partners and friends and, more importantly, the gift of life itself.

Some of the questions 3rd Ray (all Ray types) people should ask themselves are: 'Where does oxygen (life-force) come from?'; 'What enables me to breath?' (if we did not breath we could not live and work, and yet we do not even give thanks for the gift of breathing); 'Am I really in charge of my own life or am I part of a greater power/

life?'; 'Am I really in control of my life or is Life in control of me?'; 'When I or my loved ones get really ill or die can all my money and power really help?'. Humility is a quality that Ray 1, 3 and 5 types could do well to develop, for in times of great crisis this quality could be their only saving grace.

The typical 3rd Ray person, whether male or female, often has a side to their character which is very different to the one they show to the outside world. They can be self-assured and 'in charge' in the business world, but when it comes to home, family and intimate partnerships they can feel inadequate and out of control. This 3rd Ray phenomenon is well known to astrologers for it is related to the MC and 10th house (business/career) and its opposite the IC and 4th house (the home/family/upbringing). The powerful business-man/woman (10th house) who is a 'child' in the home and domi-nated by the spouse (4th house) is a common phenomenon. It is not only the 'in-control' man who turns into the child but also the 'in-control' w)man. I have had many clients, both male and female, who belong to this category. These people compensate by buying material gifts for the spouse and the children, hoping to placate them in this manner and failing to acknowledge that their real problem is a lack of feelings, emotional and body communication, sharing, and loving intimacy.

The strong pull towards hyperactivity needs to be balanced by periods of silence and relaxation (walking in nature, listening to lovely music), going on relaxing and not exhausting holidays and healthy eating and drinking. The 3rd Ray type takes their business everywhere and tends to turn social activity into business. This is often necessary because all-too-often business becomes a full-time activity, but they have to learn that everything has its rightful place and time, and business is not the ultimate aim of life. Personal ambition obviously plays a major role in their life, and competition is their mainstay. They love the competitive nature of the business world, and although they can complain about the rat-race, they like being rats themselves. Heart attacks are the disease of 3rd Ray society and a major divine reminder that it is time to slow down and live a balanced life-style. Third Ray people love talking about money (and money and money), business, organization, material acquisitions, what they possess or will one day possess, how they have succeeded or will one day succeed.

They are the pragmatists and doers of society. Their work is to put ideas, visions (Ray 1) and ideals and dreams (Ray 2) into prac-tical action; 'do it' is their keynote. They are the great philanthrop-ists who enable many charities to exist financially. They are not closed to spiritual realities and can often be quite open to them, but they want to know how these realities can be of practical significance to society. They need to realize that although the law of cause and effect (for example) may be a subjective law its embodied understanding and application makes the difference between constructive and destructive action. If one does not believe, and more importantly *know* that this law is a reality why should one be concerned about the morality of one's actions? When one truly understands that 'what one sows one reaps', one's actions change radically.

Last but not least this Ray is the integrating Ray of the three major Rays (1, 2 and 3). People/groups on this Ray therefore have the potential to integrate and balance power, love and intelligence/action. Libra, the sign of balance, is governed by it, and Saturn is exalted (gains its greatest power) in it. Capricorn is also the third and final integrating 'earth' sign, and is the MC or Midheaven (highest personal achievement) point of the zodiac. Capricorn is the sign of initiation, the 'doorway into spirit', and not simply the 'doorway into matter' as traditionally stated. When 3rd Ray activity is spiritualized than we will truly have 'the kingdom of heaven on Earth'.

The 3rd Ray has sub-influence through Neptune and the Moon (Cancer), Uranus and Venus (Libra) and Saturn (Capricorn; here we have direct dual Ray 3 influence). It also has sub-influence in Sagittarius (through the Earth), which in any case is a 'mutable' Sign and all 'mutable' Signs have automatic Ray 3 (physical activity) influence.

Light qualities: clear and powerful thinking, articulate speech, good communication, good planning, dynamic activity, great adaptability, great business and/or organizational skills, down-to-earth, pragmatic and yet deep thinking, creative manipulation of money and material energies, steadfast, can withstand and integrate conflicting energies quickly, can handle pressures and stress, can 'ground' subjective ideas and ideals, good sense of humour, can be wonderful material givers.

Negative characteristics: over-active, over-earthy, intellectual pride and arrogance, gross as far as body habits go (eating, drinking, sex and so on), very manipulative especially in terms of material resources, attachment to material objects (including action itself), attached to logical thinking, avoidance of dealing with feelings and emotions, greedy and avaricious, extremely competitive, destructive in action and use of matter, insensitive.

RAY 4 – THE PATH OF ARTISTIC LIVING

Keynotes	*Colour*	*Signs*	*Planets*	*Centre*
Harmony and beauty through conflict	Yellow	Taurus, Scorpio Sagittarius	Mercury Moon	Whole system

This is the Ray ruling humanity and human evolution on the personality level, for humanity is 'the messenger of the Gods' – the link between the three spiritual and the three material kingdoms. The task or 'labour' of humanity, and thus of each human being, is to link, network, integrate and fuse these two kingdoms, and by doing so 'bring spirit down into matter, and transmute matter up into spirit'. This process is accomplished through a succession of integrative processes referred to as 'spiritual initiations' (see Chapter 3). The 4th Ray is thus the Ray governing human initiation. The 2nd Ray rules humanity on the soul level, whereas the Ray of 'harmony, beauty and the art of living – through conflict' governs the personality of humanity. This is why humanity is always driven towards the achievement of greater and greater harmony and beauty, and also why conflict always precipitates and accompanies these achievements.

Harmony and beauty are always relative, for each level of the evolutionary spiral produces a greater and more refined degree of these qualities. Conflict entails the experience of the dualities of:

- light and dark;
- spirit and matter;
- vision and action;
- higher self and lower self, soul and personality;
- transhuman self and subhuman self;
- higher intuitive mind and lower concrete mind;
- love and fear, happiness and sadness, pleasure and pain;
- acceptance and resistance, holding on and letting go;
- future and past;
- masculine and feminine – and so on.

Harmony and beauty can only be obtained through the experience and integration of these dualities, and each initiation entails a higher and more intensive duality-fusion experience. One person's duality is another person's fusion and vice versa, and each initiation creates a higher and differing experience of duality-fusion. 'The further one ascends up the mountain the more expansive one's view (point) of the valley.' This is the Ray of 'the art of dynamic living', for true living requires an intensive experience of the polarities and their fusion into 'that which is greater than the sum total of their parts'. From a psychological perspective this might be called the art of 'holistic' living.

The 4th Ray is the great mediating or 'bridge-building' Ray, and those governed by it need to learn and understand that all creation, and thus creative experience, consists of polarity and the movement of this polarity towards greater and greater synergy. The sages of the East understood this and developed their 'yin–yang' symbol and life philosophy to communicate this wisdom. The Tao or Way of Chinese philosophy is concerned with the interaction of yin and yang energies, and the synergy that arises out of this interaction. Fourth Ray types are therefore compelled to experience life and their creativity in a very intensive manner, as they attempt (consciously or unconsciously) to 'merge the two worlds into a synergetic whole'. This is not so much the Ray of the artist but rather the Ray of the 'art of living', although many artistic people have it as their soul or personality ruler. Taurus and Scorpio people are well known for their artistic temperament, and Mercury is concerned with the communication and expression of one's inner visions and perceptions. Sagittarius, especially Rising, is more concerned with the art of creative organization, for it is also partly ruled by the 3rd, 5th and 6th Rays.

The mind in its mediating and 'travelling' dimension is the instrument which builds the bridge between the worlds of spirit and matter. This is called the 'Rainbow Bridge', and it is built of mental matter or creative imaginative thought. This 'bridge-building' links the brain, the lower rational mind, the higher abstract mind (contemplative thinking) and the higher intuitive mind. This 'thought bridge' creates an alignment between the lower and higher minds and thus the lower and higher selves, and this alignment allows a greater communication and co-operation to take place between the soul and the personality. Higher mind intuition or the 'voice' of the soul, and lower mind analytical discrimination and articulation, the 'voice' of the personality, are thereby capable of greater inter-communication and co-operation. This entire mental process is governed by Mercury.

Fourth Ray types are creative in the true sense of the word. They need to experience life to the full, and require both spiritual and material input. They can veer from intense spiritual to intense material experience, and constantly attempt to link the two in with their creative activity. This might be through art, music, dance and so on, but it is also through organization and the living process itself. They can tend to be 'devil's advocates', advocating the spiritual where there is an imbalance of the material and vice versa. This devil's advocacy is their way of expressing the need for integration of the dualities, even though the mode of this expression is often highly intense, uncompromising, and even grossly insensitive. Note the straightforward manner of expression of Scorpios and Sagittarians.

Fourth Ray types tend to appreciate physical beauty, whether this beauty is human or otherwise. They have powerful sexual desires and often regard sex as an art in itself. They recognize that the sexual act is a literal symbol of spirit–matter fusion, and they tend to approach partnerships, sex and love-making with this in mind. The sexual chakra is directly related (energy-wise) to the throat chakra, and for this reason the majority of highly creative people (throat centre) are also highly sexed. This creates great difficulties and problems with sexuality, for there will either be an overabundance of unused sexual energy contained and/or seeping into the sexual centre, or too little sexual energy as the throat centre transmutes the sex centre. Sexual conflict, confusion and perversion is often the result, and homosexuality and pornography are major 4th Ray manifestations. Paradoxically it is the 4th Ray type (with 2nd and 7th Ray influences) that can and will discover the deeper implications of sexual energy and its uses. Tantric yoga is governed by this (and the 7th) Ray, for tantric sexuality is concerned with the right use of sexual energy.

Fourth Ray types 'swing between the polarities', and this creates great emotional and mental (and sexual) stress, trauma and imbalance. There is little they can do about this factor outside of consistently, seeking, discovering, communicating and applying the lessons and wisdom of both these worlds, and of discovering the third way that lies in the fusion of the two. These people have the real capacity to dive into the underworld and fly into the overworld and discover the beauty of both; they also have the capacity to discover the secret of secrets, namely the jewel at the centre of the lotus, the experience of fusion which lies at the core of all life, and which is revealed through the initiation experience. If 4th Ray people display great imbalances, this is because they are the seekers after 'the truth and nothing but the truth', and out of their traumas (if they so wish) can arise true harmony, beauty and balance.

These people require a great deal of freedom. They need to be free to experience life to the full. They are not easy to get on with or to live with, but they provide the adventure into life which many people desire but are afraid to explore (Taurus Sun sign is much more harmonious and lazy in this respect). Above all the 4th Ray type needs self-discipline, for without it they can become too chaotic and out of order. Self-discipline could well be said to be the most potent means to an end for 4th Rays, for it allows the dualities to be focused and fused into a more integrated whole. Prince Charles with his Scorpio Sun sign has often stated that self-discipline (early to rise, daily exercise, healthy diet and so on) makes or breaks his day.

The 4th Ray type is very susceptible to drugs, alcohol, unhealthy eating patterns, extreme laziness and even criminal activity. These self-destructive patterns are manifestations of the extreme imbalances of these people, for the swing between the polarities creates a great deal of self-centredness, selfishness and confusion, which all lead to patterns of selfishness and escapism. Saddam Hussain (whose Sun is in Taurus) is typical of the 4th Ray type, as they swing from one extreme to the other. They can be quite ruthless as they descend into the underworld, and just as quickly be extremely kind and considerate as they ascend into the light. The conscious and wise 4th Ray person, while recognizing these swings and accepting and acknowledging them, also attempts to discipline and focus his or her energies so that the dualities can fuse and merge into creative activity and service. Self-forgetfulness should be the keynote of these types, because in the giving and sharing of their powerful creativity lies their doorway to harmony and real beauty.

The intuition is very active in 4th Ray people, and intuitive artistry is one manifestation of this. Without the intuition there can be no artistic living or creativity, for the intuition is the guiding voice of the higher self, and this voice is required in every aspect of life. The sacred, whether in art, music, dance, massage, healing, poetry, drama, politics, economics, or daily living, is the natural result of the intuitive mind. The sacred has been lost in modern-day creativity because the golden thread of the intuition has been left behind. The 4th Ray artists need to restore this sacredness and many are already doing so. The Soviet Union's Scorpio Sun sign evidences why their dance, drama and music are so full of passion and meaning, whereas much of the Western world's art, while technically proficient, is devoid of deeper meaning and true passion. The mythological story of King Minos, the Minotaur, Ariadne and Prince Theseus is an archetypal 4th Ray myth, for without the golden thread of the soul's (Ariadne) intuition one cannot enter into the maze of life and transform the Minotaur of greed, materialism, fear, stagnation, repression and passionless living.

Strangely enough 4th Ray people harmony and beauty, and consistently seek to embody and manifest these qualities. Even in their chaos they seek these qualities, for without them they are dead. They often seek them solely through emotional and sexual relationship and through artistic activity of some sort, and they have to learn (through much pain) that these qualities exist within themselves and need to be discovered and expressed through sacred living itself. Objective experiences are integral to the process but real harmony and beauty are internal qualities and are the result of something greater than polarity itself; the dancer must become the dance, the singer the song, the actor the act, the musician the music, the lover the love, the liver life itself. True joy, beauty and meaning are the natural result of this merger. Shirley Maclaine in her book *Dancing in the Light*, shares this type of 4th Ray creativity when she describes the sacred dimension of dance. The will to love qualifies the 4th Ray and for this reason 'love in action' is their keynote. The 4th Ray type must demonstrate dynamic love, beauty and harmony in and through their art and life if they are to feel fulfilled.

The 4th Ray has sub-influence through Mars and Pluto (Scorpio), Vulcan and Venus (Taurus) and the Earth and Jupiter (Sagittarius). It also sub-influences Aries (through Mercury), Gemini (through Mercury), Virgo (through both the Moon and Mercury, thus the conflicts in Virgo) and Cancer (through the Moon).

Light qualities: capacity to experience life to the full, highly intuitive, enthusiastic, strong affections and passions, highly perceptive mind, generous, courageous in the extreme, well-attuned to colour and sound and artistic expression, understands both worlds and thus tolerates both, great wisdom gained through life experience; straightforward, highly sensitive, make excellent astrologers, psychologists and counsellors, and are powerful healers and good communicators.

Shadow characteristics: self-centered, selfish, untidy and chaotic, lazy, immoral, subject to extreme depressions, worries and swings of mood, attached to the past and to form, very possessive, highly strung, extreme swings between the opposites, sexually manipulative and perverted, mental battles and confusion leading to extreme bias and prejudice, susceptible to addictions and escapism – sex, drugs, alcohol, crime and fanaticism.

RAY 5 – THE PATH OF KNOWLEDGE

Keynote	Colour	Signs	Planet	Centre
Concrete knowledge	Orange	Leo, Sagittarius Aquarius	Venus	Brow

This is the Ray of knowledge gained through concrete mental experimentation and exploration. It rules all the sciences, spiritual and material, but more directly those sciences which require logical thought, deduction and articulation. Psychology and astrology fall under its influence as do the other spiritual sciences (like the science of Mind), although the 2nd, 4th and 7th Rays also govern these sciences. The 5th Ray governs Aquarius and the New Era will therefore be an Age in which the mind comes into full play, and knowledge gained through mental exploration into 'spirit and matter' will replace belief (6th Ray).

Many people are surprised to find that Venus is the only 5th Ray planet, for Venus has been associated with feelings and emotions in the past. Venusian energy is really a combination of 2nd Ray love and 5th Ray knowledge, manifesting as the quality of 'intelligent love'. Mind-heart are thus balanced, and this is why Venus is referred to as the planet of balance and harmony. Spiritual science is related to the higher rulership of Venus (Gemini, and exalted in Pisces), and material science to its lower mental rulership (Taurus and Libra). Venus is the *alter ego* or higher self of the earth, esoterically called the 'Son of Mind'. It was beings from Venus who originally planted the 'germ' of mind or 'I Am' consciousness into primitive man, and it is this 'mind' that separates the human from the animal kingdom. This is the deeper significance behind Venus being a 5th Ray planet, for the lower concrete intellect is the first aspect of human consciousness. The majority of humans identify themselves with this mental aspect and feel superior to the animal kingdom because of it. Herein lies the reason for the perverted exploitation of the animal kingdom. All forms of material science are manifestations of this Ray, and these sciences have dominated society for the past 200 years or so. 'I think, therefore I Am' is the lower keynote of this Ray; 'I Am, therefore I Think' is its higher keynote.

There is a higher dimension to this Ray and that is 'higher or pure' logic or reason; this type of logic is qualified by 'intelligent love' or 'inner knowing', and this is the true quality of Venus and the higher self. This is the real factor that determines the nature of higher knowledge and of true science and scientific exploration. The scientist of the future will have to explore and use this inner dimension of the mind, for without it there can be no true discovery and no true knowledge. The secrets of the micro (atomic) and the macro (cosmic) universe open to discovery once the mind and the heart have been integrated. The failure to integrate thought and feelings has resulted in the abuse of knowledge and led to the catastrophes (atomic fission, pollution, animal experimentation) facing modern-day humanity.

Every human being is automatically a scientist of life, for intelligent love (mind–heart balance) and the voice of pure reason or inner knowing allow one to gain knowledge of the workings of life. Einstein and other authentic scientists combined these two interconnected aspects of the 5th Ray and thus balanced thought and feelings. Einstein, who was the great 5th Ray initiate of this century, stated the following:

> God does not play dice with the universe. . . . I maintain that the cosmic religious feeling is the strongest and noblest motive for scientific research. . . . Humanity has every reason to place the proclaimers of high moral standards and values above the discoveries of objective truth. What humanity owes to Buddha, Moses and Jesus ranks to me higher than all the achievements of the enquiring mind.

And to top it all:

> Nationalism is an infantile disease. It is the measles of humanity. Our schoolbooks glorify war and hide its horrors. They inculcate hatred in the veins of our children. I would teach peace rather than war. I would inculcate love rather than hate.

Scientists who work in the military, pollutant and animal vivisection industries would do well to listen to Einstein, that great and true scientist. Einstein was the living embodiment of the 5th Ray Venusian type. It should also be noted that he was a rebel and revolutionary (in the real sense) throughout his life, and obeyed his inner voice and not the lesser voices of those outside him. Quantum physics has now discovered that the observer influences that which is being observed. This puts paid to the ignorant theory that one can be a detached observer (scientist), for the experimenter influences the experiment. *The Tao of Physics* and *The Turning Point* by Fritjof Capra (Fontana) deal with these new scientific discoveries and their relationship to religious/spiritual experience.

The Master of this Ray is Master Hilarion, an incarnation of St Paul. It is he who inspires the great scientists and guides the knowledge and inventions that benefit humanity.

The 5th Ray governs lower and higher (pure) reason or logic. The use of the logical mind to penetrate into matter or into the greater mind of the universe itself is the work of this Ray. The Sagittarius Sun philosopher who has qualified in philosophy through a formal educational institution, and the Sagittarius Rising philosopher who has qualified through the university of life are two very different people. One is learning about other people's philosophies through the agency of the intellect, the other is discovering the meaning of life through the use of the higher intellect (5th Ray) and the intuition (4th Ray). The 5th Ray governs the seeker after truth who uses intellect to discover the workings and laws of matter and the truth that lies within matter. The deeper the 5th Ray scientist/mind penetrates into matter the more they come to the realization that 'matter is simply spirit vibrating at a particular speed', which is the understanding Einstein came to many years ago.

This Ray came into strong manifestation at the time of the scientific revolution, but is now in a process of objective withdrawal due to its overuse in our materially orientated society. This withdrawal will be completed by the end of this century. The result will be a far greater balance between spiritual and material science. The scientific exploration of consciousness, of which astrology and the new psychologies form the foundation, will thus become a vital part of the new world order, and the astrologers and psychologists of the future will play a key role in formulating the new 'scientific' values and attitudes that shape it.

The 5th Ray type is a 'seeker after truth'. These people use the mind in all its forms to seek, explore, discover and communicate truth as they understand it. They do not want to communicate other people's truths, but the realities that they themselves discover. They will study what others have discovered, but prefer to synthesize these discoveries within the context of their own discoveries, thus producing their own unique presentation of truth. For this reason they have a strong mental focus, well developed intellects and the capacity to articulate their findings through various forms of verbal and written expression. They also have strong mental egos, and this obviously leads to intellectual pride and arrogance, a highly critical nature which can often be quite vindictive and destructive), a powerful independent mental nature and a forceful will. They think that what they discover is 'truth', forgetting that it is but 'a drop of water in the vast ocean of truth'. This is equally true of the material or spiritual scientist, and the pride, separation and destructive criticism that manifests in the material scientific community is often evidenced in so-called spiritual circles too. Traditional and humanistic astrologers and organizations are well known for their crystallized concepts on the science of astrology, forgetting that they are studying 'the science of the infinite'. Astronomers who are studying the universe forget that the universe is studying them too, yet they see themselves as 'intelligent' and the universe as being devoid of intelligence. It is worthwhile repeating here that if it were not for the Sun's heat and light astronomers would be stone dead; the Sun does not need astronomers for its existence but astronomers sure need the Sun!

The majority of 5th Ray types are interested in the external world of 'things'. Form is their God and they are attached to the working of form. Biologists, zoologists, physicists, chemists, doctors and surgeons, nurses (although the 2nd Ray influences them too), computer programmers, archaeologists, astronomers and so on are governed by this Ray. They all desire knowledge of the material world, some for purely selfish ambitious reasons and others in order to serve their fellow human beings. There is also the higher type of scientist who wishes to explore and discover the 'science of the soul' and the interconnectedness of all things. These are the quantum physicists, ecologists and the many other types who see science as a means to an end (to serve humanity) and not an end in itself. Sir Isaac Newton, one of the Britain's greatest scientists, was such a type. Sir Isaac was also a student of astrology, and when he was asked by Haley (the discoverer of Haley's Comet) how *he* could believe in astrology, he answered: 'My dear friend, I have studied the subject, you have not.'

The science of 'mind' is also governed by this Ray, and anyone studying the relationship between the brain, mind and higher mind is involved with 5th Ray study. Materialistic scientists consistently make the mistake of assuming the brain and the mind to be one and the same thing.

The brain is part of the physical body, so how can it be equated with thought, which is non-physical? The science of the mind is directly related to the science of 'consciousness' or the soul, and this is why Venus, the sister planet or higher self of the Earth, is the only 5th Ray planet. The brain is the physical computer of the mind; it has 10 billion brain cells or computer keys. The central computer programmer is God, and the keyboard controller is mankind. Every thought we think activates one or other brain cell or group of cells, for each thought has its brain cell counterpart. Only about 10 per cent of brain capacity is being used. When Einstein was asked how to activate the other 90 per cent, he answered 'Think!' The human being is only now entering into 'creative evolutionary thinking', for it is dynamic thinking (3rd, 4th, 5th and 7th Rays) that activates the brain cells and allows mankind to become a co-thinker and co-creater with God, the Masters and the Angels. The computer age is but a manifestation of this accelerated thinking. It might be said that the accelerated thinking manifested the computer and not vice versa.

When the 5th Ray is not balanced with the 2nd, 4th or 6th Rays (by Ray composition) there tends to be a rejection, fear and suppression of anything to do with feelings, emotions, sensitivity and love. The individual becomes a cold, masculine-analytical type who tends to believe that science is the ultimate God. This creates huge relationship problems, personally and socially, for how can such a type relate correctly to his or her partner, children, friends and co-workers? In the world of science they might be successful and appreciated, but when it comes to the world of personal and intimate relationships they are cripples. The very nature of this imbalance (less evidenced than the 4th Ray imbalance but in many senses as crippling to self and society) has created massive problems for humanity and for all the kingdoms of the planet. It is no wonder that this Ray is being withdrawn, and that the UK government and other political leaders have cut back on scientific funding. It would seem that as this Ray is withdrawn its 5th and 1st Ray (politics) types are unconsciously responding to its call.

It is obvious that the 5th Ray has a greater masculine than feminine influence because it is a masculine Ray. Logical mentality is a masculine trait, and our society is largely dominated and ruled by men with strong logical minds. Politics (1st Ray), economics and business (3rd Ray) and science are all masculine Rays and dominated by men, but strangely enough even the feminine Ray activities such as education (2nd Ray), the arts and psychologies (4th Ray) and religion (6th Ray) are also largely dominated by men. It is only when the soul octaves of these Rays are activated that their finer qualities really begin to imbue their activities and the balance of masculine and feminine energies is achieved. Once again the incoming 7th Ray of 'synthesis' is bringing this about.

The 5th Ray is extremely important to humanity and the New Era for the following reasons:

1. It is the only Ray governing Aquarius and one of the two Rays ruling Leo, the opposite Sign to Aquarius.
2. It is one of the three Rays (with the 4th and 6th) governing Sagittarius, which has a very potent influence on the Earth because the Earth itself is its inner ruler.
3. It is the only Ray governing Venus, the higher self of humanity.
4. Humanity is in its 5th root race evolutionary cycle, a cycle which corresponds to the development of the 5th mental Ray. Its New Era pioneers are beginning to respond to its 6th futuristic root race in which the intuition will be the dominating factor.

The tendency amongst 'spiritually orientated' people to negate the rational mind is based more on ignorance than wisdom. The mind can either be the killer of the real, which undoubtedly the lower concrete mind has become, or it can be the doorway to the real. When the mind is used as a conscious instrument to bridge the gap between the lower self/mind and the higher self/mind it becomes what it was always meant to be, a channel to penetrate into the mind of God. It also becomes a channel to express and communicate the wonder of God's universal mind. It is the higher self or soul (Venus) that, for all intents and purposes, is the mind of God, for as the Christ stated: 'Only through Me [the Christ Self] can you reach the Father [the Monadic Self].' The aim is to fuse mind and heart and the higher octave of the 5th Ray embodies this fused energy. If God was only heart He would not have given the human being ten billion brain cells, and the corresponding 'mind' to activate them.

Fifth Ray communicators can be articulate but also very dry and non-stimulating if they rely solely upon their lower intellects for their knowledge and mode of communication. Their obsession with finding 'proof' shuts them off from the loving and magical nature of the universe, and their intuitive chord to life is cut off. The aim of course is to link the feminine intuition (2nd/4th Rays) and the articulate masculine intellect. Einstein was a master of this linkage, as are many people who are inspiring speakers. Science, religion and art (5th, 6th and 4th Rays) have been divided from one another and this linkage of Rays must be re-established. The 7th Ray of 'synthesis' rules the outer activity of the New Era and for this reason all the Rays are beginning to converge into a unified and co-operative whole.

The overriding characteristic of 5th Ray types is scepticism. They think ('think' being the operative word) that because they do not know something this something does not exist. They are atheistic because they have no logical proof that God exists. They see the Sun as a mere ball of gaseous fire.

They love intellectual arguments and tend to exhaust themselves and others with futile mind games. They regard feelings, emotions, tears and even spontaneous laughter as childish and immature, ever forgetting that repression of these aspects of human nature leads to severe imbalance and disease of many sorts. The medical scientist, proud of his or her rational qualifications and science, is consistently attending diseased and dying patients whose suffering is a result of emotional repression and other imbalanced life-patterns. They want proof that this or that complementary healing system works, and even a full explanation of the means by which it does so, before they will give it their blessing. If someone touches a scientist and he feels good and happy after being touched, how is he going to prove that he feels good? This is the danger of mere logic, and until the head is balanced with the heart the scientific community is not qualified to demand 'proof', for true proof can only be gained when logic and intuition are working hand in hand.

True scientists of life are loving individuals who are not afraid to feel. They are humble because they realize the infinity of the mystery of life. They combine inner knowing or embodied intuition with a well-attuned and strong rational mind, and are thus internally independent and outside of external control. They are honest, open and serve the greater good of humanity, and refuse to work in industries which pollute the human and planetary environment. David Bellamy and similar environmental conscious scientists are examples, as are the many medical practitioners who have chosen to combine allopathic and complementary therapies. Society is withdrawing its respect for the old logically imprisoned scientists and their irresponsible behaviour is being less and less tolerated. The new scientist is not simply the so-called quantum physicist but the human being who goes out on a limb to explore and discover life at first hand.

The 5th Ray has a sub-influence through the Sun (Leo), Jupiter and the Earth (Sagittarius) and Jupiter and Uranus (Aquarius). It also sub-influences Gemini, Taurus and Libra (through Venus).

Light qualities: well developed intellect, good memory, excellent discrimination, are not affected by emotional glamour, command of language, articulate in verbal and/or written communication, can explain abstract ideas in a logical way, can communicate facts accurately; commonsense approach to life; able to blend clear thinking with sensitivity, detachment and emotional control, good business sense, independent, responsible, perfectionist; desire to know how things work; well-ordered.

Shadow characteristics: narrow-mindedness, mental pride and arrogance, highly critical, prejudiced, ambitious and competitive in the extreme, repressed emotions and feelings, lack sensitivity and love, pedantic, attached to trivia, long-winded, insecure in personal intimate relationships (live too much in their heads), separate life into disconnected compartments, materialistic and greedy, attached to the five senses, have a deep-seated fear of the feminine side of life, serious to the extreme, lack humour.

RAY 6 – THE PATH OF DEVOTIONAL IDEALISM

Keynote	Colours	Signs	Planets	Centres
Idealism, devotion	Sky-blue, pink, rose-red	Virgo, Pisces, Sagittarius	Neptune, Mars	Heart, solar plexus

This Ray had rulership over the past age of Pisces, and its positive (soul) and negative (personality) sides were clearly demonstrated over the past 2,000 years. Its major channel has been orthodox religion, for religion and the masses are governed by this Ray. Religious idealism and devotion to God, religious figureheads/gurus and teachings have powerfully influenced this past Age. Western and Eastern religion and spirituality are both governed by this Ray, although Judaism, originating more from the Arien Era, has other Ray influences, including the 1st and 3rd.

The Master of this Ray is Master Jesus, who demonstrated the highest qualities of this Ray over His lifetime. The Hebrew race and religion was offered the opportunity to move into the Piscean Era, and many of them did, but the vast majority of Jews failed to take the Piscean initiation by rejecting Jesus as their Messiah. This was a grave error, and according to the Master DK Master Jesus will reappear to the Jewish race before the dawn of the New Aquarian Era to offer them a second opportunity. When I was networking Israel in 1979 I had a powerful revelationary dream which indicated that the Jews (of Israel) would accept Jesus this time around, but only after they had gone through a terrible purging of their national, racial and religious ego. I feel this purging is still to come. The Jewish race has a 1st Ray soul and a 3rd Ray personality, and the shadow of these Rays is pride, arrogance and a tendency to listen to no one (including each other). Their gift is the power to initiate and to pioneer, and the genius for organization. Jews are often found at the head of groups and organizations and they are natural leaders. These gifts should be shared with humanity and not kept for themselves, and this is the great defect of Israel as a nation. Israel (Jerusalem) is said to be the solar plexus centre (6th Ray) of the world, and this emotional centre must be transformed into love; this requires the Jewish race to rejoin the greater race of humanity and all religions to become part of one new world religion.

The Master Jesus demonstrated the highest qualities of the 6th and 2nd Rays – unconditional love, total forgiveness ('I tell you to forgive seventy times seven times'), self-sacrificial service and total devotion to God and the greater spiritual good of humanity. Jesus was a 3rd degree initiate when He incarnated 2,000 years ago. He had taken this initiation in His past incarnation as the Jewish prophet Elias. He took His 4th initiation at the crucifixion and His 5th Master's initiation in His next incarnation as Apollonius of Tyana, a figure well known (in the history of that time) for His dematerializing activities. Apollonius served as a spiritual mentor to a number of more peaceful Roman emperors. Later a more violent emperor sentenced Apollonius to a tribunal in a Roman arena for false crimes. When the tribunal sentenced him to death (in front of thousands of Romans) he made the following statement: 'You can take away my body but you cannot take away my soul. And you cannot even take away my body.' He then enveloped himself in the long robe that he used to wear and simply dematerialized himself.

Apollonius has resumed his original Master Jesus identity and today lives in a Syrian body. His near future destiny is to take physical command (if one might use this term) of the Christian religion and Church and move it on to a higher 'New Age' level of the spiral. He will do this by taking over the Pope's position in the Vatican, for the present Pope is the last of his line. From the Vatican he will guide the various exclusive religions towards a more inclusive world religion.

The problem with this Ray in its human manifestation is that it is the Ray of belief (as opposed to knowledge). Its adherents, through their powerful and one-pointed idealism and devotion (to the religious/spiritual teacher and teaching) become fanatically and emotionally attached to their belief system. They are then prepared to fight and die for their belief system, even if the belief system is based around peace, love and tolerance. Christianity and Islam are the best examples. On the other hand the adherents of Mahatma Gandhi and Martin Luther King and their 'peace' movements stuck to the ideal and demonstrated the great power and beauty of this Ray. The greatest disciples of Christianity have also demonstrated this one-pointed idealism and sacrificial love.

It is also sadly true that in many senses the present religions have failed humanity, and the conflicts and wars that have been a hallmark of all these religions (including Hinduism and Islam in the East) have proved to be their ultimate downfall in humanity's eyes. Mars, the planet of conflict and war, is a 6th Ray planet, and together with its peaceful 6th Ray counterpart Neptune, has contributed to the totally dual nature of the Piscean cycle. Now that the Lord of the 6th Ray is withdrawing his energy these religions are self-destructing, as are all 6th Ray groupings, institutions, nations, ideologies and activities. That which separates (6th Ray) is on the way out and that which unifies (7th Ray) is on the way in.

The 6th Ray is the energy that brings down higher will (1st Ray) love (2nd Ray), intelligence (3rd Ray), artistic creativity (4th Ray), and knowledge (5th Ray) into the astral or emotional plane. This is the most dangerous of all the planes, for it is the plane of emotional illusion, glamour and self-deception. Fear has its roots in the astral plane, as do hate, jealousy, envy, vengefulness, wishful dreamlike fantasy, illusionary ideals and fanaticism. The USA has a 6th Ray personality, and it is often said of this country that its leaders and peoples find it hard to distinguish between fantasy and reality. The Middle East and Ireland also have this 6th Ray make-up which produces religious fanaticism, and the USA has strong 6th Ray connections with these countries. The USSR's 6th Ray personality produced its 'Communistic' idealism but this USSR/East European ideal has now collapsed under the influence of Neptune's 6th Ray 'dissolving' transit. The Lord of the 6th Ray was in the process of dissolving outworn ideals and structures, and the USSR and East Europe were the graceful recipients of this Ray. The USSR's 7th Ray soul is now resuming its rightful power, and the 'death and rebirth' clash of these two Rays is causing the present but short-lived problem in that great country. The same goes for Eastern Europe. According to the Master DK (*Destiny of the Nations*, Lucis Pub.), 'Out of Russia will emerge the New World Religion.'

This Ray rules the solar plexus chakra, personally and collectively. This is the 'butterflies in the stomach' centre, for fear is its major characteristic. Either one chooses fear or one chooses love; either one chooses death or one chooses life. 'Choice' is the keynote, and it is worthwhile noting that the sign of 'choice', namely Libra, rules the final years of this century. The personality keynote of Libra is 'Let choice be made'.

The Middle East is the overall astral chakra of the world, with Israel (Jerusalem) being the focal point of this centre. It is quite ridiculous to refer to Jerusalem as the city of peace, for it is exactly the opposite. 'Re-li-gion' means 'to relink with God' and this relinking is synonymous with inclusive love and intelligent thinking. This link has been lost to the peoples of the Middle East and a 6th Ray conflict might well be necessary to purge and transform this centre. In the same way that millions of human beings are undergoing a rapid and painful transformation of their emotional and sexual nature and relationships, so will this 6th Ray centre have to undergo a similar change. At the time of writing, the Gulf Crisis has brought this to a head. It is a very dangerous but necessary situation because all three 6th Ray religions are facing one another, and stubborn adherence to one's exclusive ideals is a common factor in all three. The USA also has a 6th Ray personality.

Each of these nations and religions believes it has the only answer and the 'others' are lost and corrupt. Jews and Christians believe the Muslims are all fanatics; Muslims believe Muhammed is the highest of the prophets and everyone must be converted to Islam; Jews believe Christ was a false Messiah and the Jewish Messiah is the one true Saviour; Christians believe Christ was the only Son of God and He is coming to save humanity and especially Christians. Little do they all realize that the Christ, the Messiah and the Iman Mahdi are the same individual. There is only *one* Messiah, the great Messenger of peace and love and the adherents of these intolerant religions have perverted His message and lost touch with His Spirit. The financial and sexual scandals that consistently surface within the political and religious institutions of these countries are but a fore-taste of what is to come as these outdated religions continue to dis-integrate. A new 7th Ray World religion is being born and it will recognize One God, One Humanity and One World; it will unify rather than separate and it will rule by love and not by fear.

The spiritually evolved and mature 6th Ray type can be very intuitive, sensitive, compassionate and self-sacrificing. They can sacrifice all to help others. They are very loving, loyal, one-pointed, honest and devoted to what they serve. There is an inter-esting dual nature to 6th Ray people; on the one hand they can be passive, receptive, feminine, mystical and tolerant (Neptune), and on the other they can be active, outgoing, aggressive, projective, intolerant, combative, and fanatical (Mars). They can switch from one to the other depending on circumstances. They will listen to the words of their priest, guru or leader without questioning anything and then go out and try to convert others in a masculine fashion. Sixth Ray types are consistently trying to convert others to their views and beliefs. This is one of their worst characteristics. Neptune and Mars could be said to represent the most feminine and mascu-line of planetary forces, and this underlying duality is both a gift and a curse to the 6th Ray type. It enables abstract idealism and inner aspirations (Neptune) to be dynamically manifested (Mars), but also causes a great deal of conflict and confusion to arise within the individual as these dualities clash. A positive examples of 6th Ray energy, combined with 1st, 2nd and 3rd Ray energy, was the Band Aid recording and Live Aid concerts. Bob Geldof was inspired to bring these two great ideals 'down to earth' and with a combina-tion of will, love and businesslike organization succeeded where angels would fear to tread. His book *Is That It?* (Penguin Books) is a wonderful and awe-inspiring account of this remarkable feat.

When the 6th Ray type is let down by his or her ideal not being fulfilled they can become terribly hurt. The result may be suicide, drug addiction or alcoholism. The assassination of great figures like Gandhi and Anwar Sadat of Egypt (and many others) were the result of the assassin's broken dreams. The 6th Ray person forgets (does not wish to see) that the ideal was based upon his or her own belief system and much of it was self-delusion. They became so unified with the ideal that they were blind to all else. The dark side of fanatical idealism is all too evident in the world, but we should not be deceived by the more obvious side of this fanaticism such as terrorism (IRA, PLO and so on) for the hidden side of nationalistic and capitalistic idealism is just as corrupt and destructive. The secret service organizations of most nations have always practised terrorism behind the scenes. The USA and USSR governments committed acts of terrorism in Vietnam and Afghanistan that were nothing less than mass crimes against humanity. The USSR has at least admitted its crimes but the USA has yet to apologize to Vietnam (and Cambodia and Chile and Nicaragua) for the crimes against its peoples.

Without 6th Ray idealism there could be no push towards that which is higher, greater and more elevated. This Ray drives the individual and humanity towards greater heights, aspirations and ideals. This idealism now needs to be integrated with an inclusive higher purpose (Ray 1), intelligent love (Ray 2) and action (Ray 3), clear and discriminative thinking (5th Ray) and constructive and creative organization (Ray 7), for it is time for humanity to grow up and synthesize the many facets that compose her rainbow nature.

Mass cults and movements, ranging from the Moonies to the Rajneesh, Sai Baba and 'Rebirthing' groupings come under this Ray's influence. There are positive and negative aspects to these movements; in some there is a genuine desire to serve Spirit, to manifest love and to devote oneself to some larger purpose; in others (like the Moonies) there is a powerful bondage to past thought-forms. The Moonies are a typical 4th Ray (Moon) and 6th Ray movement, and they are attempting to bring patterns of the lunar past (the Moon) into the present. The worship of spiritual figureheads and their particular teachings and techniques is also based upon past 6th Ray patterns, for it is still a projection of one's inner selfhood. The statement that 'only when all objective figure-heads are given up can the inner self reveal its Presence' is particularly relevant in the cases of many of the above groupings. Most of these groups originate in India and the USA, which both have strong 6th Ray make-up. The 'guru' (they are all 'Masters' to their followers, even though these followers have no idea what a Master is) and/or 'techniques' for enlightenment and self-transformation all too often become a prison-house in themselves, for attachment to any objective figure or technique defeats its very purpose. The follower who keeps running back to the guru loses the capacity to listen to the true Teacher within, and the person who becomes glamorized by outer miracles (no matter how genuine) forgets that the greatest miracle of all abides within himself. This is the dangerous glamour of the 6th Ray and its great power to deceive.

Devotion in the New Era will be directed towards Spirit itself; to the Christ as the world teacher, towards one's own higher self, the true inner Master, and towards the service of humanity. This is a higher and more appropriate form of 6th Ray devotional idealism, and must replace the older Piscean forms indicated above. In the case of orthodox religions, especially the fundamental forms of Christianity (still powerful in the USA despite all the recent scandals), Islam (the most 6th Ray of all), Judaism and Hinduism these will have to be burn out through the power of Pluto as it transits through Sagittarius from 1995 onwards (Sagittarius rules religion). The self-destructive nature of the entire Middle East is already evidencing this bloody process.

As the 6th Ray moves out of manifestation during the 1990s we can expect to see a great deal of dissolution (Neptune) and destruction (Pluto). Although this will be most obvious in the religious sphere, it will also occur in the political, economic and social spheres, for outdated patterns of thinking (5th Ray) and emotional idealism need to be transformed as humanity enters its New Era.

The 6th Ray sub-influences the Moon and Mercury (Virgo), the Earth and Jupiter (Sagittarius) and Jupiter, Neptune and Pluto (Pisces). It also has sub-influence in Aries and Scorpio (through Mars) and Cancer and Pisces (through Neptune).

Positive qualities: one-pointed aspiration, intuitive, sensitive, compassionate, unconditionally loving, sincere, honest, loving, warm, devoted, nurturing, self-sacrificial, courageous, receptive, psychic/clairvoyance, capacity to endure great pain, patient, serving, all-forgiving, understanding, tolerant.

Shadow characteristics: fanatical, violent, intolerant, suspicious, deceptive, naïve, easily deceived and glamorized, emotionally imbalanced, blind to other ways, neurotic, extremely self-defensive, disorganized, escapist, susceptible to addictions, be they drugs, alcohol, sex, or crime, hypocritical to the extreme, irrational, manipulative, deceptive.

RAY 7 – THE PATH OF ORGANIZATION
AND SYNTHESIS

Keynotes	Colour	Signs	Planet	Centre
Ceremony, order, ritual, synthesis	Violet	Aries, Cancer, Capricorn	Uranus	Sacral

This is the objective ruling Ray of Aquarius and it therefore rules the New Era. This Ray links and synthesizes spirit (Ray 1 of spiritual will/power) and matter (Rays 3 and 5) into a synthetic whole (Ray 7). It builds and organizes the etheric–physical forms that are necessary to hold and materialize the will and purpose of Deity. This Ray Lord and His many co-workers, who include the Angelic Hierarchy and the nature spirits and elementals, are responsible for building the etheric and physical forms of creation. Vera Stanley Alder in her book *From the Mundane to the Magnificent* (Rider Books) describes the work of this Ray and its workers in a wonderful fashion.

Every physical form or body, be it that of an atom, an organ, a human personality, a rock, a tree, an animal, a chair, a planet, a solar system, a galaxy or whatever, has its subtle etheric body. This body is the subjective framework of the gross physical body, and is composed of millions of channels or 'nadis' through which spiritual, mental and emotional energies flow into and out of the physical body. These channels, which are invisible to human sight, converge at different points and create energy centres (centres of force) or *chakras*. The planets are the chakras of the body of the solar Logos. Various cities like London, New York and Geneva are the chakras of the planetary Logos, as are the nature chakras like the seven wonders of the world (and many more). In our septenary system there are seven major chakras, of which the seven sacred planets are the solar archetypes.

In the human being these seven centres are situated along the spinal cord and correspond physically to the seven major endocrine glands and nerve centres. There are forty-nine minor centres situated at all the joints of the human body, such as the elbow, knee, finger and toe joints. The most important of the major centres are situated at the crown of the skull (Ray 1, Vulcan), heart and centre of the chest (Ray 2, Sun and Jupiter), throat (Ray 3, Saturn), brow (Ray 5, Venus), solar plexus (Ray 6, Mars and Neptune), sacral centre (Ray 7, Uranus) and base of the spine (Ray 1, Pluto). Ray 4 (Mercury) rules the whole system for it governs the etheric body itself. It has a focus in the brow centre, for this centre and the pituitary gland are the overall governors of the etheric–physical body. The material octave of Ray 3 (the Earth) governs the spleen centre, which is the 'clearing' or recycling centre of the body. This provides a clue to the importance of the recycling efforts now occurring in many countries, for this global activity indicates that the spleen centre of the solar system, namely the Earth, is beginning to function as it rightly should. Purification and ecology are two keynotes of the Earth and Spleen Centre. Astrology works through the interaction of these greater and lesser etheric bodies and chakras, for the law of correspondence governs the functioning of all life in our universe.

When a planet (chakra) transits through the greater planetary zodiac and 'activates' a planet (chakra) in the individual birth chart (human being), this solar planet activates the corresponding centre in the individual. It also activates the corresponding endocrine gland, nerve plexi and organs related to the chakra; for example Uranus (7th Ray) transits activate the sacral centre, the gonads and ovaries, the sexual organ, plus the crown centre, to which the 7th Ray is directly linked, plus the throat centre (Ray 3) which is the higher creative centre of the sacral. Uranus transits are connected with the awakening of creative force – will, intelligence, action and sex.

The creative mind (3rd Ray) is the 'archetypal' creator or builder of this entire system, just as the mind of God is the creator or builder of His greater system. The Angelic Hierarchy are called 'the great builders' for they are the mind of God and are responsible for building the etheric blueprints of creation. The human mind (humanity is the mind of the Earth) is supposed to be co-creator in this great enterprise, but is only now beginning to play its conscious part in this creative process.

The Lord of the 7th Ray is responsible for creating the etheric body of these systems. The angels or devas and the elementals are his co-workers, the angels creating the 'blueprints' and the elementals animating and vitalizing the etheric–physical bodies or forms. This process occurs right down to the atoms themselves. Vera Alder's *From the Mundane to the Magnificent* explains how each atom is literally a miniature solar system with its own Sun (nucleus) and planets (electrons), and how each atomic life is overseen by its own god, an elemental being. Can we imagine the wonder and beauty and magic of billions of these atomic elementals working to maintain our own solar system? It is the human soul or 'angel' who is the angelic archetype or queen of this entire system, and the Monad who is the king. Such is the magnificence of each human being. The 7th Ray governs this entire organizational etheric system, and this is the deeper reason for it being called the Ray of organization, ceremony, ritual and synthesis. If we could manage our daily lives as the elementals manage their little worlds there would indeed be order and magic in the world.

The 7th Ray types are the organizers of society. Ceremony and ritual create the atmosphere for organization to take place, but these ritualistic ceremonies have to be creative and dynamic if they are to work. Dead and outworn rituals have no life-force – their elementals are largely asleep. New and dynamic rituals and ceremonial organization must arise from within, and in the New 7th Ray Era we have to create our own rituals, ceremonies and festivals to facilitate the externalization of spirit through matter. Appropriate incense, candles, flowers, dress, crystals, invocation (of spiritual forces), meditations and evocation need to be used in organizing one's daily living, work, ceremonies and so on. Chapter 7 will explain how the entire year needs to be used to facilitate intelligent rhythmic living.

This Ray synthesizes politics (1st Ray), business (3rd Ray), science (5th Ray) and religious/spiritual organization (7th Ray) for it blends all these energies. This is the essential reason for the gradual merging of all these activities over the last few years with the 'green' revolution. The 7th Ray governs 'ecology' and the true definition of holistic ecology is 'the interrelationship of various organisms to one another and to their surroundings'. The 7th Ray is the magical energy that 'weaves all life-forms into an interconnected whole'; it is therefore the Ray governing the science of 'holism'. The disconnected mind of the human ego has separated politics, business, science, the arts, religion, psychology, astrology, medicine and so on into disconnected parts. It is the connected mind of the human soul that is reconnecting all these parts and that will produce the new 'holistic' civilization, culture and world order. This is the true magic of the New Era.

This Ray is also the Ray of interhuman relationships (Uranus is the higher ruler of Libra, the sign ruling such relationship). All human relationships are being born anew, including intimate partnerships and marriage, sexual relationships and working relationships. New rituals and ceremonies have to be created to facilitate these relationships, for the old marriage ceremonies are dead and lifeless. This Ray combines individuality (1st Ray) and group-consciousness and activity (7th Ray), and its influence drives people into seeking true individual identity and creativity and into seeking group awareness, co-operation and synthesis.

It fuses centralization and decentralization, bringing about co-operation between the two. The USSR has a 7th Ray soul and this nation is now going through the experimentation stage of merging central and decentralized government. A nation or group needs to be centred within itself in order to be strong and secure; it must be part of a larger centre of which it is a co-operative part; and it must be decentralized in that it takes responsibility for its own evolution and is not controlled by outer forces.

All effective organization first has to be thought out in the mind. It is the dynamic, well-organized mind that first weaves the etheric pattern of organizational activity. 'Without vision the nation perishes' (as does the individual, partnership or group) and this vision or 'divine inspiration' is the work of the creative mind. Just as the mind of our planetary Logos has already woven the etheric body of the New Era, so each individual and group and nation has to weave their own mind and create their New Age etheric body. Co-operation and co-creation between God and humanity thus become living realities. Purpose (Ray 1), creative thinking (Ray 3), articulate communication (Ray 5) and constructive practical activity (Ray 7) all work together to create an ordered and creative existence on Earth. Since the 1960s the younger generations have been typical 7th Ray types and it will be noticed that the majority of 'green' leaders belong to this widely misunderstood generation.

Seventh Ray types are therefore purposeful and wilful, clear-thinking, practical in terms of the way they organize their lives, very active, clean and ecologically sound in their way of living (the true members of the 'hippie' generation have been eating wholefood and using ecological products for over twenty years). They are also highly sensitive and yet courageous, very intuitive and responsive to intuitive promptings, imaginative, attuned to the future and its needs, and imbued with the pioneering spirit. They can be too authoritarian and centralized in their work and are often confused as to how to integrate centralized and decentralized power, authority and government. Experience and wisdom teaches them to be patient and flexible while simultaneously being one-pointed as to their goals. They are the experimenters of life, consistently exploring (with their minds) this and that way of doing and organizing things. They can be hyperactive (like 3rd Ray types) and need to discipline their minds through regular meditation and ordered living. Seventh Ray meditation differs from traditional 2nd Ray meditation in that it combines stillness (2nd Ray) with the dynamic use of the mind to create powerful etheric thought-forms (7th Ray). Dynamic meditation is a wonderful instrument with which to 'weave the etheric web', and all networking activities belong to this Ray.

They can also tend to give too many orders to others and need to learn to do things for themselves. The balanced type takes responsibility for their rightful workload and gladly allows others to be responsible for theirs. Delegation is their strong point. At their best they aim to balance all their life activities, and try to be moderate in their discipline. (They are the 'run a little walk a little' types when it comes to exercise.) They recognize the importance of time and energy and attempt to do their best not to waste either. They are the great recyclers of material energy and hate wasting anything – be it energy itself (off with the water-heater when hot water is not needed), food (the doggy bag type) or whatever. They are the recyclers of bottles, paper, tin cans and so on. They hate to see anything go to waste as they recognize, and are sensitive to, the right use of energy. They like to live their daily lives in a ritualistic fashion, and can lack flexibility and become too rigid if they are not careful. They nevertheless like to experiment and explore new avenues of thought and creative activity, and need change and excitement to make themselves feel alive.

They are highly sexual for the 7th Ray rules the sacral centre. They are attracted to sexual tantra and wish to use sex for spiritual purposes. They can be sexually manipulative for this reason. They can swing from excessive sexual activity to celibacy but always maintain a deep interest in sexuality and its deeper meaning and purpose. It is the 7th Ray (and 4th Ray) types who will discover the true purpose and use of sexual energy, be it that this discovery will be made through their diverse sexual experiences, lessons and revelations.

The Master Racoczi, a Hungarian Master is the Master of this Ray. It is this Master who overlighted much of the Findhorn Foundation's work (Findhorn has a 7th Ray personality). His message to Findhorn in relationship to its 7th Ray activity was to learn to live with 'elegant simplicity'. This Ray (and the 4th) will bring into manifestation the new arts in the field of dance, music and drama. Colour and sound will find new and clear channels through which to work. New forms of healing will also manifest through this Ray for the violet devas hold the key to true healing.

Rays 2 and 7 together rule group consciousness and group activity. Seventh Ray types are very individualistic yet group-orientated. The Findhorn Foundation with its Ray 2 soul and Ray 7 personality has pioneered this type of group activity, and 7th Ray groups and networks have sprung up all around the planet. The new groups, decentralized networks and global network of 'light and goodwill' are manifestations of this Ray (and Ray 2). This network is the etheric body of the New Era, and for this reason it is loose, decentralized, flexible, changeable, adaptable, and ever evolving. It has certain major power points or chakras like the Findhorn Foundation and Auroville and the other larger communities, but it is nevertheless largely decentralized and has no leaders or higher authority. Its true authority is the higher self of each individual group and centre, and the Christ who is the head of the Hierarchy.

Ray 7 activity is full of ritual, ceremony and celebration. Organization and creative activity become 'magical and adventurous' with the use of enlivening rituals. Inner attunement (Ray 2) and outer action (Ray 7) interact in 7th Ray activity. This is also the Ray of magic, both 'white magic' or the correct, powerful and ordered use of the mind, and 'black magic', when the mind is used for dark purposes. The mind is a powerful creative force, and its correct use enables structural and organizational (etheric) 'blueprints' to precede physical activity. The more one-pointed and creative the mind the more successful and creative the objective form. Ray 7 types are therefore powerful and one-pointed thinkers and organizers.

This Ray has a sub-influence through Mercury and Mars (Aries), Neptune and the Moon (Cancer) and Saturn (Capricorn). It also sub-influences Libra and Aquarius (through Uranus).

Light qualities: highly intuitive, sensitive, very organized, efficient, able to synthesize parts into a whole, independent, group-conscious, co-operative and co-creative, attuned to the future, revolutionary, strong-willed, clear-thinking, practical, loving ceremony and ritual, disliking waste, ecologically aware, original, innovative, pioneering, courageous, excellent leaders, disciplined.

Shadow characteristics: hyperactive, rigid and inflexible in discipline and life-style, rebellious, authoritarian, manipulative – mentally, sexually, verbally and otherwise, chaotic and disorderly, cold and calculating, attached to physical activity; in extreme cases can turn to black magic; can repress emotions.

CHAPTER SIX

The Rising Sign and its Deeper Significance

In the first three chapters of this book we have dealt with the factors underlying the new astrology and psychology. From this point we can move on directly to the first and most important aspect of the transpersonal astrology chart, namely the Rising sign or Ascendant. The Rising sign is the zodiacal sign rising on the eastern horizon of the Earth at the date, place and time of birth. So, for example, if you were born at dawn, your Rising sign and Sun sign will be the same. It is the starting-point of any chart and without this sign the chart cannot be correctly drawn up. It is therefore the most significant factor of the birth chart, and has been largely misunderstood and underestimated by traditional, humanistic and even the majority of transpersonal astrologers. The Rising sign changes roughly every two hours, but to establish it accurately, calculations are necessary. An astrologer will be able to perform these quite easily. Any beginner's book on astrology will also give relevant instructions.

The Ascendant is in a sense the core of the entire chart, for it is the beginning or 'seed' point of the chart and, as such, embodies the entire chart within itself. In the same way that an oak seed embodies within itself (as potential) the roots, trunk, branches, leaves and acorns (fruit) of the oak tree itself, so the Rising sign embodies the overall spiritual purpose, plan and goals of the individual, group or national life. When we talk about 'potential' from a transpersonal perspective we are referring to all the above factors, for life is essentially concerned with purpose, meaning, and direction, and the mythological but very real journey in search of the Holy Grail. This 'Grail' or 'Philosopher's Stone' is one's true God self, and the quest or journey is the unique life-path along which we must walk (and sometimes run) in order to discover this self. This self has its own purpose within the larger purpose of life and the discovery and unfoldment of this purpose is synonymous with the discovery of this self. In other words the quest to discover one's true identity or self and its higher purpose, the unfoldment of this purpose and the goals and fulfilment related to this unfoldment are all interconnected, and are embodied within:

1. the energies of the Rising sign, its Cross and its Rays; and
2. its transpersonal planetary ruler and its Ray; and
3. the house this ruler is found in.

The complexities of deciphering the above are naturally the domain of the new astrologer and/or psychologist, but much of what will be shared in this chapter can be psychologically understood by anyone reading this book.

UNDERSTANDING THE ASCENDANT

The Ascendant is where one takes incarnation – where one comes into physical birth; it is where one awakens to the light of the material world. It is therefore connected to the 'awakening' process. The Rising sign is symbolically the 'dawn' point of the chart – the point of new awakening or birth into a new life. Its energy even indicates how we approach waking up in the morning; how we feel and act when we awake. For example fire signs (Aries, Leo and Sagittarius) spring into life with a fiery enthusiasm while the earth signs (Taurus, Virgo and Capricorn) will be slow to awaken; the water signs (Cancer, Scorpio and Pisces) are sensitive and emotional whereas the air signs (Gemini, Libra and Aquarius) are mentally active as soon as they awake. The Rising sign also indicates what type of birth one had – whether it was a quick fiery birth, a slow drawn-out birth, an emotionally traumatic birth, and so on. In other words, how did one awaken to the light of a new incarnation? If one could attune to the qualitative energy surrounding the birth moment (time) one could pick up the energy of the Rising sign or the planet ruling it. Stephen Arroyo (in his book *Astrology, Karma and Transformation*) describes how he picked up the energy of Saturn at the time of a birth and subsequently found the Rising sign to be Capricorn (Saturn rules Capricorn), although he had originally thought it would be Sagittarius.

This physical 'awakening' experience is directly related to the *fact that the Rising* sign is the central factor connected to spiritual awakening. We incarnate into a new life, we awake each morning into a new life; and we are born again into a new life when we awake to spiritual purpose in our lives. Spiritual awakening is referred to as 'the second birth'. According to the Master DK, the

Ascendant remains dormant until this reawakening occurs and I have found this to be true. It is only when the individual awakens to spiritual purpose – to the need to discover 'Who One Is', 'Why One is Here' and 'Where One is Heading', that the Rising sign is activated and truly begins to stream into the life of the individual. In the vast majority of cases this occurs around the age of 28–29 years, with the beginning of the fifth seven-year cycle (28–35) and the Saturn return (Saturn returns to its birth position around 29 years of age). This awakening can, and does often occur earlier than this time, but the full jolt of such an awakening usually takes place between 28 and 30 years of age. It is necessary to release and 'tie the knots' of one's past (relatively of course) before one can truly move into one's future (the 28–35-year cycle). Between 27 and 28 years of age we have what is called the progressed Moon cycle, when the progressed Moon returns to its natal position, and this cycle brings to a close the 21–28-year cycle, which is related to Cancer, the sign ruled by the Moon and connected to the past and its chains.

The final year of the fourth seven-year cycle (27–28), and the final year of all seven-year cycles (20–21, 34–35 and so on) are completion and releasing years, and the progressed Moon cycles at 27–28, and again at 55–56, are the two cycles most directly related to this 'releasing the past and cutting the chains' mechanism. Attachments to the past, to one's upbringing, conditioning, blood family belief systems, religious and cultural ties, past work and career attachments and limitations, old relationships and friendships and so on. It is worthwhile to remember the Christ's statement here: 'He who loves his mother, father, brother or sister more than Me is not worthy of My Name.' It is not love that is broken away from but rather emotional and instinctive bonds. The Moon's position indicates where (house) and how (sign) one is trapped by the past, while the Rising sign and Saturn indicate where and how one must move into the future and thus free oneself from the past.

It is for the above reasons that people go through such a turnabout when they awaken to inner realities. The Rising sign embodies the most potent energy of the chart (the seed of anything embodies the most concentrated form of energy) for the soul is the powerhouse of one's life. The Rising sign *is* the powerhouse – the central electromagnetic centre of one's life (chart) and this energy begins to be released when one awakens. This is what is called 'the reversal of the wheel', for, before one awakens, one is *involving* into matter for one only has material ambitions and is living according to the dictates of the past. When one awakens to new life one begins to *evolve* into spirit, for one's spiritual purpose, aspirations and goals begin to take hold. A new and more potent dimension of the Rising sign is activated, released, experienced and expressed at each new initiation, for one 'awakens' to new and greater realities. Astrologers will thus have to rethink what they have been taught (in the past) and move into a higher level of transpersonal interpretation.

THE ASCENDANT AND THE CROWN CHAKRA

The Ascendant is related to the crown centre or chakra, the highest and most potent energy centre of the individual, group or nation. This centre is referred to as 'the thousand-petalled lotus' because it has a symbolical connection to the monadic centre of Shambhala, the planet's crown chakra, and Shambhala itself is connected to the greater cosmic constellations like the Great Bear and Sirius. There is an eighth 'transpersonal' chakra too, called 'the Soul Star', because it is the chakra of the soul or higher self. In the individual this centre lies about 6 inches above the crown of the head and it is where one connects to, invokes and contacts (is contacted by) the higher self. The crown centre is where the will or purpose of God is known, and the Ascendant is therefore the centre where the will or purpose of the higher self is known, for the soul is, to all intents and purposes, the Godhead of the individual chart. It is said that the eyes are the windows of the soul, and the eyes are related to Aries and the Rising sign. By looking into the eyes one can physically and/or intuitively discover the Rising sign.

The head, hair and eyes are all related to the Rising sign, the crown centre and the 1st house, for this house is the initial spiritual and physical manifestation of the incarnating consciousness. Eyes, head and/or hair appearing in one's dreams can be interpreted as symbols of the 'highest' part of oneself – that is one's soul energy.

THE ASCENDANT AND ARIES

The Ascendant is related to Aries, the first sign of the zodiac and therefore the natural Ascendant of our planetary zodiac. Aries is related in turn to the New Moon cycle, for the New Moon cycle is the new beginning or 'seeding' cycle of each month, when the Sun and Moon are in the same sign and degree. The New Moon is known as the 'dark' Moon because it is invisible and hidden from normal sight. The Ascendant or Rising sign can therefore be said to represent the invisible purpose of the chart behind the persona, for its true meaning can only be deciphered by the intuition or 'single eye' and not by normal 'two-eyed' logic. The vast majority of astrologers still interpret the Ascendant from a 'two-eyed' perspective, and fail to see its deeper and hidden significance.

Most astrologers associate the Rising sign with the face of the personality that is projected out to the world. This interpretation evidences a deep lack of understanding of the true meaning of the Ascendant, and of the true nature of the soul and the personality. The soul is the reality lying behind the persona, the mask of the soul. It is the soul or higher self that comes first, as does the Rising sign. The Rising sign, the soul and the soul's purpose are therefore one and the same.

The Ascendant is plotted according to the date, place and time of birth. But what is 'birth'? Without understanding the realities behind birth it is impossible to decipher the true meaning of the Ascendant. Three major interrelated laws govern evolution, and these laws provide a deeper understanding of the true nature of birth and its hidden purpose:

1. the law of service, which is the law of the soul;
2. the law of cause and effect, known as 'karma' in the East; and
3. the law of reincarnation.

The 2nd and 3rd laws are related to the personality. The soul is a consciousness of the solar system, for this system is essentially one of 'mind' (higher consciousness) in all its dimensions – lower rational, higher abstract/intellectual, intuitive and pure mind. The soul is an immortal consciousness and is already free. Its responsibility is towards the solar system and its evolution and not simply towards the Earth. Its natural state is one of group and collective consciousness and of selfless service. Since the Rising sign is directly related to the soul's purpose it is also directly related to the above law and conditions. It is therefore connected to 'the way of service' and to the conditioning agencies of group and planetary consciousness. This is why it is said (*Esoteric Astrology*) that the Rising sign lies dormant until that time that there is an awakening of consciousness towards the above factors. This sign is activated when these conditions begin to be awakened. The will to serve is related to the Ascendant, and this will cannot be separated from group consciousness.

The laws of karma and reincarnation are related to the personality, for the soul is free of planetary karma and has no need to reincarnate. It overlights and guides the above factors but it is not subject to them. The personality on the Sun sign, and other factors in the chart which are under the overall influence of the Sun sign, are connected to cause and effect (from past lives and the present life) and thus to reincarnation – the rebirth of the personality into physical incarnation. The Rising sign is therefore not related to the personality and to personal karma, but to the soul and thus to service. The vast majority of astrologers have therefore misinterpreted the Ascendant, due to the fact that they have misinterpreted their own true identity or self and, as a result, their own true life-purpose.

Enough scientific evidence has been gathered over the years to validate reincarnation, but in the end result nothing other than intuitive perception (perception that pierces through the dualities of the logical mind) can prove the validity of spiritual realities. The true astrologer and psychologist knows that service, reincarnation and karma are real because of having taken the time, effort and responsibility to intuit these laws. If people wish to imprison themselves in their lower minds that is up to them, but they can free themselves at any time by activating their higher intuitive minds. The Rising sign informs us of our dharma or life-purpose, whereas the Sun sign indicates the stage of evolution we have reached (the Sign itself) in relationship to our earthbound karma. We reincarnate for two reasons therefore: to serve human, planetary and solar evolution as souls; and to work out karma as personalities.

Karma and reincarnation are fact and are not reliant on human belief for their existence. The higher self knows the purpose and plan for its personality (as explained in Chapter 3), and it knows the karma from past lives that has to be experienced and hopefully transformed and transmuted in the present life. The individual co-operates in all the above to the extent that they are conscious of their true nature, their potential part in the plan, and the karmic circumstances they need to face and deal with. The Ascendant is directly concerned with the purpose and plan, and the more one is prepared to attune to and co-operate with the higher self the more one can unfold and manifest the energies of the Rising sign and thus fulfil one's purpose.

THE SOUL KINGDOM AND THE ASCENDANT

It is only after the third initiation that one's consciousness begins to be transferred from the soul to the Monad. Because this book is mainly concerned with the transference of personality identity to soul consciousness (first and second initiations) – that is the transmutation of the lower self into the higher self and the infusion of the higher self into the lower self, it will only be dealing with the Monad in a generalized sense. The monadic or life thread exists in the centre of the heart, and all these threads extend and link up to the planetary monadic centre called Shambhala, the centre 'where the will of God is known'. Shambhala is where the Lord of the World dwells, and it is He who might be called the God of our planet. Shambhala is where the greater purpose of God is known; likewise it is the Monad that knows and embodies the greater purpose for each individual, group, nation, planet and so on. Our crown centre at the top of the head (= the Godhead) embodies this purpose.

A portion of the soul is anchored in the area of the pineal gland; this is called the consciousness or soul thread. All these threads are linked to the collective soul kingdom of the planet, namely the spiritual hierarchy or inner government of the Earth. It is the heart energy centre of our planet. The hierarchy embodies the love and wisdom of God, and the Christ or Lord Maitreya, the lord of this centre. Likewise the soul or higher self is the Christed self of each individual, an integral member of this inner hierarchy. The 'will' of God is passed down from Shambhala to the Hierarchy, who in turn pass it down to humanity for external manifestation. The Rising sign and the soul purpose triangle is the embodiment of this will from its triangular perspective – the pure or overall will of the soul (Rising sign), its manifestation into and through higher conscious-ness and finally its manifestation in and through human conscious-ness and activity (see the soul purpose triangle–diagram 20). This is

Rising Sign

Soul Purpose Triangle

Soul Ruling Planet of Rising Sign

Soul Ruling Planet of Sign the Ruler is in

Diagram 20

why it is said that 'for all intents and purposes the will of the soul *Is* the will of God'.

All the pineal 'soul threads' extend and link up to the heart centre of our planet – to the 5th kingdom of souls, to the Spiritual Hierarchy and to the Christ Himself. The personality thread is anchored in the area of the pituitary gland, and is linked to the 3rd Ray energy centre of the planet, namely humanity. At the head of this centre is the Mahachohan or Lord of Civilization and Culture, also known as the Master Racoczi. Personalities embody the quality of active intelligence (intelligence or mind as the building force of material creation), and, as such, are the 'hands and feet' of God on Earth. Humanity, the collective personality kingdom of the Earth, represents the mind-brain of God, and is therefore the co-creator with God of human and planetary evolution. The aim of course is for humanity to become a conscious and intelligent co-creator, rather than an unconscious destroyer, but this co-creatorship can only come about by humanity linking back to its original incarnatory purpose. The personality and the soul must be consciously interconnected on an individual, group and collective basis. The Rising sign, conscious evolution and initiation are directly related to this fusion process.

Without these threads of 'life and consciousness' there could be no life as we understand it, for the personality is reliant upon these threads for its existence. In other words the consciousness and life that we call 'humanity' has no life outside of these energy threads and their link to the heart and power centres of God. This is the new, intelligent and even practical way to explain the reality of God and the reality of the unity and inclusiveness of all life. The relationship between the personality and the higher self and between humanity and the 5th kingdom of souls is part and parcel of one's purpose, path and plan. This linkage work is called 'the building of the Rainbow Bridge' and will be dealt with in the final chapter of this book.

The Rising sign might be called 'the straight and narrow path' for as long as one is on this path one is on the right path. We all deviate from this path as our minds, emotions and the physical pressures of life sway us to and fro. But we can refocus our energies by constantly recognizing our Rising sign, repeating its spiritual keynote and reorganizing our lives accordingly.

THE RISING SIGN AND THE SUN AND THE MOON

The Sun sign is directly related to the present, for it is determined by factors from the past. Esoterically it is said that the sign (month) in which a person leaves the physical body is the sign in which they will incarnate in their next lifetime. The Sun sign is therefore a karmic carry-over from the past life in terms of when one passed on; it indicates the stage one reached at the completion of this past life-cycle. I have noticed that a good number of spiritually unconscious people pass on in the same month (sign) as the one in which they were born. I would therefore sense that once one has become conscious one evolves into the next sign (in the anticlockwise zodiac). According to the Master DK (*Esoteric Astrology*) the initiation process accelerates one's evolution through this zodiac; in other words initiation forces one to 'complete or perfect' one's evolution in the Sun sign one has incarnated through. This is why conscious evolution entails such an intensive experience of the energies of the Sun sign, for one is perfecting one's experience of this sign, in terms of both embodying and manifesting its energies and of working out karma.

The Rising sign is said to remain the same for seven lifetimes, for it takes far longer to perfect the energies related to this sign than it does the Sun sign. It should be remembered that it takes effort, time and much calculation to discover the Rising sign. One has to find out the exact time of birth, which is often an effort in itself, for only a few countries register this on the birth certificate. One has to consult one's parents and very few parents take careful note of this time.

Astrologers sometimes 'rectify' the chart to try to discover the birth time. The best way to find this time is to ask one's higher self in meditation, for it obviously knows this time and it will reveal it in whatever way possible. One does this by projecting the consciousness up to the soul (crown) and asking the question. (One may have to do this several times to focus the mind. The answer usually comes in telepathically conveyed words or images. The Ascendant is a line of strong resistance (very much like the Moon's North Node) for it takes much effort, time and dedication to attune to and work with the soul and its purpose, path and plan.

The Sun sign embodies the overall personal identity, make-up and expression of the individual, group or nation – mental, emotional–sexual and physical/material. It is essentially concerned with the present lifetime and its karmic necessities – that is the lessons one has to learn, the karma or life-patterns one has to experience and the energies one has to embody, develop and manifest. It is a line of least resistance because one is naturally one's Sun sign. It takes no effort to know this sign for one can simply look in the newspapers to discover it.

The Moon sign is directly related to the past but in a different sense to the Sun sign. The Moon is a dead planet for its Logos left its body during the Lemurian Era. This definition of the Moon might annoy some people (especially women, who tend to identify with the Moon) but if anyone tried to identify themselves with a dead human body they would be regarded as rather strange. The Moon's old and decaying energies, mainly of a lower emotional and instinctive sexual–physical nature, filter through our planetary system and are the cause of much of our instinctive reactive attachment and bondage to old and deadening patterns of behaviour. This is putting it mildly for much of this behaviour, be it personal or collective, is of the nature of evil. 'Evil' spelt backwards is 'live', and the emotional–instinctive energies of the Moon are not alive but dead: they in fact deaden us to the true life of the personality (Sun sign) and the higher purpose and life of the soul (Rising sign). What is past is past. As the Jewish saying has it, 'What was was, what is is [the Sun] and what will be will be' – if we walk the path of the soul, which is that of the Rising sign.

There are many women who revere the Moon, claiming it to be a symbol of the feminine principle. This is a degradation of this principle in its true sense, for it is the dark side of the feminine that is related to the Moon. The Earth is the true feminine, for it is a living planet, Mother Earth, the nurturing and manifesting principle of Father Space. The Moon is but a satellite of the Earth, a symbol of its bygone past, when humanity lived through its 'mass' instinctive nature. The dark or shadow side of the feminine is that aspect of self which is attached to the past, and which puts blood before spirit. It lives its life according to the dictates of others, be they parents, 'blood' family, friends and society, culture or religion (and atheism is as much a religion as anything else). By the very nature of this life-pattern, it worships mass subjugation and fear (the Moon) and not personal intelligent thought (the Sun) and loving, intuitive service (the Rising sign).

It is true to say that women, and the feminine in man, have great difficulty in breaking away from their instinctive attachment to the past and to the physical body (both ruled by the Moon). This is a very tricky subject and one much avoided by both men and women, but avoidance only enhances the problem. It is always fascinating to note how unconscious people are of this area of their lives. When I interpret this aspect of the chart the majority of clients are largely unconscious of its influence, and yet the major conflicts in all relationships, including intimate partnerships, are related to the Moon's influence. It is our attachment to parents, family influences, childhood conditioning, schooling and hereditary brainwashing in its various dimensions that creates our monstrous conflicts with one another. This is true not only for individuals but for nations too. The USA's Moon in Aquarius creates her childish idealism about her great democratic society, an idealism which she projects unconsciously onto the world at large. That her society is riddled with political, economic and social injustices seems to pass her leaders and people by, for this inherent idealism is largely an unconscious (lunar) factor.

The only way to break the 'ties that bind' is to go to war with them. This entails a war within oneself, for the problem is essentially an internal one, but also includes a war with those agencies (such as parents, friends and so on) who in their ignorance and fear attempt to hold one back from moving into the future. How is it possible to break the bonds (two-way) to the past and to one's heredity if not through conflict, battle and war. This is the true holy war, and it is for this reason that Pluto and Mars, the planets ruling Aries and Scorpio (the signs of battle) are connected to the experience of 'the burning ground' – the destruction of the past and its chains. The child at the teenage and/or adult level must confront the parents and revolt against their authority and assumed power. They must break away from their influence (the Moon) and establish their own sense of priorities, personal identity and creativity (the Sun sign) and their own direction, life-purpose, path and goals (Rising sign). If the child is afraid of this battle, is afraid of hurting the parent, they will give in to their will, and then fear, and not love, will be the result. At a deep unconscious level, the child feels a deep sense of bitterness and even hate, and this leads to all manner of self-destructive habit patterns.

Many people on the so-called liberal or spiritual path tend to reject battle as an antithesis to what is 'good', but those who do not enter into conscious battle with the powers of the past will become the prisoners of these powers, and the pain of this imprisonment is far worse than the pain of the battle itself. When one sees the terrible consequences of personal diseases like AIDS and cancer and collective diseases like crime, drug epidemics and war, this tragedy becomes self-evident. The Moon is concerned with belief systems (it rules Cancer) whereas the Sun is concerned with personally acquired knowledge. The Rising sign is concerned with knowledge of a higher spiritual order.

The Moon acts as a veil or channel for the Seven Rays of the Sun, the masculine principle of individualization, and for the energies of the transpersonal planets, Uranus (higher mind and the etheric body), Neptune (higher feelings/aspirations) and Vulcan (higher will/action). The monthly lunar cycle is determined by the position of the Moon in relationship to the Sun and the Earth. It is the Sun's energies which essentially enter the Earth and not the Moon's, for all the planets live by the grace of the Sun (the Solar Logos). The Moon does have a powerful influence on the three lower instinctive centres (self-preservation, sexual desire and emotional reaction) and the transmutation of this lunar influence is a lifelong struggle. The Moon and the Sun's dual influences are especially powerful at each Full Sun–Moon, and I will deal with this in Chapter 8.

The Rising sign, Sun and Moon form a triangle relating future, present and past, and personal-centred astrology has tended to confuse their respective meanings. I have read books by well-known astrologers in which they have stated that the Rising sign is related to the personality, the Sun to the inner self (or true identity) and the Moon to the soul. This is simply not true, and it is easy to see why if one studies the information on the Monad, soul and personality.

At the beginning of each new seven-year cycle a new soul impulse is potentially available. A new input of soul energy, that is the energy of the Rising sign, can be attuned to and unfolded over the seven-year cycle.

THE ASCENDANT AND THE 12TH AND 1ST HOUSES

The Rising sign is the mediating point between the 12th house (Pisces) and the 1st house (Aries) in the astrological chart. The 12th is the realm of collective superconsciousness – of the divine whole, namely the Spiritual Hierarchy and Shambhala, the love and will chakras of the planet. This is why the 12th house is related to selfless service, and why Jupiter and Neptune (2nd Ray) and Pluto (1st Ray) rule it. It is also where Venus (2nd Ray and 5th Ray) has its exaltation, for Venus is the higher self of the Earth, and the planet connected to selfless service. The 12th is associated with prisons and with isolation, but it is the prison of the lower ego and not the soul, for the 12th is the natural and exalted home of the soul. Pisces is related to 'the unity of all life' and this unity is the natural quality of the higher self and the Spiritual Hierarchy.

Shambhala, the Hierarchy and the 5th kingdom of souls form the spiritual kingdoms of our planet, and the Christ, who is associated with Pisces, is 'the Master of Angels and Men alike'. Sanat Kumara is the Lord of the world and the Christ is his 'Son' for they form the head and heart centres of the inner government of the Earth. All souls serve the Christ, and the 12th house is thus the burial, death, dissolution and crucifixion ground of human egos. This is why

Pluto (death) and Neptune (dissolution) rule the 12th, and why Jupiter (the Christ) and Venus (the soul) also rule here.

Placements in the 12th house (and the ruler of the 12th house cusp) need to be given over to intelligent loving service. All three planets of love, namely Venus, Jupiter and Neptune, rule the 12th, and all these planets embody different aspects of Christ or Love–Wisdom consciousness. The 12th is the final or completion house of the present life-cycle and also the completion house of the past life. Planets in the 12th that lie near to the Ascendant often indicate what karma one has carried over from this past life. This could be extremely positive and graceful (Jupiter, Venus or Neptune) or negative and restrictive (Saturn, Mars and so on) in the sense that one (the ego) has to learn to accept such limitations and use these energies for the greater good of humanity. Love, forgiveness and selfless service are the quickest and most constructive ways to dematerialize and dissolve (Neptune) past-life karma. Karma is also 'burnt up' through Pluto, and the 12th is thus related to 'the highest and the lowest' (superconscious and unconscious) aspects of life.

The 1st house is where we move from the collective superconscious, the greater purpose and plan for humanity and the planet, to individual consciousness (birth/incarnation) and the purpose and plan of the individual entity. The Rising sign is thus the interconnection point between the collective and the individual, and it thus embodies the very purpose, path and plan for incarnation.

The final statement of Jesus on the Cross – 'Father, Father, Why hast thou forsaken me? – is archetypal of Piscean crucifixion. When the lower self is dying one always feels deserted – and this is typical of all crucifixion experiences in life. Jesus then stated: 'It is finished – into Thy Hands I commend my spirit.' This 'death–rebirth' experience is typical (in its relative sense) to 12th house experiences, for only after the ego has died a relative death can there be a rebirth of new and expanded consciousness of the soul. For example Bob Dylan has a number of 12th house planets and his life and music attest to this, for his music was a channel for collective revelation and transformation. His pain and suffering has largely been due to his lower ego undergoing dissolution and transmutation. His periods of isolation, chosen or forced (by his motor-bike accident and so on) have led to his regeneration and newfound inspiration, and this is also 12th house experience.

INTERPRETING THE SOUL'S PURPOSE

The Rising sign represents the overall will or purpose of the higher self, the life-purpose that has to be perceived, unfolded and fulfilled.

It is essentially concerned with the archetypal idea, or vision of this purpose. The spiritual keynote of this sign provides the inner key to this purpose and vision (see 'keynotes' in Chapter 7). Other factors to be taken into consideration in interpreting the Rising sign are:

1. What Ray(s) rule this sign? What are their psycho-spiritual qualities?
2. What is the transpersonal or soul interpretation of the sign? In other words what is the essential purpose and what are the qualities of Leo (for example), rather than what are the characteristics of Leo. Characteristics are the material manifestations of the personality, and these belong more to the Sun sign and personal planets. Purpose and quality belong to the soul.
3. What element rules the sign (fire, air, water or earth), and how do we interpret it from a soul perspective? The elements are the four aspects of higher consciousness, namely the fifth element, ether, in manifestation.
4. What decanate is the sign in? This brings in the potential sub-influence of another elemental sign. For example if the sign is 23 degrees of Leo (ruler: the heart of the Sun) then there is a sub-influence of Aries (the 3rd decanate of Leo) and of Mars, the ruler of Aries. I would also suspect that Mercury, the inner ruler of Aries, is a sub-influence because we need to take the trans-personal ruler into consideration when dealing with the Rising sign.
5. What planets, if any, conjunct the Ascendant in either the 12th or 1st house? These planets sub-influence and condition the sign. It should be stated though that the sign always has overall signi-ficance, no matter what the planet.
6. What aspects (geometrical energy formations) does the sign have to other placements in the chart? Conflicting, challenging aspects (like the 90° square, 180° opposition or 150° quincunx) will create pressure, stress and conflict in unfolding the sign's energies (which forces the will to be developed), whereas har-monious, flowing, inspirational aspects (60° sextile, 120° trine or 72° quintile) will allow for a non-restricted and easy-going unfoldment.
7. What is the sign on the Descendant (opposite the Rising sign)? This is the Rising sign's balancing sign/energy and also the area (7th house) where the sign's energy needs to manifest itself through interhuman partnerships of an intimate, platonic and social nature (and national–international nature in national charts).

8. The cross of the sign, namely the cardinal (will-power/activity), fixed (love–intuition/consciousness) or mutable (active intelligence/mind) cross. Leo is on the fixed cross (along with Taurus, Scorpio and Aquarius) and is therefore concerned with the development and unfoldment of will (1st Ray), love–intuition (2nd Ray) and knowledge (5th Ray) through the central agency of consciousness itself, for the fixed cross is the cross of love–wisdom.

The transpersonal planetary ruler is the conditioning or focusing placement of the soul's purpose (Rising sign). In Leo's case this would be the heart of the Sun, which is obviously in the same position as the Sun. The second point of the triangle is essentially concerned with the development and unfoldment of *'consciousness' in relationship to the Ray of the ruling planet.* In Leo's case (the heart of the Sun) this is the 2nd Ray. The following factors need to be considered in interpretation:

1. The transpersonal interpretation of this planet. For example the heart of the Sun is related to the heart or soul of Leo, and this is related to one's higher (soul) identity, one's individuality (and not personality or 'personal' identity), one's inner heart-love consciousness and one's inner work/activity. This planet is referred to as the Lord of the chart.
2. The Ray of this planet. This is referred to as the ruling Ray or Ray Lord of the chart. In the Sun's case this is the 2nd Ray of love–wisdom, the Ray of unity, inclusiveness, intuition, and loving-wise service. It is the Ray of the Christ Himself. Its colour is deep royal blue to midnight blue. This colour is the ruling Ray colour of the chart, and should be used to foster one's soul colour.
3. The sign that the planet is in and its transpersonal meaning.
4. The house that the planet is in. This indicates the sphere of *inner* and outer activity that the planet's energy will manifest in and through.
5. The aspects of the planet to other placements in the chart (see aspects of Rising sign above).
6. The speed of the planet orbit around the zodiac. This informs one of the time-frame of the planet's functioning. The Sun moves one degree per day, through one sign per month and takes one year to evolve around the zodiac. The evolutionary process is therefore quite rapid, and in this particular case every new birthday (when the Sun returns to its birth chart position) will be of great significance. Uranus takes seven years to orbit through one sign, and those with Libra rising (Uranus ruling)

will be powerfully affected by the seven-year cycles of Uranus, Uranus transits to birth chart placements and especially the Uranus opposition at 39–40 years of age.
7. Transits of any planet (or planetary progressions) to this ruling planet. The transiting planet will obviously determine the effect upon this planet.

In Chapter 7 I will be dealing with the Rays, signs and planets more extensively, and this will provide a deeper comprehension of the Rising sign and its rulerships.

CHAPTER SEVEN

The Transpersonal Zodiac:
The Twelvefold Journey of the Soul

In this chapter we will be dealing with the twelve signs of the zodiac and their overall influence on human evolution. These influences will be dealt with in relationship to astrology and psychology in general, to the astrological birth chart and also to the annual astro-psychological cycle (the Sun's yearly transit through the planetary zodiac from Aries to Pisces). The twelve astrological signs and their Ray and planetary rulerships plus their corresponding twelve houses (objective or material spheres of influence) should therefore be applied not only to the birth chart but also to the whole annual astrological cycle from the spring equinox (Aries) to the completion of the winter solstice (Pisces).

Everyone can apply the living principles of astrology to their personal, group and social life, and the evolution of the Sun through the twelve signs of the zodiac over the annual cycle provides the most constructive means by which to do this. The New and Full Sun–Moons which occur at two-week intervals are the focal points of each month/sign, one seeding the energies of the sign the Sun is in and the other ripening or illuminating its energies. It is especially advisable for groups to meet over these two cycles.

Astrologers are capable of applying transpersonal astrology to the birth chart. The vast majority of people interested in using astrological knowledge in their daily lives can call upon astrologers to interpret their birth chart (at whatever intervals), but are themselves incapable of birth chart interpretation. Birth chart interpretation is highly constructive but at the same time limited by time (about two hours is the limit for most astrologers) and the consciousness of the astrologer and client. By applying the information in this chapter to the corresponding twelve months/signs of the astrological cycle, people can experience astrology as a living science, and use it to benefit themselves, their friends and co-workers, their groups and organizations and humanity and the planet itself. I would like to emphasize in the above regard that it is impossible to separate astrology, psychology and meditation, for the three are intrinsically interconnected.

I will not be repeating comprehensive information on how the Rays work through their respective signs in this chapter because the reader can refer to Chapters 4 and 5 in this regard. This Ray information can then be integrated with the rest of the information on these signs found in this chapter. There are many fine books which provide comprehensive information on the signs of the zodiac and their traditional planetary rulers and there is no need for me to repeat this information. I am more concerned with interpreting the deeper purpose lying at the core of each sign and the qualities or consciousness (or soul) of the sign and its transpersonal ruling planet. By applying this core information to the birth chart and to the living unfoldment of planetary and human evolution over the annual (and seven-year) cycles, we can turn astrology once again into a dynamic, living and practical science.

The Labours of Hercules (Lucis Trust Pub.) by Alice Bailey and the Master DK provides a wonderful example of this twelvefold journey or search for the Holy Grail of truth, light, love and purpose. Each sign embodies the dualities and their potential synthesis and can thus be regarded as a labour of effort, struggle, change, transformation, understanding, gained wisdom, synthesis and evolving fulfilment. It takes seven lifetimes to fulfil each Rising sign and one lifetime (from the perspective of conscious evolution) to fulfil each Sun sign. Patience, persistence and service to humanity (and those to whom one is nearest) are therefore the keynotes of wise evolution.

ARIES	1st sign of the zodiac.
Keynote	I come forth and from the plane of mind I rule.
Symbol	A ram roaming the high mountainous regions.
Rays	1st and 7th.
Rulers	Mercury (inner) and Mars (outer).
Festival	Spring equinox and the Festival of Rebirth or Resurrection.
House	1st of one's spiritual purpose, path, direction and goals.
Elemental	Cardinal fire.

Aries is the first sign of our planetary zodiac. The spirit of Aries initiates the first cycle of outer manifestation. The movement of the Sun into the energy field of Aries on 21 March (spring equinox) results in the initial manifestation of spirit into matter. The 1st and

7th Rays work through this sign, for Aries is concerned with the initiating and pioneering impulses of God's will or purpose (1st Ray) and the manifestation of this will through organized, rhythmic and ritualistic activity (7th Ray).

The archetypes, ideas or inspirations related to creative pioneering activity seek manifestation through the sign of Aries. All creative activity originates in the realm of ideas, for ideas are the archetypes of all objective material creation. Carl Jung coined the word *archetype* to signify the original energy pattern or model lying behind creation. *Archos* means first and *typos* means model. The archetype or idea behind all microcosmic or macrocosmic creation is its soul, for the soul of any form is the perfect idea or pure consciousness lying behind that creative form. All forms (material creations) originate in these archetypal planes through the agency of divine thought or ideas, and through directed streams of intelligent energy acquire substance as they are reproduced or unfolded upon each subsequent plane, finally reaching the dense physical plane where they acquire physical bodies. The soul of every form of creation is thus to be found on these archetypal planes; the soul or higher God self of each human personality is therefore the perfect(ed) self, idea or archetype of the human self. This is likewise the case for humanity collectively and for the planet itself, for each in turn has its perfect archetype, as does each and every aspect of creation.

Energy is generated and initiated in the cardinal signs, and fire is the element of the mind in its intuitive and inspirational nature. When Aries is Rising (soul's purpose) or the Sun sign (personal identity and expression) and when the Aries cycle is in manifestation (21 March to 20 April) the task is to perceive, embody and manifest archetypal ideas in the fashion of the pioneer. In other words the archetypal ideas related to the purpose of divinity, the Hierarchy or the soul seek manifestation during the Aries cycle of each year, and through those with Aries Rising or the Sun in Aries.

Mercury is the transpersonal ruler of Aries, for Mercury is a sacred (soul-based) planet related to the mind. Mercury is the messenger of the Gods, for the mind is the messenger of the soul, the Spiritual Hierarchy, the Christ and all agencies of divinity. The mind has three aspects to itself and this is why Mercury has a threefold symbol ☿. It has its higher receptive, intuitive nature which is capable of identifying with and receiving audio-visual imprints from divinity; it has its higher contemplative nature which is capable of 'thinking-into' the realm of the intuitive mind and of embodying the imprints from the intuitive level: it has its lower rational nature which is capable of embodying, discriminating and communicating the imprints received from the higher mind. Finally there is the physical brain (10 billion brain cells), the central nervous system and the muscular system of the body which manifests these imprints in the material world. Mercury is related to this entire inner and outer communicative system, a fact which many astrologers fail to realize. Mercury is a 4th Ray planet because mental harmony and beauty are achieved by integrating this threefold system, and this integration can only come about through the conflict of this internal intercommunicative process.

Mars is the outer ruler because Mars rules the objective system required to manifest these imprints into the emotional and physical material world. Mars is a 6th Ray non-sacred planet working with dynamic devotional idealism, for a dynamic and powerful idealism is required to manifest divine imprints into and through the emotional planes and finally into the physical plane. Mars also rules the red (active) blood corpuscles, the muscular system, the sex chakra and corresponding sexual organs and thus sexual desire and activity. Mars and passion go together and without a 'passion' for things there can be no manifestation of ideas and ideals.

The major need in Aries is to focus and control the mind, for without this control the mind cannot attune to, receive, embody and communicate the consciousness of the soul. Dynamic meditation rather than passive meditation is vital in this regard, for dynamic meditation uses the mind to focus one's energies. One of the major faults of the Arien is the tendency to expect others to manifest his or her ideas and to become angry and bitter if they fail to do this; one of the major spiritual laws is that if one 'catches' an idea one must unfold and manifest it oneself. Only after this has been adequately accomplished can others help in the process. Ideas are the imprints of the higher self into its personality, and these ideas are attuned to the purpose and path of that particular individual. A scientist receives scientific imprints, an artist artistic imprints, a psychologist psychological imprints, and so on. Once the individual (Aries and the Ascendant rule individual consciousness) has taken full responsibility for the imprint and its manifestation then, and only then, can he or she expect or invoke another individual to partake in the ongoing work. Libra, the opposite and complementary sign to Aries, is the sign of partnerships, and a partnership is the first stage of group relationship.

Many ideas are lost (return to their source) because people fail to realize the above fact, or because people lack the courage and tenacity to 'hold and manifest' the idea. *Every action, no matter how small or large, starts with an idea.* Creation itself is the originating idea of God and the ideas that enter our minds are the archetypes that set our creation into motion. It is impossible to be truly creative unless one has dynamic ideas and the willingness to manifest these ideas in form.

Aries and the Ascendant of any chart are concerned with self or individual consciousness, and with those ideas which are related to the higher purpose of the individual (or group or nation or event). The gift of Aries is the capacity to grasp and manifest these ideas in an initiating, pioneering and catalysing fashion. This takes great courage, tenacity, one-pointedness and a passion to serve the purpose and plan of God/the Christ/the soul. The Aries shadow is extreme self-centredness, impulsiveness, insensitivity, mental and emotional fanaticism, personal wilfulness and ambition, aggressiveness and the failure to anchor abstract ideas into objective and practical manifestation. Further 'light and shadow' qualities and characteristics of Aries, Mercury and Mars as they manifest through human agencies can be understood by referring to the section on the 1st, 4th, 6th and 7th Rays in Chapter 5.

©FELICITY KEEFE 1991.

TAURUS	The 2nd sign.
Keynote	I see and when the eye is open all is light.
Symbol	The bull of desire and one-pointed 'single-eyed' aspiration.
Ray	The 4th.
Rulers	Vulcan (inner; Ray 1) and Venus (outer; Ray 5).
Festival	Wesak/Festival of the Buddha; 2nd phase of spring.
House	2nd of focused and grounded spiritual aspiration, emotional–sexual desire and material–financial values.
Elemental	Fixed earth.

The archetypes of Aries seek their next phase of manifestation through Taurus. From the mental plane these ideas must move into and through the emotional or astral plane (Taurus) and finally into the etheric (Gemini) and physical (Cancer) planes. Spiritual aspiration and emotional–sexual desire are the two facets of the astral plane, and both are activated in Taurus. Aspiration means 'to breath towards' and comes from the Latin *ad* – to and *spirare* – breath. There must be a burning aspiration or higher desire and a fiery determination and one-pointed dedication towards the goal if one wishes to succeed in any great task, and the fulfilment of one's life-purpose in relationship to the divine plan is the greatest task of all.

One's values determine one's aspirations and desires in life, for values are the 'worth' one puts upon things. This is especially the case when it comes to the worth one puts upon the material world and its objects. Money is the most concrete form of material energy for it is the physical exchange mechanism of the material world, and the way we value money therefore becomes the determining agent for all our material values and the life we lead in the material world. Taurus and the 2nd house rule this value mechanism, for the spiritual archetypes/purpose of Aries (and the individual Rising sign) require emotional and material manifestation in Taurus, a fixed earth (physical elemental) sign. The questions that need to be asked in Taurus are:

1. What is money?
2. What is the purpose of money?
3. How is money to be earned or acquired?
4. How is money to be used?
5. How do we manifest the divine plan in the material world?

The basic answers to the above questions might be that:

1. Money is the energy of spirit manifesting in matter (the material world).
2. Money is the agency of exchange in the material world; it allows the process of giving and receiving and supply and demand to take place in relationship to spiritual and material need.
3. Money needs to be earned in any way that constructively benefits the individual, society and the world; money also needs to be psychologically earned through developing trust and faith in the laws of divine manifestation – this is the law that states that 'when one attunes to and serves the will of one's soul, all one's needs will be perfectly met' – at the right time and in the appropriate fashion.
4. Money is to be used to serve the greater good of humanity and the planet and this does not exclude the needs (not to be confused with 'wants') of the individual or group.
5. The spiritual plan needs to manifest on Earth and this requires money and material needs. Finances and material possessions, and this includes one's home, car and even one's partnership/

marriage, do *not* belong to one but rather 'have been given to one' to serve this plan. The *intelligent* discriminatory use of one's material possessions is required in this regard.

In Taurus material energy not only includes money and material objects but also emotional and sexual energies. There is of course a direct interrelationship between the forces of the mind, emotions, sex and money in all human relationships including intimate part- nerships. The way we value and use all material forces acts as the determining agent for true harmony and beauty in individual, group, national and collective relationships. Conflict will always be the doorway we have to enter to achieve this harmony (the 4th Ray rules Taurus), for emotional, sexual and financial desires are highly complex issues and are powerfully influenced by factors of upbring- ing and conditioning, and by personal fears, desires and/or needs. The second year of any seven-year cycle brings these Taurian issues to the fore.

Venus is traditionally related to harmony and beauty but its lower rulership of Taurus (and Libra) indicates that intelligence (3rd Ray) and knowledge (5th Ray) are required if any real harmony and balance (between spirit and matter) is to be achieved. Taurians often get trapped by material or objective beauty and fail to see that outer forms are but the temple of subjective consciousness. They need to use the material world to anchor, house and beautify spir- itual ideas while not getting attached to these forms. This is an extremely difficult task for sensuality (relationship with form) has the capacity to anchor spirit into matter and/or to trap it into form. Sensuality is at its most potent in Taurus and this is why Venus rules this sign. The opposite sign of Taurus is Scorpio and Venus is in detriment (losing power) in this sign, for in Scorpio sensuality can only be sustained for short periods of time before it comes under the purifying fires of Pluto and Mars.

After one has received the archetypal ideas and inspirations in Aries one has to aspire towards the goal of fulfilling these ideas. This is the great work in Taurus. The sacral (desire/sex) and the throat (creative thought-activity) centres are activated in Taurus. This creates a conflict and interflow of energy between the use of energy for higher creative enterprises and for the desire for emotional–sexual gratification. There is of course a powerful inter- connection between these two passions, for creative expression stimulates emotional–sexual desire and emotional–sexual fulfil- ment stimulates one's higher creative potential.

There is a powerful down-to-earth pragmatic approach to life in this sign, and one result of this is a very strong attachment to physical plane objects and activities. In many senses material desire and attachment are strongest in this sign, and this creates great problems for people with Taurus Sun or Taurus Rising, but especially for those with the Sun, Moon or Venus in Taurus. Material possessiveness is at its strongest in Taurus (and Cancer) and all too often the 1st Ray energy of Vulcan is the only force capable of breaking these attachments. 'What one holds on to with excess force will be taken away from one with similar force'. It is of interest to note that Neptune, the planet of dissolution and transmutation of material energy, is at present transiting through the 2nd house of the chart of the USA, and the Gulf Crisis and the present banking and financial crisis are manifestations of this. The 2nd house is related to material attitudes, values and possessions, and thus to financial institutions.

Vulcan is the soul ruler because it is the planet channelling the 1st Ray of power or will in its constructive building form, although it is part of the nature of the 1st Ray to destroy form. It provides the energy of one-pointed aspiration and dedicated will and has rulership of Taurus when this sign is Rising. Vulcan is also the planet of 'illumination and enlightenment'; Buddha was enlightened at the time of a Full Moon in Taurus, and this is why the Buddhist festival of Wesak is celebrated during the Taurus Full Moon. Venus rules the personality and influences both the rational commonsensical mentality and the sensual nature of the Taurian ego.

Arien ideas require physical bodies or 'temples' in which to anchor and stabilise themselves. These bodies are provided in Taurus, and 'beauty and harmony' become the essential quality that they possess. This beauty and harmony is nevertheless created through conflict (the 4th Ray), for all true beauty and harmony is a result of the clash of the dualities. Aspiration and desire-attachment are the dualities in Taurus and these will be powerfully experienced if one has Taurus Sun or Rising and also in the Taurus cycle from 21 April to 21 May each year. The great gift of Taurus is the offering and building of material forms to house the mental seeds of Aries. Spiritual purpose (the Ascendant) is an abstract vision and it requires a physical body/temple in which to house itself. The human body is such a temple housing the soul, and Taurians are well noted for their beautiful bodies. Every soul-inspired idea requires a beautiful temple and Taurus (and Cancer and Virgo) are meant to provide this.

Taurus stabilises and consolidates what has been achieved in Aries. It provides the capacity to move forward steadily, slowly and surely towards the goal. If Taurians stick to the goal ahead they can succeed in their task but they often tend to get bogged down in the material world. Stubbornness is their worst characteristic. It is the shadow of one-pointedness. Hard-headedness is the masculine shadow of Aries and stubbornness is the feminine shadow of Taurus. Further 'light and shadow' qualities and characteristics of Taurus can be gained by studying the section on the 4th, 1st and 5th Rays in Chapter 5.

© FELICITY KEEFE 1991.

GEMINI	The 3rd sign.
Keynote	I recognize the other self and in the waning of that self I grow and glow.
Symbol	The twins of the higher and lower mind/self.
Rays	The 2nd.
Rulers	Venus (inner; Ray 5) and Mercury (outer; Ray 4).
Festival	Festival of humanity or goodwill; 3rd phase of spring.
House	3rd of higher-lower mind alignment, perception,

	intercommunication, knowledge and objective communication.
Elemental	Mutable Air.

The archetypal impulses of Aries descend from the emotional plane of aspiration–desire (Taurus) into the etheric body in Gemini. I have explained a good deal about the etheric body in previous chapters. Suffice it to say that it is the subtle 'blueprint' body of the gross physical body of all creation. It is the linking and communicative agency between the monadic, soul, mental and emotional bodies of the individual (group, nation, planet and so on) and the physical body and its various glands, nerve systems and organs. The etheric body is thus the intercommunicative system of creation, and this is why it is connected to Gemini and Sagittarius, the two signs of communication.

The etheric body is also the agency which synergizes polarities, for it receives, transforms and distributes energies into and out of the physical body of creation. Gemini is the sign ruling all polarity systems and their evolutionary synthesis because its energy is directly related to the etheric body. Gemini rules the polarities of:

spirit	matter
higher self	lower self
soul	personality
higher mind	lower mind
the spiritual kingdom	the human kingdom
left brain	right brain
the yang energy system	the yin energy system
right eye/ear	left eye/ear (and all the body polarities)
in-breath	out-breath
left lung	right lung

The blueprint or causal foundation of all these polarities lies in the etheric body which is their controlling agency. When we breath in we take in energies from the etheric body and when we breath out we give out energies into the etheric body. There is a direct relationship between the mind (the way we think), the breath, the nervous system, the lungs and the physical body, for the mind is the controlling agency of the etheric body. As we think so we become. The above interrelationship is directly connected to Gemini, which is why Geminians have so many problems with their minds, their nervous systems, their breathing and their lungs. The 3rd house of Gemini is also connected to the above. Correct thinking and correct breathing (for example filling the lower stomach, diaphragm and lungs with the in-breath and breathing out in the opposite fashion are essential to alleviate these problems.

The impulses of Aries and Taurus enter the etheric body in Gemini in order to bring the polarities of spirit, mind, emotions and the physical body into relationship. These impulses (ideas, inspirations, visions) only enter the physical body in the fourth sign of Cancer, four being the number of matter or material manifestation. It is for this reason that Geminians swing between the opposites, for their essential task is to experience the polarities and to work at synergizing or integrating them into a unified whole. The 2nd Ray works through Gemini and this Ray is the energy of love–wisdom; love and intuition are the qualities which blend polarities into a unity.

Venus is the inner ruler because Venus is Earth's 'twin sister or soul'. Earth is essentially a lower mind planetary system (a non-sacred 3rd Ray planet) whereas Venus is a sacred or higher mind planetary system (5th Ray). Venus represents the soul quality of pure reason or embodied intuition (inner knowing) which is the embodiment of soul-consciousness. The higher self and higher mind *knows*, whereas the lower self or mind *believes*. Belief is based upon mental duality or lower reason whereas true knowledge is based upon mental synthesis where the knowledge of the higher mind (of the soul) is blended with the lower mind. This is the deeper reason for Venus being called the planet of intelligent love, for the energy of Venus is a fusion of higher mind (intelligence) and the heart (love). Gemini Rising most embodies this Venusian quality.

Mercury is the outer ruler because Mercury in this sign rules the lower rational mind and the etheric–physical brain and nerve impulses from the brain into the body. Venus is concerned with subjective communication from soul to personality and from soul to soul (the 5th Kingdom of souls is one interconnected whole), whereas Mercury is concerned with objective communication from lower mind to brain to nerve system to body and from personality to personality. This is why the 3rd house is related to communication between soul brothers and sisters (Venus) and blood brothers and sisters (Mercury). It is also related to short-distance mental travel (lower mind to higher mind) and to short-distance physical travel and communications (Mercury).

Gemini is the sign ruling human evolution and for this reason a deep understanding of the relationship between Gemini, Venus and Mercury is of immense importance. The great significance of the mind in its twofold nature and its relationship to the left and right brain, the seven endocrine glands, the yin–yang nerve impulses and the body with all its dualities is revealed in this sign. There are ten billion etheric–physical brain cells and each contains millions of units of information. This 'in-formation' is the totality of universal knowledge contained within the microcosmos of the ten billion brain cells. The question of course is how to activate this knowledge, how to bring it into consciousness. It is dynamic, creative, innovative thinking that activates the brain cells, and it is this form of thinking that is so lacking in the individual and in society.

The Gemini Full Sun–Moon festival is called the festival of humanity. It is said to be the one time annually when the Christ blesses humanity. The Christ or Lord Maitreya (Iman Mahdi to the Muslims) is the head of our planetary hierarchy or spiritual kingdom. He is the Master of all the Masters, a fact which all the world religions and many spiritual groups fail to realize. Because Gemini rules human evolution and humanity it is also most directly linked to the Christ, who stands at the apex of humanity. The esoteric wisdom states that Christ was the first of humanity to become fully enlightened; Krishna was an incarnation of the Christ. Gemini is the festival of goodwill, of the reception and giving-out of intelligent love.

Gemini completes the spring cycle. By the end of the Gemini cycle (21 May to 20 June) the seed impulses of Aries have entered the etheric body of the individual, group, nation and humanity. There is always a crisis at the end of each triplicity cycle (Aries to Gemini, Cancer to Virgo, and so on) because the energies related to each cycle seek a final integration before the advent of the next triplicity cycle. This crisis of integration is a kind of death and rebirth experience because all that has been accomplished during the threefold cycle of Aries, Taurus and Gemini reaches its highest potential fulfilment as the Gemini cycle closes down. This entails a transformation (death and rebirth) of what has been accomplished. The last five degrees of each sign are also crisis degrees but crisis degrees of the mutable signs (Gemini, Virgo, Sagittarius and Pisces) are the most extreme because they complete each triplicity cycle. This is significant for people who have placements in the final five degrees of a sign and also for the evolutionary process of the annual cycle from Aries to Pisces. In other words when the Sun is in the process of completing its cycle through Gemini, Virgo, Sagittarius and Pisces there is a sub-cycle death–rebirth experience.

Gemini is a mutable sign with great flexibility and adaptability for it rules the dualities and their movement towards integration. The above qualities are its gift for Geminians are capable of great flexibility, change, movement and growth, and the clear articulation of ideas and perceptions. The shadow of this sign is dissipation of mental, emotional and physical energy and the tendency to get caught in lower intellectual perceptions and facts. Dynamic meditation, higher–lower mind alignment, correct breathing and clear and creative communication are required to create balance and integration of all the diverse energies that manifest through this sign. Further 'light and shadow' qualities and characteristics can be understood by studying the section on the 2nd, 5th and 4th Rays.

©FELICITY KEEFE 1991.

CANCER	The 4th sign.
Keynote	I build myself a lighted house and therein dwell.
Symbol	The crab, capable of living in water and on land; the bee colony and its hive.
Rays	The 3rd and 7th.
Rulers	Neptune (inner; Ray 6) and Moon (outer; Ray 4).
Festival	Summer solstice and Full Sun–Moon.
House	4th of the inner and outer home and family; the unconscious memories and influences of one's upbringing/conditioning.
Elemental	Cardinal water.

The seed inspirations of Aries enter the gross physical body of the individual, group, nation and humanity through the doorway of Cancer, the 4th, earthing, sign of the zodiac. Cancer might be regarded as the doorway into matter, for the physical incarnation of consciousness takes place in this sign. It is also the sign directly related to 'Mother Earth' and to the womb of material existence. Cancerians are well known for their love of Mother Earth and nature, for their capacity to work with physical matter and for their deep and dark depressions when they feel trapped in the womb of matter. There is often a feeling of being entombed in the womb (of matter) in this sign, and it is this feeling which leads to depression, scepticism, negativity and even suicidal tendencies. This feeling is part of the experience of the Cancer cycle in the astrological year (21 June to 21/22 July), for this is the time when the conceptional (mental) seeds of Aries are taking root in the physical body of the individual and the Earth.

The 3rd and 7th Rays work through this sign and these are the Rays connected to matter itself; the 3rd is related to the physical body and to physical activity and the 7th to the etheric body and organizational activity. Cancerians are very active on the physical plane and are exceptionally good organisers when they put their mind to it.

Cancer is related to the home and family, the base or physical foundation of existence. Everyone needs to have a home or base in order to feel secure and stable. Likewise everyone needs a family to feel part of a greater whole. Whereas Aries or the Ascendant has to do with personal identity and one's unique individual purpose in life, Cancer or the IC (the foundation point of the zodiac/chart) has to do with the anchoring of this identity and purpose into a stable home environment and family situation.

In the past the home and family have been associated with blood relationships and with the nuclear family unit. This is connected to the outer ruler of Cancer, namely the Moon, the planet which rules blood-ties, or material/traditional home–family relationships. Since the Moon is a dead planet with no life-force of its own, it symbolizes that which is dead and gone, for 'blood' relationships have no reality outside of the consciousness of the soul. All physical forms exist by the grace of the life-force (*prana* or *chi*) of the spirit (or Monad) which is anchored in the heart and circulates through the blood. We have become so attached to 'blood', the symbol of material existence, that we have forgotten that it is the life-force within the blood that gives life to all creation.

There is of course no doubt that the past has a massive influence on the present and that upbringing and conditioning within the sphere of the blood family, culture, religion, society and nation impinge upon the present and future. Most of these memories and influences are unconscious, instinctive and habitual and create what might be called 'one's chains to the past'. All the above are connected to the subterranean influences of the Moon, and to the base and sexual chakras. Breaking these chains requires consciousness and the application of love, light and will. This entails:

1. A breaking-away from one's blood family, home, traditions, culture and religion and their physical, emotional and mental influences. Love, light (knowledge) and the use of the will are required in this regard for the attachments related to the above (child to parents and vice versa) operate in both a gross and subtle manner.

2. A continual transformation of these attachments and unconscious influences. The position of the Moon in the chart is a direct indicator of these influences. The Moon's influence is unconscious and instinctive and the vast majority of people (including 'New Age' people) are largely unaware of these lunar pulls towards the past. As one awakens to one's Sun sign (personal identity) and Rising sign (individual purpose and path) one becomes more and more aware of one's shadow or attachments to the past, because the brighter the Sun the more evident the shadow.

3. The breaking of emotional attachments does not mean the breaking of love between family members. Love is not an emotional force but an all-encompassing energy. 'Love loves for itself' and not for reward, and love is the great energy that neutralizes karma from the past and clears the path into the future.

My experience in chart interpretations is that very few people are aware (to any great extent) of how powerfully the Moon's position influences them and all their daily relationships. It is often the small negative habit-patterns of life (inherited from the past) that create the biggest problems, and these patterns surface on a daily basis because the Moon is the fastest-moving planet, taking only two and a half days to move through one sign and a month to transit through the zodiac. The home (4th house of Cancer) is the central area where these habits surface, and the major conflicts of life most often occur in the home/family environment. The Moon's influences have more to do with the feminine mother shadow, whereas Saturn's influences (10th house of Capricorn, opposite to the 4th house) have to do with the masculine father shadow.

Many women are extremely self-defensive about the negative

influences of the Moon (they wish to see the Moon as a positive feminine influence). Unconscious and instinctive self-defensive mechanisms are related to the Moon's position, for this position indicates where one feels insecure and emotionally out of control of one's life. It is far more difficult for women to break the Moon's chains (I have found that gay men have the same problem) as the will to detach from matter is less developed in women as a whole, and attachment to the past and to form is far stronger in women than men. Men are more self-defensive about their Saturn position (Saturn and the Moon rule opposite signs and houses) as this has to do with one's career and position of power and influence in society, and with the capacity to control oneself and one's environment in a rational way.

The most positive aspect of the Moon as a feminine principle is the capacity of women (or men) to act as channels of service for divine incarnation. This is why the Moon is the higher ruler of Virgo, another Mother sign, for in Virgo the Moon, the symbol of matter (the Mother principle), becomes a sacrificial channel for the birth of the Holy child, the Sun or higher consciousness. When a woman gives birth to a child she is demonstrating (consciously or otherwise) this sacrificial process, for self-consciousness has been given up in order to serve a greater cause – the birth of a solar child through the womb of matter. Men can only accomplish this by giving birth to their inner children and by serving and nurturing this birth in others.

Neptune is the inner ruler of Cancer. Here we see the transference and transmutation of 'blood' into 'soul' relationships. The home and family become spiritual concepts; the home on the one hand becomes an inner rather than an outer reality (the h-OM-e within the cave of the immortal heart) and this enables one to be 'at home' wherever one finds oneself. The physical home itself becomes the base for spiritual activity – it becomes a centre of light, love and purpose. The family becomes 'the family of souls', and one is with one's family (in the inner and outer sense) wherever one finds oneself. On a collective physical basis the Earth becomes one's home and humanity becomes one's family. This Cancerian transformation is being accelerated through the grace (strangely enough) of the greenhouse effect and the ozone layer break (and so on), for these negative planetary influences, inherited from our ignorant past (the Moon), are forcing humanity into a global consciousness, and into a recognition that 'all things are interconnected'.

Neptune is the planet most associated with unconditional love and forgiveness, which is the central quality of Christ-consciousness. Neptune is a sacred planet and is therefore essentially concerned with 'the consciousness of unity' – that is the unity that governs the entire 5th kingdom of souls and the Spiritual Hierarchy. One's highest spiritual ideals and dreams (6th Ray) are ruled by Neptune, and thus it is Neptune that rules Cancer, and not the Moon. For a good example of this Ascendant the Neptune–Saturn conjunction of 1990 (see Chapter 8) had Cancer Rising. Neptune was placed in the 6th house (of Virgo). The two remarkable results of this 1990 conjunction were the collapse (Neptune) of the Eastern European dictatorial (Saturn) regimes, and the 'green' ecological uprising (Neptune in the 6th house) in Western Europe and around the world. Cancer Rising people have very high abstract ideals and they need to discover how to anchor these ideals into material form. The spiritual 'home and family' is vitally important in this regard, and some form of community living is often an important factor in this area. Their dream is to contribute towards the greater ideal of 'one humanity and one planet'. They can best serve this ideal by building the new 'home–family' forms that can embody and nurture this dream. This h-OM-e must first be established within (the heart) and then within matter (the New Age Light Centre/Community).

Summer solstice is when nature begins to blossom and bloom, for the Earth is giving birth to its offspring. These offspring include the human kingdom (which we often tend to forget), who also begin to blossom during this solstice cycle. The summer solstice (21 June) is also the blossoming of the spiritual fulfilment attained in Capricorn and the winter solstice (21 December), for Cancer is the opposite sign of Capricorn. This is a very important fact which needs to be remembered and taken into consideration as one evolves through the annual cycle.

The Sun, the macrocosmic representative of the soul, begins its return journey into the 'light' after the winter solstice, the time of the longest night and shortest day of the year. The Capricorn Full Sun–Moon is when we reach the height of annual fulfilment and the summer solstice (the longest day and shortest night of the year) and the Cancer Full Sun–Moon is when the results of this fulfilment 'flower' into the objective world. Capricorn is symbolically 'midnight' and Cancer 'noon' in the chart and annual cycle. The summer solstice should be the most joyous and expansive of the seasonal celebrations. If possible it should be held outdoors and should include activities like folk/circle dancing, nature walks, an evening bonfire, a communal buffet and so on. Its aim is to celebrate community and global consciousness and to establish a direct link with nature and Mother Earth.

Cancerians need to serve spirit in matter (like Taurians, Virgoans and Capricorns). They need to build the forms or physical bodies that will give birth to the archetypes of Aries. They provide the nurturing, caring and healing 'space' for divine ideas to anchor themselves. Their homes need to become the 'Light Centres' of the New Era. They have a strong connection with the mineral, animal and vegetable kingdoms of the Earth, and Cancerians therefore make wonderful farmers, smallholders and house builders. Organic farming is an extremely good outlet for their creative energies. This 'Mother' energy is their gift.

Their shadow is their tendency to attach themselves to form and to try to possess these forms. The unconscious manipulative 'mother', unwilling to free her children, is thus the archetype of this dark side of Cancer. These attachments are often extremely subtle and instinctive, and bind the emotional body of the child to the parent and vice versa. This chaining situation not only occurs in blood families but in spiritual families/organizations too. The 'mother' guru can be an actual mother-figure and/or the organization too, and this 'mother' can bind and entrap her children in just the same fashion as the blood mother-figure. The attachment of the disciple to the guru-figure is often a projection of his or her attachment to the blood father or mother. The follower tends to become emotionally bonded to the guru-figure's authority. The 'mother' guru is often more deceptive than the 'father' type because her power is far more subtle and concealed.

The negative results of these parent–child emotional chains are far-reaching and many of society's major problems have their foundation in these subtle and unconscious bondings. Traditional blood family relationships are regarded as the stabilising factor in modern-day society. Margaret Thatcher and Ronald Reagan, plus all traditional political and religious leaders, constantly expressed this viewpoint. Bloodline relationships are more the destabilizing factor in society for they worship the past (matter) rather than the future (spirit/the soul) and create huge emotional and psychological problems in the child in its early and later years. One should remember the words of the Christ in this regard: 'He who worships their mother or father or brother or sister more than Me is not worthy of My Name.' One cannot have two Masters at the same time for if one worships one master (matter/the bloodline) one cannot worship the other. By aligning to one's own higher self (see the meditation at the end of the book) and to the higher self of one's parents and family one can learn to trust the powers of this loving self rather than the illusionary powers of the lower fear-ridden self.

The gift of Cancer is its nurturing, healing and hospitable self; its capacity to build and organize the physical forms and structures to nurture spirit; its staying power when it comes to fulfilling its higher ideals and dreams; and its vivid and creative imagination in its expression of its inner life. Emotional instability, hyperactivity, attachment to form, to rational knowledge and to the limitations of the past are the Cancerians shadow. By studying the section on the 3rd, 7th, 6th and 4th Rays one can better understand the 'light and dark' side of Cancerians.

©FELICITY KEEFE 1991.

LEO	The 5th sign.
Keynote	I am that and that I am.
Symbol	The lion or lioness, king and queen of the beasts.
Rays	The 1st and 5th.
Rulers	Heart of the Sun (inner; Ray 2) and corona of the Sun (outer; Ray 2).
Festival	2nd phase of summer; Full Sun–Moon.
House	5th of personal identity, power, knowledge and creative expression.
Elemental	Fixed fire.

Leo and the number five are the sign and the mathematical note of individuality and of the processes of individualization. The archetype of the Ascendant (Aries) incarnates into its physical body in Cancer, the sign ruling Mother Earth, mass consciousness and belief systems. In Leo this archetypal purpose moves out of the womb of the Earth in order to individualize itself and establish its own unique identity and creative expression. The Sun and the 5th house are directly connected to the above, as is the Leo cycle (23 July to 22/23 August) during the astrological year. It is during this Leonian cycle of each year that the individual and group discover their unique identity and creative potential, for the energies of Leo and the Sun are directly influencing the planet at this time. As always the Full Sun–Moon is when this discovery reaches its peak.

The 1st and 5th Rays work through Leo. These are both masculine Rays concerned with will (power/purpose) and experiential knowledge gained through the faculty of the rational 'I must prove it to myself' mind. The Sun channels the feminine 2nd Ray of love and intuition, and this is why Leo has a wonderful yang–yin balance. Leo is the sign of true individual 'flowering', although Capricorn is the sign in which individuality reaches its highest peak or fulfilment. The fifth year of each seven-year cycle (25–26, 32–33 and so on) is the 'flowering' year of that cycle.

The heart of the Sun is the inner ruler. The heart represents the soul or inner self of the individual, whereas the corona represents the outer self or lower ego. The lower ego sees itself as a separate entity and displays itself as such. It works from a position of material ambition and the desire to be recognized as better or more creative than others. It forgets that it is but one micro solar system within the greater body of the galaxy with its myriad solar systems, each having its own unique identity and purpose. Our modern-day entertainment industry with its so-called 'stars' and 'superstars' is one of the best and worst examples of this Leonian ego. It is a breeding ground for corrupt competition, selfish desire, greed and ignorance. Modern-day media and arts exemplify this egotistical ambition, although the latter half of the 1980s has seen the emergence of a new type of celebrity who is interested in the welfare of others and the planet. Live Aid and Band Aid were the turning-point in this area.

True individuality belongs to the soul, for the soul is an entity of light/higher knowledge, love, intuitive understanding and divine purpose. As such the soul is an agent of giving and of unconditional loving purpose. It gives for the sake of giving and this is true creativity. Creativity is not simply a type of objective expression but is concerned with the inner 'quality' lying behind objective activity.

'Giving' of any nature is true creativity, and the giving of love and wisdom is the highest (human) creative gift. Leo Rising (ruled by the Sun's heart) has the greatest capacity to exemplify this inner–outer creative gift.

Most astrologers make the mistake of giving the Sun greater spiritual significance than the Rising sign and its inner ruling planet. The Sun and the 5th house (Leo) are the outer expression of Aries and the 1st house (Ascendant), and it is the Ascendant or Rising sign which embodies the essential inner purpose or archetype of the chart. The seed embodies the essence of the flower and not vice versa. The Sun is exalted in Aries and the 1st house because the Sun in this sign or house has the greatest capacity to channel the Ascendant archetype directly.

The Sun is the central focusing point of any individual's life. It is the conscious channel (the Sun is not a planet but a 'light' or channel) for spiritual energies from the cosmos to reach our solar system. The Sun in the chart and its ruling 5th house are therefore the channels through which the Rising sign (spiritual purpose/ energy) manifests its energies. The Sun is the individual star that receives, embodies and distributes energy into its macro and micro solar system. For this reason the Sun sign informs us of the major personality channel through which the higher self is seeking manifestation. The house in which the Sun is found informs us of the particular sphere where this manifestation needs to occur. If the Sun is in the 7th house this needs to be through partnership; in the 10th through one's career; in the 4th through the home, and so on.

Leonians gifts are their open-hearted giving nature, their positivity and natural self-confidence and their capacity to express life in a loving and electromagnetic creative fashion.

Their shadow is their pride and their exclusivity, and their tendency to give in order to be recognized and acknowledged. By studying the 1st, 5th and 2nd Rays one can get a far better understanding of the dual nature of Leo.

The 5th house of Leo is associated outwardly with children. Placements in the 5th tell us about our relationship with children. Children are the outer manifestation of our creative energy; they are born through the act of creation, that is the merging or fusion of two opposite forces – spirit–matter, yang–yin, male–female, man– woman. This gives us a clue to the secret of all true creativity or creative expression, that is 'the expression of the Creator/God'. There is only 'beingness' at the beginning, at the centre or seed of all life. This core is the Monad, the spirit of life, the Being lying behind all creation (represented by Aries, the first sign of the zodiac).

Out of 'Being/the Monad' (Aries) emerges consciousness or the soul, the first creative manifestation of spirit. The One manifests through the two, through initial duality. This provides a clue to the enigma of 'twin souls' (see the section on Venus in Chapter 3). There are indeed 'twin souls', the twin consciousness(es) of original Being as it manifests itself through the consciousness of the solar system – through souls. There are masculine–feminine twin souls, the perfected children of father (spirit) mother (earth) God. In esoteric terminology they are called 'Solar Lords' because they are Lords of the solar system. Twin souls are nevertheless integrally part of one collective group soul, and this 5th kingdom of souls is sub-divided into seven groupings under the rulership of the Seven Rays.

The above provides the clue to why Leo, the 5th sign, is the second fire sign after Aries. Aries is the Monad, 'the flame at the core of our being', the essential identity of self. Leo is the soul, the child of Aries, the Monad. This is why the heart (soul) of the Sun is the transpersonal ruler of Leo, for the soul (heart) of all life is the true creative expression (child) of God, the Spirit. Christ was not the only Son of God – all perfected or 'Christed' souls are the sons and daughters of the Spirit. In Leo we are asked to reidentify with the soul, our higher selves, our true creative self, the true Christ child of our Father, the Monad. Thus the Leo keynote, 'I Am That and That I Am'.

All children that are born are children of God because they are essentially (truthfully) spirit manifesting through soul (higher consciousness) and soul manifesting through personality (lower consciousness). Thus the three rulers of Leo are the core, heart and corona of the Sun.

There can be no true creativity without soul consciousness – without higher purpose (Ray 1), love, wisdom, warmth, group consciousness and service (Ray 2) and self-gained knowledge (Ray 5), the Rays ruling Leo. Most of modern-day creativity is self-centered, selfish, ambitious, and rejective of higher reality. The true creative human being is qualified by a capacity to love, to give (selflessly), to share inner and outer resources, to know that they are but a 'part of the greater divine whole' and are only giving back to life what they have already received from it. The meditation at the end of this book includes an 'identity' affirmation that helps one to embody this higher creativity.

In our society partners are expected to have children because collective society is out of tune with the reality of the true inner child, the soul, and the manifestation of the soul's love and power and knowledge into the world. Any activity which manifests this triune nature of the higher self is creative – love itself is the greatest creative act. When love, will and knowledge act in unison (a revealing word) then we have true creative genius.

Planets in the 5th house (and in Leo) inform us of the potential quality of our creative expression. The Ray of the planet reveals this quality. There is of course a direct relationship between the Rising sign (essential identity and life-purpose) and the 5th house sign and planets (soul manifestation of this purpose). There is also a connection between one's 'physical' children and one's own inner children/ creative energy. This connection and the corresponding relationship between parents and their children can be seen through the energies of the 5th house. If Venus is in this house there is a positive loving 'knowing' (5th Ray) connection; if Mars there is a conflicting, idealistic, dynamic, wilful (and perhaps sexual) connection (Ray 6); if Mercury there is a mental, communicative (and argumentative) and 'harmony through conflict' (4th Ray) connection and so on.

Leo is therefore concerned with the discovery of one's unique identity and creative expression, which is individualized and yet interconnected with the whole of life. Individualized identity and creative expression (Leo) need to be shared with and distributed to the group and humanity as a whole (Aquarius, Leo's opposite sign), for true creativity is always the manifestation of the mergence of the opposites. Creative expressions are one's inner children (the inner meaning of the 5th house) and they require as much attention, nurturing, caring and correct up(out)bringing as outer children do. Many couples in the New Era will find that they have little need (or desire) to have children because their inner children are being born through them at a rapid and fulfilling rate.

As the energies of Aquarius enter the world they automatically activate the energy of Leo. Individuality and group-collective consciousness, identity, creativity and responsibility go hand in hand. The gifts and problems that this dual energy brings can best be seen in countries like the USSR and Yugoslavia, where various ethnic entities are rediscovering their unique identity, culture and so on. As they do this they desire to separate themselves from the greater whole (the larger nation) of which they have been part. The dilemma of how to integrate the individual and the collective into a co-operative and co-creative whole is one of the major challenges of the New Era and the New World Order.

VIRGO	The 6th sign.
Keynote	I am the Mother and the Child – I – God I – matter am.
Symbol	The virgin holding three sheaves of corn.

©FELICITY KEEFE 1991.

Rays	The 2nd and 6th.
Rulers	The Moon, channelling Vulcan (inner) and Mercury (outer).
Festival	3rd phase of summer; Full Sun–Moon.
House	6th of day-to-day structured living and soul–personality integration.
Elemental	Mutable earth.

In Virgo the soul and the personality seek integration. Six is the number of higher and lower self-integration in which the triune nature of the soul (light, love and purpose) and the personality (body, emotions and mind) need to interconnect and seek manifestation through daily existence. The mother is the symbol of matter or physical form and the child is the symbol of consciousness or the soul. In Virgo, matter becomes the vehicle or channel for the manifestation of higher consciousness. Mother Mary was thus the channel for the birth of the Christ, and esoteric tradition confirms that she had to undergo a preparatory training and purification before she was able to give birth to Jesus, the Christ child.

Virgo is the sign most directly related to the first spiritual initiation, namely the birth of Christ or soul-consciousness within the cave of the heart. This might be called the first conscious step on the path back home. This step entails an accelerated purification and integration of one's threefold personality, and the integration of this self with the purpose, love and light of the higher self. The physical body is the major focal point of this initiation, and this is why the purification of the body through health/whole foods and exercise (yoga, Tai Chi, running and so on) plays such an important role in this initiation. The worship of some spiritual figurehead or guru also features strongly (in the majority of cases) in this initiation, for bodily form is still being worshipped at this early stage of the path.

Virgo's two Rays are the 2nd and 6th, both feminine Rays. The energies of love and devotional idealism feature strongly in this sign. First degree disciples have a tendency to be both loving and inclusive (Ray 2) and fanatically idealistic and exclusive (Ray 6). The worship of the objective teacher and his or her school of teaching is also a 6th Ray characteristic. Love and unity rule the soul while emotional idealism rules the personality.

The Moon and Mercury are both 4th Ray planets, and this is the reason why the higher harmony and beauty aspired to in this sign is only attained through much conflict and struggle. The ego (symbolized by the Moon) needs to subjugate itself to the will or purpose of the soul (Vulcan). Vulcan is the great forger – in mythology Vulcan forges the shield of matter (the body) into a fit and beautiful instrument for the soul. The 1st Ray of creative forging works through Vulcan. Mercury is the outer ruler and represents the lower concrete mind, the brain and the central nervous system. In Virgo the logical mind is required to express and communicate the will, love and light of the self in a practical, down-to-earth and day-to-day manner. The lower mind either becomes the instrument of the soul or it blocks off higher consciousness by limiting its perception to logical thought, knowledge and communication.

Virgo and the 6th house are related to day-to-day structured living and to health and wholeness. True health only comes about through the integration of mind (thought), emotions and the etheric–physical body, and the alignment of these bodies with the higher self. The movement towards this integration is a daily and lifelong process, and holistic health and healing must therefore be seen in this light. There is no such thing as a holistic healer or a holistic healing technique, for 'holism' from a personal perspective means the full integration of the lower and higher selves. The self becomes whole, and thus healed, over a long stretch of time, and no

© FELICITY KEEFE 1991.

complement and balance itself through the agency of partnership (Libra) and vice versa. Libra is the sign or archetype of balance and equilibrium, for it sits in between the first six signs and the last five signs of the zodiac. It acts as a balancer or mediator between:

subjective	objective consciousness
inner reflection	outer activity
personal consciousness/activity	transpersonal consciousness/activity
past	future
spirit in matter	matter transformed into spirit
individuality	group and social consciousness
the light of day (consciousness)	the dark of night (unconsciousness)
the masculine/yang	and the feminine/yin forces

The Sun's movement into Libra (23 September) is the time of the autumn equinox, the cycle in between summer (light) and winter (dark). The autumn season brings a balance between expansion and contraction, heat and cold, spirit in matter (summer) and spirit at its centre (winter). Libra is the descendant point of the zodiac/chart and this point corresponds to dusk, the time of peace and equilibrium between day and night. Libra is also associated with that point of stillness in between the in-breath and the out-breath, which is one (and not the major) goal of meditation. If the ultimate goal of meditation was stillness and peace then Libra would be the last sign of the zodiac.

Libra is the sign of rest, for it exists in between the two conflicting signs of Virgo and Scorpio. Bringing spirit/higher consciousness into matter (Virgo) and transforming and raising up matter into spirit (Scorpio) are both labours of struggle, conflict and pain. The 4th Ray has strong rulership in Virgo and Scorpio. In between these two signs sits Libra, for its energy is that of balance itself. This does not mean that Librans (Rising or Sun) are always in a state of peace and harmony, but that these qualitative energies are available to Librans.

According to the Master DK (*Esoteric Astrology*) the last quarter of the twentieth century is overruled by the spirit of Libra, and this is a guarantee that there will be a balancing of forces as humanity moves into the twenty-first century. This will prevent major catastrophes. If one examines the present-day global situation (with the 'inner eye') one cannot but notice that a balancing of forces is taking place. The balancing of yin–yang forces, of capitalism and Communism, of individuality and group-consciousness, of masculine and feminine energies, and so on, is self-evident. It should be remembered that every sign is in truth a great spiritual life, and the spirit of Libra is that great cosmic Life which brings about balance between the opposites. Astrologers are also aware that Saturn and Jupiter had their triple conjunction in the sign of Libra in 1980/1, and this conjunction has effect for twenty years, until the next one occurs. If the planet of restriction, containment and objective consciousness (Saturn; 3rd Ray) and the planet of expansion, abundance and subjective consciousness (Jupiter; 2nd Ray) conjunct in Libra, the sign of balance, then we can see why all forces are in a cycle of balancing.

The 3rd Ray works through Libra. This is the green Ray of creative or active intelligence. It is also the Ray of ecology and the Green movement (see Chapters 4–5) for ecology is concerned with the interrelationship of all natural forces which produces balance and harmony. The major work of the Green movement is to help bring about a rebalancing of spirit/yin and matter/yang energies. The Green movement emerged into the foreground in 1989, just as the Jupiter–Saturn conjunction cycle reached its ten-year midpoint.

The 3rd Ray is the Ray of activity itself and this is why so many Librans are hyperactive. Hyperactivity might be said to be the Libran's greatest problem, for the 3rd Ray, together with the 1st and 7th Rays of Aries, are all masculine activity Rays. The Libran tends to swing between hyperactivity and extreme laziness. This swinging between the polarities and the attempt to find a point of balance between these opposites is typical of Libran experience.

The 3rd Ray at its best integrates purpose (1st Ray), love and intuition (2nd Ray) and creative action (3rd Ray). From the highest perspective the 3rd Ray is the Ray of balance, adaptability and intelligent activity, for it integrates the energies of the higher triangle of the soul. Ray 3 types have the capacity to integrate and manifest power, love and intelligence, and this should be the goal of all Librans, especially those with Libra Rising.

The Libran cycle of the year (23 September to 23 October) provides a wonderful opportunity to rest, balance and recharge one's energies. It is the best time to take a holiday in order to rest and heal one's entire system, for the six-month cycle from Aries to Virgo taxes one's system to the full. Scorpio, the 8th sign, is a cycle of reorientation and intensive transformation (the changing of mental, emotional and etheric–physical forms to suit a higher mode of consciousness). The Libra cycle is therefore the best time to recharge one's batteries, and thus to prepare for the five signs/months to follow. This is a very good example of how to use astrology as a living science.

Uranus is the inner ruler of Libra. Uranus works with the 7th Ray of ritual, ceremony, organization and synthesis (of will and action). Uranus rules Aquarius and thus the future and its unfoldment in the present. It is the planet of accelerated awakening of consciousness, vision, innovative ideas and freedom-orientated thinking and activity. Uranus transited through Libra from late 1968 to late 1975 and this seven-year cycle initiated the accelerated breakdown of the old marriage system and the start of a new and experimental system of partnership. 'Living together' became an essential part of young people's lives.

Traditional marriage is no longer working and the divorce rate is living proof of this fact. New experimental forms of partnership and marriage have become the norm amongst the younger generations. New rituals and ceremonies are being developed by partners themselves, and marriages are being conducted within a new and freeing atmosphere. Uranian energy inspires freedom of choice and a breaking away from traditional norms such as religious institutions, priests, marriage laws and ceremonies. Individuals are inspired to choose their own mode of behaviour, ceremonies, rituals and so on. It should also be noted that the most constructive time to get married is on the Libra Full Sun–Moon, for the energies at this time are the most appropriate for partnerships and marriages – that is for the balancing of the opposites. My partner and myself married one another at a Libra Full Sun–Moon. It might be of interest to astrologers that our marriage chart has a six-pointed star formation, the aspect related to the linking of the higher and lower triangle.

The central aim of partnership, from the perspective of the soul, is for two individuals to join together, combine their energies and work together in serving the divine plan and their greater purpose. This is the essential purpose of partnership or marriage, and true partnership is therefore a sacred relationship. 'Sacred marriage' belongs to the realm of Libra–Aries, for it entails not only the sacredness of partnership between two individuals (Libra) but also the unification of the opposites within each individual themselves (Aries). The lower self and the higher self seek union within the individual (Aries) and within the partnership. Partnerships are therefore an intensification of the process of individualization, for a partnership is simply a 'space' in which two individuals can share their spiritual and material resources for their own greater good and for the good of the greater whole. Sacred partnership is a commitment by two individuals to serve the will of their souls and the greater plan of the Christ and God. Every other aspect of partnership is only a by-product of this dedication.

Partnership is a battleground for it is simply a combination of two individuals' energies. These two polarities seek a point of balance and harmony through their dynamic interrelationship, but such a balance is only attained through 'the swinging of the scales'. In Libra inner life and outer life must be combined, and purpose, love and intelligent action require integration and manifestation. The partnership needs to integrate itself within a larger group energy too, because Uranian energy works best through group activity. The best partnerships will fail unless they serve some greater group and collective purpose, and participation in group activity of some sort or other is necessary if any partnership is to contribute towards the divine plan.

Venus and the 5th Ray are the outer rulers. It is interesting to note the difference between Libra Rising and Sun Libra. Libra Rising people (when awakened) are highly intuitive and revolutionary in their thinking and activities (Uranus), whereas Libra Sun people are very logical and pragmatic, and desire traditional security in their relationships (Venus and the 5th Ray of the concrete mind). Harmony and beauty might be associated with Venus traditionally, but these qualities are more related to the 4th Ray as it works through Mercury and the Moon and to Neptune. Venusian harmony and beauty in its lower rulership of Libra (and Taurus) is all too often materially based and lacks spiritual purpose and direction. I have seen many Libran–Venusian type marriages which contain great material beauty (purchased with money) but which lack the true inner beauty of the spirit. This type of marriage is being replaced by the Uranian-type partnership. Uranus brings constant change and 'change' must therefore be seen as integral to the new partnerships. Astrologers must therefore look to the placement of Uranus in the chart in interpreting the inner significance of Libra and the 7th house.

The tendency to avoid all potentially conflicting situations tends to be one of the worst sides of the Libran character, especially Libra Sun, Moon, Venus and even Mars (Mars loses power in Libra). Librans tend to avoid conflict and confrontation at any cost, and this often leads to more conflict in the end. Problems grow if one avoids rather than faces them. Choice is another great problem because they desire to walk in between the two extremes, being afraid (in the very real yet often unconscious sense of the word) of the conflict inherent in any one extreme. Choosing the path of true balance requires not a rejection but a synthesis of the two extremes, for spirit and matter, yang and yin and all opposites require one another if they are to experience true harmony, beauty and unity.

The capacity to find the middle path between the extremes and to choose the path that leads in between spirit and matter is the gift of Libra. Libra provides the energy of balance, harmony and right human relationship. Librans have the wonderful capacity to swing back to the centre after swinging to either extreme and this allows them to understand the two sides of every story and the third and balanced side too. By studying the 3rd, 5th and 7th Rays we can gain a deeper comprehension of the workings of this sign.

SCORPIO	The 8th sign.
Keynote	Warrior I am and from the battle I emerge triumphant.
Symbols	The scorpion, the serpent and the eagle.
Ray	The 4th.
Rulers	Pluto (inner; 1st Ray) and Mars (outer; 6th Ray).
Festival	2nd phase of autumn; Full Sun–Moon.
House	8th of personal(ity) reorientation, transformation and regeneration.
Elemental	Fixed water.

© FELICITY KEEFE.

After the resting and balancing cycle of Libra comes Scorpio, the great sign of testing, trial, battle, transformation and final triumph. The energies of Libra are an integration of the first six signs of the zodiac, and this creates a balancing of soul and personality forces in which neither takes the upper hand. Libra balances the spiritual and material forces of life. In Scorpio the forces of the lower self reawaken and reassert themselves, and the individual (group, nation) is required to descend into the underworld of this self to transform and raise it up to the soul.

In Virgo the higher self in its triune nature seeks birth into the material world through the triune nature of the personality (thus the three-armed symbol of Virgo focuses the energies of the soul into the Earth). In Scorpio the soul seeks entrance into the three-fold material world in order to raise up the lower self into its own world – thus the three-armed symbol of Scorpio focuses itself into the earth and then ascends into space. This symbol hides the great secret of Scorpio and the secret of initiation, for it is only by descending into (and fully experiencing) the underworld that one can transform and raise it into spirit, which is the essential purpose underlying incarnation into matter.

The 4th Ray rules Scorpio and this is the Ray ruling initiation. Initiation is the process of step-by-step integration of the personality and the soul, and later of the soul and the Monad. The results of initiation are a greater and greater degree of purpose, love, knowledge, harmony, beauty, integration, fusion, freedom and service of humanity. Harmony and beauty are only attained through conflict – that is through the experience of life and all its dualities. There are greater and greater degrees of harmony and beauty, for each initiation occurs on a higher level of the evolutionary spiral. The 4th Ray is the linking energy of spirit and matter and of the higher and lower selves. It is this linking or fusion that underlies the processes of initiation (see Chapters 3–5). Astrologers should note that Chiron, the planetoid discovered in 1978, is ruled by the 4th Ray, and thus its position in between Saturn (personal self) and Uranus (transpersonal self), and its 51-year orbit (5 + 1 = 6, the number of soul–personality integration). Chiron's discovery signalled the advent of an accelerated linkage of these two selves, individually and collectively.

One of the major manifestations of Chiron was the great expansion of 'networking' – the linking-up of people, events and information on a local, national and global scale (see the section on Sagittarius for more details on this subject). This in turn resulted in the accelerated integration of higher and lower consciousness on a personal, group and collective level. This is all part of the initiation process which is bringing the Spiritual Hierarchy and humanity, the 5th and 4th kingdoms of the planet, into a greater degree of communication, co-operation and unification. This in turn is bringing about the birth of a new spiritual dispensation into the material world. This 'birth' is ruled by Virgo, and Chiron is said to have dual rulership of Virgo (with two 4th Ray planets) and Sagittarius, a 4th Ray sign.

Scorpio rules the second initiation in which the emotional and sexual nature (solar plexus and sacral centres) are transformed and raised up to the soul centres, the heart and throat chakras. This entails a twofold process because the energies of the soul descend into these two lower centres of force in order to stimulate them into heightened activity, and this stimulation forces the person (or group, nation and so on) to experience their lower self in a highly dynamic and forceful fashion. Thus the intensity of all Scorpionic or 8th house experience, be it mental, emotional, sexual, financial or otherwise. The will to experience the world of desire to the full is the Scorpionic experience, but unlike the Taurian who loves desire for its own sake the Scorpionic person is intent (whether they realize it or not, and they often do *not* realize it) on experiencing their desires in order to transform and transmute matter into higher consciousness.

The great problem with this process is that the experience of matter (sensuality) tends to create attachment to matter. Taurians desire the attachment (Venus) whereas the Scorpio type tends (consciously or unconsciously) to destroy any attachments (Mars and Pluto) by the very intensity of their energy. The great challenge in Scorpio is to learn the art of replacing material attachment with spiritual detachment and love, but this has to come about in Scorpio through experience itself and not through words and avoidance of such experiences.

Pluto and Mars co-rule Scorpio and these are both non-sacred planets ruling the base, sacral and solar plexus centres. The entire physical, emotional, sexual and mental sides of oneself are forced into the battleground and burning ground of Scorpio. Although Scorpio is a water sign and therefore governed by the water (emotional–desire) elementals, fire is the central agency which brings about this required transformation. Pluto and Mars are both fiery planets and the 4th Ray also works with fire. Fire is the great agency of transmutation; water is transmuted into steam through the agency of heat or fire and internal fire acts in the same way in transmuting human consciousness and forms back to their higher source. Astrologers give great emphasis to the element that rules each sign, but this element only rules the material aspect of the sign. The Rays govern the spiritual and psychological aspects of each sign, and the Rays and elements have to be integrated in interpretation.

Pluto, the Lord of the Underworld, is related to Kundalini fire or the dynamic life-giving energy that dwells at the core of the Earth and in the core of the base chakra. Pluto is the feminine Shakti force who is the consort of Shiva, the masculine Godhead related to Vulcan; Vulcan and Pluto are the two 1st Ray planets (Vulcan is the inner ruler of Taurus and Pluto of Scorpio). When the light of Vulcan enters any system it illuminates and enlightens that system and automatically awakens its counterpart Pluto. The entrance of light and its illuminating power (Vulcan and Uranus) awakens that which is dark or unconscious (Pluto and the Moon). This is the deeper relationship between Taurus and Scorpio; it is also the deeper reason why Uranus is exalted in Scorpio and why the Moon is in its Fall in this sign, for Uranus rules the future and spiritual law and order while the Moon rules form life and the past and its illusions and deceptive influences. The Moon's exaltation in Taurus creates the necessary forms (physical bodies) to house the spirit, but it also creates the terribly strong attachments to form that those with Sun, Moon or Venus in Taurus tend to have.

In Scorpio the will or purpose of the soul seeks to impress itself upon and into the innermost depths of the personality – right down to the very core. The purpose of this higher will is to enter the mind, emotions and etheric–physical body and to anchor itself into the core of the Earth itself. This is the deeper reason why Scorpionic people have an intense desire to experience life to the very core, and enter into all life experiences with intense purpose, will and desire. When any consciousness enters into the life of its personality with such intensity its light awakens that which is dark and unconscious, and the sleeping serpent or Kundalini is activated. A twofold process thus begins in which the light, love and will of the soul enter the lower self and the desires of this self are activated in order to be experienced to the full, for that which has not been experienced (to whatever relative and necessary degree) cannot be transformed.

Mars is concerned with the objective experience and active dynamic projection of one's inner desires and ideals (6th Ray) and in its true nature is not a malefic planet. Without Martian force one could not project one's consciousness, ideals, dreams and desires into the outer world. Mars gives one the will to enter into the world of matter, and this will can be used for constructive or destructive purposes. The intent and the purpose determine whether Martian force will be used for selfish or unselfish purposes. In Aries Martian force drives one into material experience because the soul requires incarnation into matter. In Scorpio Mars drives one into material experience in order to transform the material world so that the soul can expand its light, love and purpose into matter. Mars has the same influence in Capricorn because it is exalted in this sign. Martian force is wilful, fiery and conflicting because it breaks up old crystallized patterns of behaviour (forms) in order to allow a greater inflow of spiritual energy into matter.

Pluto (the Goddess Kali in Hindu terminology) is related to the Kundalini fire which, from the human point of view, is an unconscious and hidden force. Kundalini is spirit in matter and this spirit is automatically activated by the descent of Vulcanian or Uranian light into matter. A relative degree of Kundalini fire ascends up the spine and brings to the surface (of consciousness) memories, hurts, anger, frustration and bitterness that forms part of our crystallized mental, emotional, sexual and physical habit pattern. These patterns are largely unconscious and require transformation and transmutation for they form 'blocks' in our life system and restrict our capacity to fulfill our purpose and serve the divine plan.

Each initiation is different in the above regard for each initiation releases a greater amount of Kundalini force. Kundalini pundits (East and West) tend to be ignorant of this fact. In Scorpio the Kundalini fire sweeps through the emotional/astral body, which is the most difficult body to cleanse and transmute. If Kundalini (Plutonic force) ascended right up the spine to the crown chakra (as these pundits claim) the person(ality) would go mad, for this 'burning ground' experience only takes place at the 3rd initiation – the transfiguration on the mountaintop (related to the highest level of Capricorn).

The great paradox about Plutonic force is that it is both transmuter and regenerator simultaneously. Transmutation is an extremely painful process, for recognizing, facing, accepting, transforming and integrating one's past and its negative habit patterns is a very difficult and time-consuming process. The millions of people who are involved with this process know this all too well. The demons and ogres that the hero/heroine has to face and overcome are not that easily defeated as in the myths, for stories are but stories. Real life is a little different (to say the least). The paradox is that it is these demons and ogres, symbols of one's fears, desires, jealousies, ignorance, attachments, pride and lack of will, that entrap and imprison one's consciousness in the 'hell' of one's own making. The transmutation and defeat of these demons allows individual and collective consciousness to expand its light, love, wisdom, purpose, joy, inner peace, creative activity and service of the divine plan. This is regeneration, for regeneration is the result of the transmutation process. It might be said that transformation, transmutation and regeneration occur simultaneously, for death and rebirth intertwine with one another.

Owing to its periodic retrograde motion, Pluto always makes three transits (sometimes five as in 1989–90), and each transit is experienced in the above manner. It is only after the final transit that the third death–rebirth process occurs, but it takes at least one year (and often many more) to integrate the experience in one's consciousness and new life patterns. The USSR had Pluto transiting its Sun and Mercury over 1989–90 and it will take at least one year before the nation can integrate the huge purging, transforming and regenerating experience. It might be of interest to note that 1991 is the final 'Libran' (seventh sign) year of the global seven-year cycle, and this seventh year is a cycle of final integration of the past seven years (1985–1991). Gorbachev came to power in 1985 and initiated the massive transformation of Soviet society. The positive results of this amazing feat will only be witnessed (objectively) by the end of 1991.

There is nothing more deadly than mental, emotional and/or physical stagnation and complacency. After the Libran cycle of October–November there tends to be a great deal of stagnant energy because stagnancy is the shadow of balance and harmony. The Scorpio cycle is therefore a time to activate the hidden forces of the personality (the sleeping Kundalini) and to transform, transmute, regenerate and reorientate one's consciousness. The Scorpio cycle each year and Scorpio people, groups and nations (the Findhorn Foundation has Scorpio Sun, as does the USSR, Czechoslovakia, and Japan has Scorpio Rising) have this Scorpio task. This is 4th Ray activity, for the higher and lower selves are in a process of direct and intensive interaction, leading towards fusion (initiation) and a greater degree of union and directed purpose. If we look at Scorpio in this fashion we can see the deeper significance of its power and influence through those that it governs.

True 4th Ray types desire to experience both worlds with intensity. Note the Scorpio and Sagittarius (especially Rising) types and note the Russian people. The second initiation is the most difficult of the first three initiations, for the emotional–sexual bodies are the most difficult to transform and transmute. Humanity's line of least resistance is its emotional–sexual body, for fear is the major characteristic that rules the reactive and compulsive influences of these bodies. Material and financial security and greed are in themselves manifestations of emotional fear. We fear we will not have enough money; we fear we will not have enough sex; we fear we will not have enough love; we fear we will not have enough power. It is no wonder that the ancient Egyptians gave the name Set to the devil, for Set means fear. It is important to study the 4th Ray to get a deep understanding of Scorpio and the path of the Scorpionic type, for this Ray has a direct and powerful influence in this sign.

Pluto and Mars have rulership in Scorpio, Pisces (Pluto) and Aries (Pluto and Mars), and all three signs are therefore involved with the death–rebirth experience.

It is absolutely necessary to be adequately armed to face this battleground. In all the mythological legends the hero is 'armed' by the Gods before entering the underworld (their own lower self); in some cases they are given a sword or club (will), a shield (love and wisdom), a helmet (knowledge) and special shoes (practical gifts/ work). During the various stages of this holy war the armour is lost or has to be given up. The hero is often accompanied by three friends or warriors who are also killed along the way. The three friends symbolize traditional material security, emotional desires and the rational mind or personal will, the three-faced personality.

Sometimes the hero fights a three-or nine-headed monster, also symbolizing the lower self nature. In the labours of Hercules we find the hero fighting a nine-headed monster (*The Labours of Hercules* by Alice Bailey, Lucis Trust Pub.). Aries and Scorpio provide much of this armour because they embody and distribute the energies of potent one-pointed will and courageous and passionate idealism. Pisces is armed with the power of unconditional love and self-sacrificial idealism.

The great problem with 4th Ray and Scorpio types is that they become so caught up in the battle within themselves that they tend to forget its deeper purpose. This intensive self-centredness often leads to a great degree of plain selfishness, negative self-destruction and unnecessary conflict with others. I say 'negative' self-destruction because the aim in Scorpio is to transform and raise up the self and this implies its own self-destruction. The paradox is that it is impossible to destroy the self because it is the instrument of the self in the material world. The self has to become a conscious, intelligent, co-operative and co-creative channel to transform itself and the world. There is often a thin red line between negative and positive self-destruction and it takes a good deal of experience, trial and error to decipher the difference between the two.

All forms of psychology, astrology, counselling and all techniques and activities related to self-awareness and self-transformation fall under Scorpio. The science of symbols and their interpretation is also governed by this sign although this is also the domain of Sagittarius. Scorpio is more concerned with the symbols of the unconscious whereas Sagittarius is concerned with the language of the superconscious.

Scorpio types not only test themselves but are constantly testing others. They have the capacity to see into the dark corners of their own psyche and into the darkness of other people's and society's psyches. The intensity of their perception, feelings, emotions and experiences often causes them to project their darkness onto other people. 'Projection' is a major characteristic of the shadow nature, for people, nations, religions and races are consistently projecting their fear, prejudice, frustration, anger, envy and ignorance onto others. 'We see in others what exists in ourselves' although this is often an unconscious projection. The American–Russian 'enemy' projection is now largely over (thanks to Gorbachev) and the white–black projection in South Africa is gradually reaching some resolution, but the Arab–Israeli and Greek–Turk projections (and many others) are as strong as ever.

Taking responsibility for one's own shadow is an extremely difficult process demanding great courage. The Scorpio type will often force other people to awaken to their dark and hidden motives and desires because the work of Scorpio *is* to awaken these hidden forces. One cannot change what one does not recognize, and few people wish to recognize what they dislike in themselves. When the Iraqis rocketed Tel Aviv during the Gulf War the Western powers and the Israelis pleaded shock and horror. Civilian casualties in the Israeli bombing of Lebanon were completely forgotten, as was the American bombing and use of 'agent orange' in Vietnam. The Gulf War is a perfect demonstration of age-old projections and the destructive consequences of this unconscious behaviour. Scorpio forces one to face oneself and one's projections, and war, be it internal or external, is often the only way to bring this situation about. The more that people go into inner war with themselves, the less will humanity be required to go into outer war. Martian force can either operate unconsciously and be projected through outer war or it can operate consciously through inner battle. It might be of interest to note that the chart of the Gulf War (for Baghdad) has Scorpio Rising with Pluto just above the Ascendant, for Scorpio (and Aries) rules the transformative power of the battleground.

A deep study of the 4th, 6th and 1st Rays can supply a great deal of constructive information on the Scorpio labour.

SAGITTARIUS	The 9th sign.
Keynote	I see a goal, I reach that goal and then I see the next goal.
Symbol	The centaur, half-animal (horse) and half-man, aiming his arrow(s) towards the heavens.
Rays	The 4th, 5th and 6th.
Rulers	The Earth (inner; Ray 3) and Jupiter (outer; Ray 2).
Festivals	3rd phase of autumn; Full Sun–Moon.
House	9th of the focused and expanded spiritual path; communication with and guidance from one's soul and other spiritual sources via dreams and audio and/or visual telepathy; spiritual of life education.
Elemental	Mutable fire.

After the descent into the underworld of Scorpio comes the ascent into the light of Sagittarius. In Scorpio we explore the underworld and in Sagittarius we explore the overworld, the world of the soul or the 5th kingdom of souls. Humanity is the 4th kingdom or 'centre of force' in nature after the mineral, vegetable and animal kingdoms. In Sagittarius the 4th and 5th kingdoms enter into a more direct interrelationship, for humanity is the mediating kingdom

© FELICITY KEEFE 1991.

between the 5th kingdom of souls and the three lower kingdoms of nature. The kingdom of souls is in turn the mediating centre between the 6th kingdom of the Christ and the Masters of the Wisdom (the senior members of the spiritual hierarchy of the Earth) and humanity. The spiritual hierarchy is the mediating kingdom between Shambhala, (the Monadic Centre of the planet) and the soul of humanity.

This interrelationship between the higher and lower selves is continually evolving during the cycles of the first and second initiations – that is between Aries through to Virgo, Libra and Scorpio and Sagittarius. The first initiation creates an initial fusion of the crown (will) and base (gross physical) centres and transmutes (relatively) gross material attachments such as financial greed and dietary and health patterns. Vulcan and Pluto (1st Ray) govern this initiation, plus Mercury and the Moon, rulers of Virgo. The second initiation, which is far more drawn-out and complex, fuses the solar plexus (emotional–desire) and heart (love) centres, and transmutes (relatively) the emotional/astral body and subtle desires such as envy, jealousy, hate and of course their king-pin, fear. Jupiter (Ray 2), Venus (Ray 5) and Neptune (Ray 6) govern this initiation – that is all three planets associated with the quality of intelligent love, plus Mars and Pluto, rulers of Scorpio, and the Earth, ruler of Sagittarius.

Sagittarius expands the second initiation to include a far more direct 'vertical' relationship with the higher self in its individual, group, national and planetary context, for the 5th kingdom of souls is in truth one interconnected whole. This expanded contact also occurs on a 'horizontal' cross-national and cross-cultural human level. In other words the fusion between the two worlds now takes place at an expanded, accelerated and inclusive level, rather than simply on a personal and exclusive level. First degree initiation groupings are exclusive to a large degree (my/our guru or teaching or technique is the best) and second degree initiation groupings are exclusive in a more subtle manner; they communicate inclusively but nevertheless think and act exclusively to a greater or lesser degree.

The major instrument of this inclusive expansion is the higher mind, for it is this mind that is activated in Sagittarius. The higher mind consists of two interconnected parts: the abstract contemplative or 'pondering' mind (higher manas) and the intuitive or 'all-knowing' mind (Buddhi). These are part of the mind of the higher self (see the soul triangle in Chapter 2). In Sagittarius one's consciousness expands into the mind of God, which is the world of the soul, and one begins to identify one's consciousness with this twofold mind. In Gemini, the opposite and complementary sign, the higher (Venus) and lower (Mercury) rational mind governs and this leads on to the higher abstract and intuitive mind(s) in Sagittarius.

In order to contact the intuitive mind one first has to 'think into' the world of the soul. One has to study and ponder upon the higher purpose and laws that govern the life of the soul, the means by which this purpose and these laws can be understood, and the goals that are necessary for the manifestation of this purpose on Earth. This type of thought is not philosophical thinking as taught by conventional educational institutions, but rather the philosophical wisdom that is gained through the dynamic use of the mind by the free-thinking individual. The mind spirals upward and penetrates into the world of higher consciousness. It becomes 'at one' with the mind of the soul – it creates and builds a path into the realms of the 5th kingdom of souls.

This path is called 'the rainbow bridge' or *antakarana* and it is the bridge that links the brain and the lower mind (Mercury), the higher logical mind (Venus) and the higher abstract mind (Jupiter) with the intuitive mind of the higher self. The higher self can then relay its wisdom and guidance (which is always right) via the intuition and the rainbow bridge to the consciousness of the thinker. This process sets up a vertical intercommunication system between the human self and the higher self, and co-operation and co-creation between the two kingdoms now become possible. This can and should take place on an individual, group, network and collective level in the sign of Sagittarius (and the 9th house) because this sign expands energy vertically and horizontally.

The journey into higher thought has its great advantages and its corresponding disadvantages (as does everything). The stimulation of the higher mind naturally tends to abstract one from the physical realities of the world (one gets 'spaced-out'), and for a certain period of time it is extremely difficult to be grounded in physical plane realities. Sagittarians, Aquarians and Pisceans (all Jupiter-ruled) suffer most directly from this experience. This type of thinking also tires and exhausts the mind–brain, which in turn exhausts the nervous system and body. Sagittarius Rising people, who have the major purpose of working with the higher mind, are highly dynamic and creative thinkers, great visionaries, born leaders, and fiery initiators, but suffer from frequent bouts of mental and physical exhaustion.

The information and knowledge gained from the higher mind needs to be mentally integrated and then put into a practical working context. This is exhausting work for it not only taxes the entire mental body but also the emotions and physical body. This work is also transpersonal in the sense that it is not simply personal but involved with group, network and collective activity, for Sagittarius interlinks all these levels into a connected whole. Much of this work is futuristic in vision and context too and all these factors add up to a very heavy workload. It should be remembered that the 4th, 5th, 6th, 3rd and 2nd Rays are all focusing through this sign and its ruling planets, and Sagittarians (especially Rising) have a great diversity of energies to integrate and synthesize.

Networkers and the work of networking are largely governed by this sign. Thus the discovery of Chiron (in 1978), a co-ruler of this sign, for Chiron is the great networker of the two kingdoms of the soul and the personality. True healing can only come about when the higher and lower selves are linked up, communicating and co-operating together. Chiron is associated with the 'wounded healer' in mythology but the 'wound' is the split between the soul and the personality and only the unification of this split can heal the wound. Chiron is related to the higher mind (the mind beyond Saturn) because it is only the higher mind that can bridge the gap between the two worlds. The position of Chiron in the chart indicates how (sign) and where (house) this linkage and corresponding healing needs to occur. A great deal has been written about Chiron and much glamour has developed around its image. Dynamic meditation and intelligent dynamic living are the two major keys to healing the split between higher and lower consciousness, and the building of the rainbow bridge is paramount in this regard.

The intuition reveals reality directly, and it simultaneously synthesizes duality (logical thought) into unity. The intuition (or Buddhi) and the higher abstract mind are interconnected, because what one thinks about is what is revealed to one intuitively. One cannot intuit or know something unless one is thinking about it and this is the secret of intuitive revelation. If one wants to know something one must 'think into' that something; as one increases the tempo of one's thinking one's consciousness penetrates into the realm of the intuitive mind and (hey presto) a revelation occurs. This dual nature of the higher mind and the intuitive revelation that results from its linkage is the gift of Sagittarius.

Another gift of Sagittarius is the secret of the language of symbols. Scorpio reveals the language of symbols via the collective unconscious whereas Sagittarius reveals the language of symbols via the superconscious. Both of these symbolical languages are required if we are to have access to the dual world of the unconscious and the superconscious. They are like brother and sister to one another. Sagittarius reveals the spiritual realities lying behind the symbols of the superconscious, and the application of these symbols to intuitive daily living, for every life-experience is an outer symbol of an inner reality.

In Sagittarius it is necessary to integrate the psychology of the unconscious and the psychology and symbology of the superconscious. By understanding the symbology of astrology, numerology and various other symbols of life, and by integrating this knowledge with intuitive comprehension, one is able to interpret the hidden meaning behind objective experiences and phenomena. Objective experiences or situations, whether personal or collective, are then capable of being interpreted in a new, meaningful and spiritual light. The spiritual path or the path of life thus becomes all-encompassing, for every relationship, experience and situation is a living symbol embodying an inner spiritual meaning. The path and the goal are one – indeed the Path is the goal.

Sagittarius is the only sign besides Capricorn that channels three Rays, the 4th, 5th and 6th. This makes for its intensity and complexity. Note especially the lives of Sagittarius Rising, for the Rising sign works with the Rays far more directly. Harmony and beauty and the art of living – through conflict, concrete knowledge gained

through personal exploration and experience and abstract devotional idealism all work together in this sign. Sagittarians therefore
have to work with and integrate all three Ray energies plus the 3rd
and 2nd Rays. The study of these five Rays provides a deepened
understanding of the Sagittarian labour.

The rulers are Jupiter (2nd Ray) and the Earth (3rd Ray). There is
a good balance of masculine (3 and 5) and feminine (2, 4 and 6)
Rays, and this can be recognized in many Sagittarian types. Jupiter
creates the expansive, inclusive, positive, loving and generous
personality of the Sagittarian, although the tendency to over-
expansion and over-indulgence is its shadow. Jupiter and Uranus
are the two planets most associated with vision, intuitive revelation
and the future (they co-rule Aquarius). Jupiter also governs the
abstract mind and its capacity to transcend barriers, and as the personal ruler of this sign it governs the connection between the lower
and higher selves and communication with and guidance from the
higher self through the intuition, dreams and actual life-experience.
Long-distance travelling and cross-national and cross-cultural
communication and the work of networking are also governed by
Jupiter. Jupiter is the soul in its most positive, inclusive, loving,
joyful and humorous mode, operational in both the abstract and
material world. Giving, sharing, trust, faith, abundance and the
manifestation of one's needs are also the gift of this great planet
(Ray 2).

The Earth is the higher ruler. Very few astrologers use the Earth
in the chart. The Earth is placed opposite the Sun in the birth chart,
because the Sun is symbolically the masculine giving principal and
the Earth the feminine receptive principle. What we are as a giving
individual (Sun) needs to be given, shared and physically manifested by the Earth (and its placement in the chart by sign and
house). The Earth is a dark, gross, polluted non-sacred planet and it
requires cleansing and transformation, and for this reason it is one
of the unconscious ('shadow') planets in the chart. Here lies its complexity in Sagittarius, for a non-sacred (personality-focused) planet
is the inner (soul) ruler.

Food, drink and sex are directly associated with the Earth and
with the earth elementals. The spleen chakra is the focal point of
the Earth's energies, for it is the cleansing centre of the etheric–
physical body. The Earth can therefore be said to be the spleen
centre of the solar Logos and its system – Earth is the cleansing
house of our solar system. The spleen centre receives, absorbs and
distributes the vitalizing energy (*prana* or *chi*) of the Sun via the
etheric body into the physical body. If the spleen centre becomes
blocked through impure diet it begins to malfunction. This leads to

exhaustion because prana is not being correctly distributed to the rest of the system, especially the solar plexus centre (the whole digestive system) and sacral and base centres (sex and activity systems). A great number of Sagittarius Risings suffer from this problem, and the slightest deviation in their diet (heavy or allergy-producing foods, alcohol, drugs and smoking) creates a major loss of vitality. A light and pure diet is vital for them although this is difficult because of the great amount of energy they use in their fiery work.

The five Rays working through this sign create an abundance of differing energies, and the work of integrating them all is extremely difficult. The 3rd Ray creative centre (the throat) and its lower counterpart the sacral centre are activated strongly in this sign, and this is another reason why sex plays such a powerful role in their lives. Sex(uality) is a major characteristic of the Earth (Ray 3 in its non-sacred mode) and this sign (with its strong 4th Ray influence too), especially Rising, has the task of resolving the dilemma of sexuality and finding solutions to its new and upgraded usage. This is part of its great 4th Ray battleground. The USA has Sagittarius Rising and the worst and finest aspects of sexuality are evident there. Sagittarius forces the sexual issue into the foreground of the person's consciousness where it can be seen, explored and hopefully resolved. This results in some of the worst and best manifestations of sexual energy, for the Mutable signs display the polarities at their extreme. It is up to the 4th Ray signs (Taurus, Scorpio and Sagittarius) to resolve the sexual issue, and the harmony and beauty of this resolution will only come about through intense internal conflict. This is another facet of the Earth as the inner ruler, for the Earth as a collective system has to be purified and healed through collective activity, such as environmental protection work (a 3rd Ray activity), and it also has to be healed through each individual healing their own micro Earth system.

There is nevertheless a very positive side to the Earth's ruler-ship and this is the strong links that Sagittarius (especially Rising) has with the Earth itself. There is no sign that has a more direct link with the soul of the Earth. Sagittarius Rising, with its ruling planet the Earth (Ray 3), has the task of cleansing and lighting up the Earth. 'Light' is the essential quality of the 3rd Ray, for light is the inner energy of the higher mind (Ray 3) or 'creative intelligence'. Networkers and the work of networking are essentially ruled by this sign because the purpose of this work is to assist in bringing light (Ray 3) and love (Ray 2) into the etheric–physical body and into the minds and hearts of humanity. Networking is concerned with:

- creating a direct link between the Spiritual Hierarchy, the world of souls and humanity through the agency of dynamic meditation and imaginative thinking;
- creating links between individuals, groups, networks and nations in order to merge and strengthen the network of light and love around the globe;
- helping to form 'New Age' groups and networks so that people can function in group formation and learn to evolve, work and co-operate as group units; and
- prepare the Light Network and humanity overall for the entry into the New Era and for the return of the Christ, the world teacher, and the emergence of a new world order, culture and civilization.

'Think globally and act locally' has become one of the major keynotes of this Network. This keynote originally emerged through the 'Planetary Initiative for the World we Choose' which was initiated by Donald Keys of Planetary Citizens in 1981, the year that Uranus (the awakener and synthesizer) moved into Sagittarius for its seven-year cycle.

The gift of Sagittarians is their one-pointed yet flexible vision towards the discovery and application of truth, love and light. They are born leaders and inspirers who lead from the front and are capable of seeing 'the forest *and* the trees' simultaneously. Their Jupiterian humour is a blessing to themselves and others. Their shadow is their failure to stick to the vision, the avoidance of responsibility, immature idealism and over-expansion and over-indulgence.

CAPRICORN	The 10th sign.
Keynote	Lost am I in light supernal yet on that light I turn my back.
Symbol	The goat climbing the mountain; the unicorn standing on the peak of the mountain.
Rays	The 1st, 3rd and 7th.
Rulers	Saturn (inner and outer; Ray 3).
Festival	Winter solstice; Full Sun–Moon.
House	10th (MC or Midheaven) of one's highest aspirations and goals and the larger work (career/vocation) by which to achieve these goals.
Elemental	Cardinal earth.

Sagittarius leads us goal by goal to the mountain of initiation which is ruled by the 10th sign, Capricorn. Sagittarius might be regarded as the spiritual path that leads one to the doorway into the spiritual

©FELICITY KEEFE 1991

kingdom. Capricorn and the Midheaven is this doorway, for Capricorn is called 'the doorway into spirit'. Ten is the number of the completion of the individualization process, for completion entails the unification and resolution of personal(ity) duality into the greater unity of the soul. Many books refer to Capricorn as the sign of ambition, but the true interpretation of this word is never given. The true meaning of 'am-bi-tion' is the integration of the polarities ('am-bi') within the totality or wholeness of life. The highest ambition or aspiration ('to breathe towards') in life is to integrate or synthesize the yang–yin dualities of the lower self and to become 'at-one' with the higher Christ self and the 5th kingdom of souls. This is finally achieved at the third initiation which is symbolically referred to as 'the transfiguration on the mountain top', and Capricorn rules this initiation.

Capricorn is the natural MC or Midheaven point of the zodiac/chart, the MC being the highest point or 'mountaintop' of the zodiac (which is opposite the IC or Cancerian 'base' point). The MC is the 'doorway' into spirit for the mountaintop is obviously the nearest point to open space, the symbol of spirit or the soul. The MC in the individual chart is therefore the indicator of:

- the highest ambitions, aspirations or goals that one is aiming to achieve in this lifetime;
- the 'doorway' of initiation that one has to enter and pass through in order to fulfil one's spiritual or life-purpose (indicated by the Rising sign); the position of Saturn in the chart is also related to this fulfilment as Saturn is the natural ruler of the MC/Capricorn; and
- the full-time work, career or vocation that one needs to undertake in order to objectify and fulfil one's life-purpose.

The sign ruling the MC, its ruling Ray(s), the position of its planetary ruler, plus the position of Saturn, the normal ruler of Capricorn, have to be interpreted in the above regard. Many astrological texts give a simplistic materialist slant to this sign without realizing that it is the actual sign ruling spiritual initiation. It should be remembered that Jesus and many other Solar Gods (3rd degree initiates) were born into Capricorn. The arguments as to when Jesus was actually born are superfluous when one understands this fact. Christmas is of course celebrated in the Capricorn cycle and has unfortunately become associated with the physical birth of Jesus rather than the birth of Christ-consciousness 'within the cave of the heart', which is its true celebratory meaning.

If one understands that Capricorn is the doorway into the higher kingdom of the soul or Christ self, and that this entrance symbolizes the birth of Christ-consciousness in and through the personality, then one can understand that Christ Mass (or Soul Mass) is the time when individuals, groups, families, nations and humanity overall should be celebrating the reality and birth (manifestation) of love, light, joy, purpose, community, sharing and goodwill. It is an inner celebration of Christ-consciousness and not the celebration of the birth of the physical form of Jesus. The Christmas tree itself is the symbol of 'the tree of consciousness'. This tree has seven lights (the seven chakras) and at the top of this tree is a five-pointed star or angel, both symbols of the higher Christ self. This self is actually referred to in the ancient wisdom teachings as 'the Angel of the Shining Presence'. How far we have deviated from the original and true meaning of Christmas! It has even reached the stage where Christmas has become the time when the greatest number of marriages break up due to financial pressures and conflicts (as reported in the *Guardian* newspaper of December 1990).

The winter solstice begins the Capricorn cycle (21 December). This is the time of the longest night and the shortest day of the year, for the Sun has reached its nadir – its lowest position in its annual cycle through the zodiac. It is thus the darkest point of the year – the symbolical and literal 'dark night of the soul'. Directly after the winter solstice the Sun begins its new six-month journey back to the light of day, a journey that culminates at the time of the summer solstice when the Sun enters Cancer, the symbolical zenith or noon point of the zodiac. These two cycles or festivals, together with the two equinox cycles of Aries (spring) and Libra (autumn) are the four focal points of the Sun's journey through the zodiac, and should be celebrated as such by groups and communities alike.

The movement of the Sun after the winter solstice can be related to spiritual conception because it is only at the spring equinox (Aries) that mental–physical conception occurs. The entire winter cycle of Capricorn to Pisces is an inward cycle of personality withdrawal and spiritual conception. It can therefore be a time of personal negativity and depression, for the soul is at its ascension (so to speak) and the lower self at its descension. The winter cycle is therefore the most spiritual time of the year for it is the quarterly cycle in which we are attaining the highest degree of individual fulfilment (Capricorn), and in which we are also sharing what we have attained and received (Aquarius and Pisces).

The Capricorn cycle is the time of the year when the mental seeds of Aries (Spring) have reached their highest degree of spiritual flowering. Physical and spiritual labour both take nine months, with birth occurring in the tenth month (Capricorn).

The Sun is the living symbol of the soul, for it is the heart centre of our solar system. The Sun is the living channel through which cosmic and solar energies enter our planetary system. Its journey or path through the zodiac represents the journey of consciousness through the circle of life. By following and attuning to this solar journey we automatically follow the path of the higher self, for 'as above, so below'. If we want to follow or worship (put worth upon) a teacher, then who better than the Sun, the centre of our solar system. The soul is our microcosmic Sun in our individual journey through life.

This is the reason why astrology is referred to in the wisdom teachings as 'the royal science', for the Sun is royalty at its grandest (Leo, the sign ruled by the Sun, is the sign governing royalty).

There is of course a grand paradox in the winter solstice cycle. This is because Capricorn is the 'highest' sign of the zodiac (the MC) when the Sun in truth reaches its zenith and not its nadir. The paradox comes about because the Sun reaches its physical or objective zenith in Cancer (noon, when the Sun's heat is at its most extreme), the 'doorway into matter', and its spiritual or subjective zenith in Capricorn (midnight, when the Sun's heat is absent), the 'doorway into spirit'. It is only at the darkest moment (midnight) that we are born into spirit. Summer is our highest, most joyful, most sunny and extroverted time of the year, but this is an outer material experience. In winter we are at our lowest, most depressed, most cold and introverted time of the year, for material objective energy (the personality) is at its lowest, and spiritual energy (the soul) is at its highest or 'peak' point. Before the light must come the greatest darkness and the winter solstice is this darkest point before the light. It is an established psychological fact that every major 'light' experience is preceded by a time of great darkness; darkness or death always precedes light or rebirth from both a psychological or physical point of view.

The Capricorn Full Sun–Moon cycle of each year is the time when we reach the height or mountaintop of the year's achievements. This is why 21 December to 20 January is such a profound and yet difficult time of each year, for not only does one have to climb the final stage of one's mountainous path (which is always the hardest) and reach the peak (which is always relative), but one also finds oneself beginning the initial stage of a new journey down the very mountain one has just climbed. This is the other divine paradox of Capricorn, for the only reason one aspires to reach the mountain-top of achievement and fulfilment is to come down the mountain (into the valleys of the world) to share, teach and give out the wisdom that one has gained. Thus the Capricornian keynote, 'Lost am I in light supernal yet on that light I turn my back.'

In relationship to the above it might be of interest to note that the transits of Neptune (1984–98), Uranus (1988–95) and Saturn (1988–90) through Capricorn signal the time for this twofold achievement. This achievement and descent down the mountain is especially relevant as a planet reaches its final transit through this sign, for the final decanate of Capricorn is sub-ruled by Virgo, the sign of spirit manifesting through matter on a daily basis (the sub-decanate rulers are given at the end of this chapter).

Traditionally Capricorn is said to be a feminine polarized sign and yet all three of its ruling Rays are masculine. Ray 1 (power/will), 3 (active intelligence) and 7 (organization and synthesis) are all 'activity' energies. This is why Capricorns are eternally busy and why business, politics, economics and organizational activity are ruled by this sign. The capacity to generate and initiate energy (Ray 1), to think creatively and dynamically (Ray 3) and to act and organize things practically (Ray 7) are the integrated gifts of this sign. The intelligent capacity, willingness and courage to bring spirit(ual purpose) into the material infrastructures of society and the world is the gift of Capricorn. First and second degree initiates do this in their own small way through business, organizational ventures and projects and work in the political and social spheres. Third degree initiates are those people who help to bring about major changes in national and even global consciousness and socio-political infrastructures. Vaclav Havel of Czechoslovakia, de Klerk and Nelson Mandela of South Africa, the late Anwar Sadat of Egypt and others of this calibre are the finest examples. Gorbachev is another example although he could well be an initiate of a higher calibre.

A third degree initiate is someone who has consciously or unconsciously fused the three bodies of the personality and the three aspects of the soul. They therefore 'stand' in the centre of the six-pointed star of soul–personality integration. Essentially they have fused the lower and higher minds and have blended the heart and head chakras and in so doing have reached the mountaintop of personality ascension. They therefore serve that which is greater than themselves or their group for their consciousness has become collectively focused. Jesus was a third degree initiate when He incarnated 2,000 years ago. He had achieved this status in His past life as Elias, the Jewish prophet. He retook the first three initiations (birth, baptism and transfiguration) to demonstrate their reality and finally took the fourth initiation (crucifixion or the great renunciation). He took His 5th Master's initiation as Apollonius of Tyana in His next life. The film *The Last Temptation of Christ* was a basic depiction of the four initiations. The Church was critical of the depiction of Jesus as a normal human being. But one is in truth a 'normal' human being until the third initiation, for it is only at and after this initiation that one gains entrance into 'the kingdom of God' or the Spiritual Hierarchy (Capricorn is the doorway into the kingdom of God).

Saturn is the inner and outer ruler and it also works with the 3rd Ray. This Ray has double influence in this sign and Capricorn is therefore the major 3rd Ray sign. Saturn is a hugely complex planet and I recommend a deep study of Liz Greene's wonderful book *Saturn – A New Look at an Old Devil* (Aquarian Press) in this regard. The placement of Saturn in the chart is a vital indicator of the doorway one must go through to fulfil one's spiritual purpose. Saturn is thus the 'doorkeeper, guardian of the gate or dweller on the threshold' as depicted in mythology and the esoteric teachings.

Saturn is also 'the lord of karma', for its placement is the indicator of the restrictive karma (cause and effect) we have inherited from past lives and have to face in the present lifetime, and the 'dharma' (lifework) that we are destined to fulfil (if we so wish) in this lifetime. Saturn is where we have our greatest weaknesses, inadequacies, complexes and fears yet simultaneously where we have our greatest potential strength, power and capacities to achieve true inner security and fulfilment. The above makes up for its complexity.

The 3rd Ray is essentially the energy of the mind in its dual nature because this Ray is the causal body of the personality and the first aspect of the soul (creative intelligence). Saturn is therefore a planet associated with the mind and not simply with the physical body and objective activity. It is the focused and intelligent control of the mind (thought) that leads to success or failure in our ventures. During the first two initiations the mind is not under our control for the focal points of one's endeavours are the physical and emotional bodies. The mind is being stimulated and expanded but it is not under focused control. Saturn's position indicates where and how we have to focus and control the mind, for there can be no success unless this is relatively achieved. There is a great deal of energy interflow between the throat chakra (Saturn) and the sacral chakra (Moon and on a higher level Uranus) when it comes to create activity. Saturn is concerned with higher creativity which has creative thought as its basis (throat centre) whereas physical creativity (sexual activity and procreation) has its foundation in the sex centre. One cannot but notice that if one is tired or unfocused during creative mental–physical activity one's energy slides down into the sacral centre, further diffusing one's focus and control.

Control does not mean a repression of feeling and its expression which is the negative side of Saturn's placement. The masculine 'father' principle which is associated with Saturn has its dual nature of intelligent and controlled use of the mind (with an added touch of humour) and a cold, detached, unfeeling nature. The 3rd Ray is concerned with the plan – that is the structural mental blueprint of the plan one has to potentially fulfil. The plan is the mental (blueprint) and physical structures and practical organizational activities that are a manifestation of one's overall purpose. The Ascendant and Midheaven are connected in this way. Saturn and the MC are related to this 3rd Ray plan, but the first thing that is required is to blueprint these working structures in the mind. The mind must first 'think' this plan into creative form on the higher abstract and lower mental planes. The physical organization of this mental blueprint will than follow suit, *but* it is the dynamic creative thought that precedes outer activity. Creativity starts in the mind and then proceeds downwards. Saturn is the planet governing this process and this is why it is said to be the doorway into spirit (3rd Ray) and also the doorway of spirit into material activity, for it and the 3rd Ray 'stand midway between the soul and the personality'.

Saturn is also the 'tester and teacher' for we are tested and trained for discipleship by Saturn. Saturn could be called the testing-training principle of the soul, remembering that the 3rd Ray is the first and most objective aspect of the soul. It is the major area where we have to develop mental, emotional and physical self-discipline for this is the area where we will also be put under the greatest tests, trials and pressure in the work that we have chosen to do. Work and responsibility always put us under extreme pressure for we have to be responsible for our own actions and for the actions of those we work with or supervise. There is a continual process of training taking place to prepare us for this responsibility, and the Saturn placement indicates how and where this training and testing occurs. Since Saturn is the masculine principle women will find it more difficult to deal with than men, and the 'father–daughter' relationship is indicative of this difficulty.

'Fathers' (in the vast majority of cases) embody the Saturn principle and project it onto their children. If these principles were taught in a constructive fashion it would be fine but they are usually taught in a negative projective way due to the unconsciousness of the father and/or mother. These negative projections of authority, power, responsibility and logical-mindedness tend to disempower the child (daughter or son) and make them feel inadequate and inferior. The child either gives in to this projection by following the path of the parent and living up to their ambitions (for the child) or attempts to negate everything related to the parent in order to escape from their power and influence. Both avenues disempower the person because in neither case is there a positive (be it conflicting) confrontation with the parent. The fact is that there are very important lessons to be learnt from the father/mother concerning the Saturn principle, and the best way to confront the parent is often to accept and acknowledge the best of their truth while moving steadily ahead along one's own individual path. Light, love and will (and humility) are required to accomplish this.

There are two types of careers or vocations; one is the material career which has little purpose outside of self-centred achievement, recognition and material–financial gain. This is Saturn's outer rulership of Capricorn. The second is our true and higher vocation. This is the fulfilment of our life-purpose through intelligent creative service to the whole. This is Saturn's inner rulership. One is a purely material testing area and the other a spiritual and material testing area.

One of Saturn's laws is organic growth and unfoldment. This

requires great patience (and more patience), perseverance and persistence, the three keynotes of Saturn. Organic development entails the fact that there are steps on the path up the mountain, and each step or experience and lesson leads on to the next step. 'The path is part of the goal' and this is especially so in the case of Saturn and the MC sign. One is not allowed (by spiritual law) to bypass any step, for each experience and lesson, no matter how small and insignificant, is essential for the next stage of the journey. True recognition and success comes when one has released all need for recognition and success. True fulfilment comes when one does what one has to do without expectation of return or recognition. The reason that so many New Age projects fail is because this lesson is forgotten. 'Go slow and go steady' is the Saturnian keynote. 'Keep on keeping on' is another.

One more factor should be mentioned in relationship to Saturn. If there is any position where we will experience cycles of inner pain and loneliness it is Saturn's position. Struggle, effort, frustration, anger, fear of failure and failure itself (if there is such a thing), inner suffering (and sometimes outer suffering too), loneliness and desperation are Saturn's testing ground. No matter how many times one falls down one must get up and keep on going on. 'If you fall on the ground use the ground to get up' is yet another Saturn keynote. Why is loneliness associated with Saturn? Because there is one major area in our lives that only we (as individuals) can work at and fulfil and that is our chosen Saturnian work. No one else can help us directly; indirect support is possible but not direct help. This creates a sense of inner aloneness, but the more and more we get used to the idea and accept it with understanding, grace and thanks (which is vitally important) the more and more we begin to feel good and secure in this area. This takes time and much effort but it is an essential part of the path. True inner security thus becomes our chosen lot and this is the security that provides a sense of inner strength and fulfilment.

Saturn is also associated with leadership, which always requires a good deal of personal responsibility, self-reliance and loneliness. In the larger context of the above I would like to recommend two wonderful books. The first is *In Search of Identity* by Anwar Sadat, the late and great President of Egypt (who had the Sun in Capricorn), and the second is by his magnificent wife Jehan Sadat, *A Woman of Egypt* (Coronet Books). These two books are a Capricornian gift to humanity. They give accounts of the lives of two great human beings who deserve humanity's highest respect.

Capricornians are best when they aspire towards the achievement of their highest life-goals. Their gifts are their pragmatic down-to-earth nature, their wonderful dry humour, their ordered activity and sense of responsibility towards others and their capacity to bring spirit down into the very infrastructures of society. Their shadow is their personal ego-centred ambitions, their pride and arrogance, their tendency to see everything in terms of work and money, their manipulative use of power and authority and their tendency to see the dark and dismal side of life as the only reality.

By studying the 1st, 3rd and 7th Rays we can gain a deepened understanding of this complex sign.

AQUARIUS	The 11th sign.
Keynote	Waters of Life am I poured forth for thirsty humanity.
Symbol	The water-carrier pouring forth the 'waters of Life'.
Ray	The 5th.
Rulers	Jupiter (inner; Ray 2) and Uranus (outer; Ray 7).

Festival   2nd phase of winter; Full Sun–Moon.
House   11th of group, social and global consciousness,
                  activity and service; futuristic visionary ideas and
                  organizational activities.
Elemental   Fixed air.

After reaching the mountain peak of personal achievement in
Capricorn and 'turning one's back' on this light in order to use it for
the greater good, one enters the eleventh archetypal doorway of
Aquarius, the constellation that will rule planetary evolution for
the next 2,500 years. In Aquarius personal energy is transcended
and left behind for the energies related to this sign are focused
through group, community and collective consciousness and
activities. Human beings cannot order the functioning of the signs.
The signs are living and dynamic energy systems, that is spiritual
Lives, with their own will or purpose (Monad), higher consciousness and qualities (soul) and personal characteristics (personality).
Aquarius is the sign of group energy, and group energy is related to
higher consciousness because the soul and the 5th kingdom of souls
is one interconnected group conscious being. Uranus, the personal
ruler of Aquarius, is itself a group-focused planet because the 7th
Ray of 'synthesis' blends and merges individualized streams of
energy into a greater whole.

There is a grand paradox in Aquarius and its ruler Uranus in that
it takes 'individuals' to work in group formation. The opposite sign
of Aquarius is Leo, the archetype of individualization, and its ruler
the Sun is also concerned with the individualizing process. Uranus
is known for its powerful individualizing effects although, as a
transpersonal planet, it influences collective consciousness and
brings about changes on a planetary scale. These dual influences
create a situation in Aquarius whereby individual, group, social
and planetary consciousness are stimulated simultaneously. The
results of this stimulation are positive and negative because the
person(ality) that is becoming far more individualized is attracted
to group activity and yet has to learn to become depersonalized
within the group itself. Strong individuals have well-developed
egos and this creates many difficulties in the evolution of groups,
especially in the new groups working with the incoming energies of
Aquarius. The art and science of integrating individual and group
consciousness is still in its infancy and represents a major challenge
for the future. Individuals and groups that have been working with
this challenge over the past fifteen years or so are the pioneers in this
field.

The older type Piscean groups and organizations, be they religious, spiritual, political, economic or social, still have the powerful leaders or gurus at their head. Members of these organizations are not allowed to take an equal share in group decisions because this is the prerogative of the leader. They must constantly look up to the leader for guidance and direction, and are not encouraged to look within themselves for the same qualities. This allows one to project one's personal and spiritual responsibilities onto the leader, party or organization and inhibits the individualization process. Cancer, the sign preceding Leo, governs the masses, and is ruled by the Moon, the planet governing instinctive emotional attachments to the past and its outdated belief systems. When one is attached to objective belief systems one automatically projects personal responsibility onto these systems and their leaders. There are many fine leaders in the world today and this is not to decry the importance of such leaders, but the projection of individual responsibility onto these leaders in no way helps oneself or for that matter the leaders themselves. The Moon is in detriment (losing power or influence) in Capricorn, the opposite sign of Cancer, for Capricorn is concerned with emotional detachment and personal responsibility.

The new groups and organizations are very different to the better-known older groups. They might be called 'New Age, New Era, Service, Networking, Synthesis or Synergy' groups (for want of other names) because they are, to whatever degree, attuning to Aquarian energies flowing into the planet at this time in history. Some of the major characteristics of these groups are:

• They are composed of people of any gender, age, race, religion (or no formal religion) or nationality who are, to whatever degree, individualizing themselves, and who are intent on serving humanity and the planet.
• They do have leaders but these leaders operate in a way which differs largely from the old leadership. The word 'leader' is often not used due to its old connotation and has been replaced by words such as 'facilitator, focalizer or co-ordinator'. These words imply the 'facilitating or focusing' of the energy of a group or organization rather than 'leading' it. These facilitators are usually the one, two or three people who initiated the group or project and who have some degree of experience in this work. Decision-making is by consensus ('agreement by all the units of the group') so that everyone feels an integral part of the purpose and decision-making process.
• They work at integrating the spiritual, human and material aspects of each individual and the group itself. Creative

meditation, human communication and sharing, personal transformation and various forms of creative service-orientated activity form an integral part of the group's work. This triangle
integrates the three facets of higher consciousness, namely purpose or attunement to higher will, love–wisdom and intelligent
activity.

- While the integrity of each individual is respected and honoured
the individuals themselves need to respect and honour the larger
purpose and good of the group. This conscious interactive process entails a new experiment in human evolution.

- They work at integrating and maturing themselves as a group
while realizing that they are part of a far larger 'network of light'
spread around their local community, nation and the planet. The
group attempts in whatever way possible to link up with this
network and to co-operate in its larger work of human and planetary service and transformation. 'Unity in Diversity' becomes
the keynote. This linking and co-operation needs to be intelligently applied. Over-idealistic and simplistic perceptions on the
lines of 'Let's all work together because we are all one' more often
than not create problems rather than solutions. Non-interference
in the work and responsibilities of other groups and networks is
vital in this regard. The transit of Saturn into Aquarius (1991–3)
will provide a new and updated ground for this co-operative
adventure.

There are already tens of thousands of these groups around the
world and they will continue to expand and grow as we enter more
directly into the New Era. These groups are not simply 'New Age'
groups as many people understand the term, but are focused in the
political (Ray 1), educational (Ray 2), economic and business (Ray
3), artistic (Ray 4), scientific (Ray 5), religious (Ray 6), ecological
and new spiritual (Ray 7) spheres of human activity. This 'Network
of Light' is referred to esoterically as 'the New Group of World
Servers' ('the invisible Church of Christ' in Christian terminology)
and is the intelligent, loving and purposeful human chalice through
which the energies of Aquarius and the Spiritual Hierarchy can
manifest themselves. It will eventually comprise 144,000 major
groups each focused by a third degree initiate, and thousands of
other groups facilitated by second or first degree disciples. This
Network, under the direct guidance of the Christ and His Masters,
will lead humanity into the New Era.

The 5th Ray works through Aquarius. This is the energy of concrete knowledge – of knowledge gained through personal experiment and exploration. This differs greatly from the 6th Ray, which

ruled the Piscean Era and influences 'belief'. Knowledge is not belief; it is the result of a direct personal experience of life and its realities. This Ray might be called the Ray of 'the science of life', for it rules spiritual and material science and the knowledge gained through these inner and outer sciences. These two interconnected sciences are entering a merging ground as spiritual science becomes more accepted, practical, self-evident and visible, and material science becomes more metaphysical and invisible. Fritjof Capra's two books *The Tao of Physics* and *The Turning Point* (Flamingo Books) are the classics in this regard. According to the Master DK (*Destiny of the Nations* – Lucis Trust Pub.) the reality of the soul will be discovered and revealed by French scientists. France has a 5th Ray soul and its gift to humanity is its scientific genius.

The 5th Ray is a masculine polarized Ray as is the 7th Ray ruling Uranus. With the 2nd Ray ruling Jupiter, the inner ruler, Aquarius has a wonderfully balancing energy system. Knowledge (mind), love–intuition–wisdom (heart and higher mind) and organization–synthesis (will–intuition–creative activity) all merge to create a masculine–feminine synthesis of energies. This is the major reason why this balancing is occurring in the individual, in groups, society and the world at large, and why 'the battle between the sexes' (the yang–yin polarities) is reaching a climax of conflict and resolution.

Aquarians are often regarded as rather strange people (in the nicest sense of the word) and are much misunderstood. They are automatically attuned to the future and its needs and have an intuitive knack of predicting future trends that will affect themselves and the rest of humanity. Aquarian children are natural oracles. This is their blessing and curse, for they have to live with these revelations and see them unfold before their very eyes. As a Sun sign Aquarius I have had this gift since I was a child. My intuitive promptings have always proved to be uncannily accurate. I have often been given (for this is the only way I can describe it) dreams in which I have been shown the unfolding future. Uranus is the planet of the future and Aquarians (Sun and Rising) are thus capable of comprehending the future before it materializes. They have the opportunity to prepare themselves and others for this future through their visionary ideas and activities.

The blueprints of the future are embodied and revealed by Uranus, for the 7th Ray rules the etheric body of creation, and the etheric body is the inner blueprint of physical creation. Aquarians and people attuned to Aquarius–Uranus are thus capable of catching imprints of the etheric blueprint before it manifests externally. This enables them to be psychologically prepared for the future and to prepare and organize the necessary material infrastructures. The 7th Ray is concerned with organization – that is the structuring of the 'organs' of the mind–brain and body to fit into the needs of the greater whole. The organizations of the future are 'networks'. As an Aquarian, I began to communicate the reality and needs of these organizations ten years ago, as did a number of individuals around the planet. It took three to five years for this planetary imprint to penetrate the collective.

Aquarians tend to be positive outgoing people but they are subject to deep and dark depressions which turn their energies inwards. They sense the future to a large degree and have very high ideals when it comes to the betterment of human conditions. They are the true visionaries and humanitarians of the world. Their problem is twofold: their visions and ideals can be too abstract and impractical and they thus become abstracted from day-to-day realities; or their visions of the future need are valid and practical but they find themselves having to 'go it alone' – with or without one or two like-minded co-workers.

They are often able to sense (intuitively and/or through personal experience) the inner light, love and purpose and fears, suffering and pain of others and the collective and their work is often dedicated to the alleviation, transformation and potential resolution of these pains, and the greater unfoldment of spiritual consciousness for the good of the whole. They need to live in and serve the present while dedicating themselves to the future, for they can tend to forget that 'in serving the small parts one also serves the larger whole' (Sagittarians tend to have the same problem).

They might well show a cold and detached exterior but inwardly they are extremely sensitive. Many 1st and 7th Ray types seem cold and insensitive but are in fact highly sensitive to the pain and suffering in others, the world and in themselves. They often hide this pain and find it extremely difficult to share their feelings with others. Like the Scorpio type they prefer to have a few very good friends rather than a larger number of superficial acquaintances. They nevertheless have a remarkable capacity to communicate with all sorts of people, from the beggar to the millionaire, and from the housewife/husband to the world leader.

Aquarians have a fine balance of masculine–feminine energies due to the Ray composition of this sign. This balance can result in a well-integrated human being or it can result in a sense of confusion about one's gender identity. Many Gay people (of both sexes) are Aquarians who are confused about their identity. The problem in this regard is that if one identifies solely with one's lower ego an identity crisis will obviously ensue because the lower ego is not one's real identity. This confusion manifests in the three lower bodies and can potentially create objective bisexuality. It is only by transferring one's consciousness to the higher self and thus one's true identity that one can integrate rather than confuse polarities, for true balance and healing is related to soul–personality integration. The vast majority of bisexual and Gay people I have met and talked to (including clients) are polarized in their lower selves. This is their essential problem and of course the essential problem of the orthodox heterosexual community too. For homosexuals to talk about heterosexual people being 'straight' is non-sensical and a crude form of escapism, for 'straight' people are people polarized in their lower egos and thus in ignorance and escapism. If one does not wish to be 'straight' (that is 'trapped') one must transfer one's consciousness to the higher ego, the soul, start working at integrating the higher and lower selves, and open oneself to serving the needs of others.

In many senses Aquarians and Pisceans do not really belong to this world, and they feel this lack of belonging quite strongly. The Earth as we understand it is a personality-focused world, whereas Aquarius and Pisces are focused in the world beyond this persona – that is in the transpersonal and collective world. Aquarians must therefore work with energies that are not natural to the normal world, and this provides clues to their personal dilemma and transpersonal gifts. I have found that many Aquarians even find it hard to find (and wear) clothes that 'fit' their bodies. They need loose, flexible and natural fibre clothing that is often extremely difficult to find. For this reason they often wear strange and futuristic ('other world') clothing. This is not simply due to their revolutionary nature but to the fact that their energies are not attuned to the world of matter. Science fiction clothing might well be the Aquarian dress of the future.

Aquarians have strong intuitive and rational mental natures and this creates one of their major conflicts. Aquarian Sun or Moon (and Mercury) have to learn to integrate the higher and lower minds if they wish to function in balance. There are three distinct types of Aquarians. The first is polarized in the lower intellectual scientific mind and is fearful of life beyond logic (the shadow of the 5th Ray). The second is polarized in the intuitive mind and is generally 'spaced out' and afraid to deal with the practical realities of life (the shadow of Ray 2). The third is involved with integrating both the higher and lower minds and in organizing the practical structures to manifest their spiritual inspirations. They are well-balanced (in a non-traditional sense) and strong individuals intent on serving spirit and humanity (Rays 5, 2 and 7). Mercury is exalted in Aquarius because its placement in this sign leads to a linking of the higher and lower minds. Aquarians need to get on with what needs to be done and forget what others say, for the work of this sign is to seed in the future and its diverse needs. If they can organize their visions into practical service-orientated activity they will slowly but surely succeed in their chosen task.

Many astrologers claim that Saturn has rulership in Aquarius. This is incorrect. Saturn rules Capricorn and personal goals and achievement, and no longer holds sway in Aquarius. The confusion comes about for two reasons. The first is that astrologers have not been aware of the 5th Ray of concrete mind and science ruling this sign, for it is this Ray that gives the well-known scientific bent of Aquarians (science is normally associated with Saturn). Secondly Saturn sub-rules the 1st decanate of this sign and placements in the first 10 degrees of this sign have a strong sub-Saturnian influence. Astrologers who use Saturn as a ruler in this sign limit the scope of its greater potential and Uranus must always be seen as the true outer ruler.

Jupiter is the transpersonal ruler of this sign. The fact that our solar system is a 2nd Ray system (in other words 'love–intuitive wisdom' is the essential nature of the soul) and Jupiter and the heart of the Sun, rulers of Aquarius and Leo, are also 2nd Ray planets, implies a very important fact. If the Ray of the soul or Christ-consciousness rules both these inner (soul) rulers then the power of love–wisdom, of which group-consciousness and inclusive service are keynotes, is guaranteed to sway the present–future evolution of humanity. Jupiter is the great benefic, the planet that bestows an expanded awareness, intuitive understanding, future revelation, the aspiration to serve and give to others on a selfless basis (it also rules Sagittarius and Pisces), joy, humour and abundance. Outside of its tendency to create over-expansion and over-extention in people/nations (as in the USA and in Sagittarians) it is the most beneficial of all the planets. This is why the keynotes of love (Jupiter) and light (Uranus) have become the natural keynotes of the present era, for heart and mind are blended in Aquarius.

When Jupiter is in Aquarius or in the 11th or 12th houses it is in its best position for its soul-based energies can operate most spontaneously. Its position in the chart indicates where the greatest expansion, joy, sense of unity, service and giving and abundance can occur. Jupiter takes 11.8 years to circle the Sun so it works in an approximately twelve-year cycle. It therefore takes just under a year to move through each sign of the zodiac. Seven times twelve years = 84 years, the time cycle of perfection in a human incarnation. Each twelve-year Jupiter cycle corresponds therefore to each of the first seven signs of the zodiac. Birth to 12 = Aries, the first sign; 12 to 24 = Taurus, the second sign, and so on. Jupiter is essentially concerned with the spiritual or 'life' educational process, and this process unfolds in twelve-year cycles. The third Jupiter cycle, between 24 and 36, corresponds to Gemini, the third sign, and will be focused around a great deal of reading, studying, interhuman communication, the development of the intellect, the experience of the dualities and their gradual synthesis, especially the link between the higher (Venus) and lower (Mercury) minds and between the individual and his/her environment (Gemini). Between the ages of 21 (new seven-year cycle) and 24 (Jupiter return), the soul appropriates the mental body and the cycle of adult mental development and knowledge begins.

The cycle between 36 and 48 corresponds to Cancer, the 4th sign, and is related to the development of family and home/community consciousness in the broader spiritual sense of these terms. Each year of the cycle in turn corresponds in meaning to each of the signs of the zodiac. The first year (12 to 13; 24 to 25; 36 to 37 and so on) corresponds to Aries, the first sign. In these years the initiating seeds of the cycle are unfolded. The second years (13 to 14; 25 to 26) are Taurian in nature and consolidate and stabilize the cycle. Material resources and needs often manifest in this second year. When it comes to education in the broader sense of the word Jupiter provides the clues to this unfolding and expanding process. By studying each sign and applying it to the cycle it rules we can get a wonderful understanding of the work of Jupiter. Jupiter's Ray 2 energy is directly related to the consciousness of the soul and to the Christ, the Lord of this Ray. Unity in diversity, group-consciousness, world service, unconditional love, open-heartedness, spiritual humour, manifestation of need, and intuitive wisdom are therefore the great qualities of the Aquarian soul. Aquarius Rising has direct access to this Jupiterian energy.

Uranus was discovered in 1781. Some of the repercussions of this discovery were the Industrial Revolution, the French and American revolutions and the discovery and use of electric light. All of these events resulted in astronomical changes in the lives of millions of people and transformed the socio-political and economic climate of the world. Electric lighting was probably the greatest human discovery since fire, for it lit up the dark face of the planet in an incredibly short space of time. The Logoi of planets only allow their planets to be discovered at the right time, and one of the major effects of Uranus is its capacity to accelerate evolution to a vast degree through the stimulation, lighting-up and awakening of the mind, the thinking faculty of humanity. It is known for its lightning bolt and 'speed of light' effects which break through and break down old patterns of thinking and behaviour and bring in new revolutionary thinking and activity. The 'breakdown-breakthrough' syndrome is thus a Uranian (and Neptunian and Plutonic) influence. Uranian transits (especially oppositions and squares) are often experienced as 'inner' earthquakes, for they shake up the crystallized foundations of the persona and open the door to whole new life experiences.

The Uranus–Pluto conjunction of 1962–9 instigated the present change and turmoil in the individual, groups, society and humanity at large. 'Change is changeless' says our dear friend Uranus – learn to trust, change and move in the moment (literally) for all your needs will be perfectly met in the moment. This capacity and need to *know* that everything is unfolding as it should and to trust in the perfect manifestation of one's needs (in times of change) is integral to life in the New Era.

Uranus also rules microchip, computer, radio, TV and satellite technology. The information age has also changed the face of the planet in a short space of time, and this is bound to change even more rapidly as we approach the twenty-first century. Although many of these technological discoveries might seem to be destructive, the Band Aid concerts of 1985 and many other similar events since have proved that these Uranian technologies have their purposeful and constructive use. TV is becoming and will become one of the major channels for the communication of New Age consciousness and this will culminate in it being used by the Christ to broadcast His message to humanity.

The material manifestations of Uranus correspond objectively to its inner functioning, for Uranus is essentially concerned with the activation of the higher creative thinking faculties. It is these faculties which reveal or 'discover' the scientific (5th Ray) basis for such discoveries. The human brain is the most powerful computer known to man. It is a hugely powerful microchip containing 10 billion units of microcosmic and macrocosmic information. It is nevertheless 'thinking' that activates these cells, and Uranus activates those cells containing information related to the spiritual order of the universe. The science (5th Ray) of astrology (1st–7th Rays) is ruled by Aquarius–Uranus. The computer is a copy of the human brain as are all software packages (of course, for it is the human mind that designs and creates them).

Uranian energy activates the higher intuitive faculty. The intuition is a fascinating faculty which is hardly touched upon in conventional education. It is the mind of the soul ('only through Me can you reach the Father'), and the soul is the doorway into the larger whole ('the Father' or Cosmos). In 'a flash' the intuition grants us entry into the mind of God, for this flash of divine vision or inspiration embodies within itself a great bookload of information. Uranian intuition is different to Neptunian intuition for it is mentally polarized. It often comes in response to one's deep pondering thought about some aspect of the spirit. This 'thinking' penetrates into the realms of the soul and the soul responds by 'flashing down' its answer (to the questioning human mind) through the faculty of the intuition. The bookload of information contained within the 'flash' will then unfold itself as time goes on. Uranus channels the 7th Ray of organization, ritual and ceremony and spirit–matter synthesis. If one combines Uranian intuition with 7th Ray creative activity one can understand the great gift of Aquarius.

Because Uranus is the outer material ruler of this sign the capacity to be highly intuitive and to organize this intuitive knowledge into creative action is available to Aquarians and to humanity in the Aquarian Age. Seventh Ray organization requires ritual and ceremony because these two interrelated activities provide the chalice for spirit to enter and merge with matter. Ceremonies and rituals in the New Era need to be discovered, initiated, explored and unfolded by individuals and groups themselves. They should not be based upon rituals and ceremonies of the past, whether these be of an orthodox or unorthodox religious nature. The vast majority of these old rituals have lost their significance and power for they were part of the energy system of Pisces with its different Rays and zodiacal and planetary energies. Many people turn back to the past to seek the old ways of the Druids, American Indians, Buddhists, Hindus and so on. They become caught up in the nostalgic glamour of these old religions, races and cultures and forget that one must live in the present. The new rituals and ceremonies exist within each individual and group, not outside themselves.

Ritual and ceremony can best be used to celebrate the sixteen most important festivals of the year. These are the four seasonal festivals, the equinoxes and the solstices, and the twelve New Age Full Sun–Moon festivals, of which the first three, Aries (Rebirth), Taurus (Wesak) and Gemini (Humanity) are the most important. Creative forms of meditation, sacred dancing, sacred drama, music, singing, the right use of colour (attuned to the Rays and signs and planets of each month) in relationship to clothing, flowers, crystals and candles, wholesome food (shared in community-style buffets) and much more can be included in each of these festivals. These festivals are essentially group and community-orientated, although the Full Sun–Moon cycles are global celebrations because there is an automatic linking of the entire global Network, spiritual and human, at these times. The colours to be used at these times are shown in Table 7.1.

Table 7.1: Sign colour associations

Sign	*Colour*
Aries	Red, violet, yellow and rose-red
Taurus	Yellow, gold, red, orange and green
Gemini	Royal blue, dark blue, orange and yellow
Cancer	Green, violet, sky-blue, pink, yellow
Leo	Red, orange, deep blue, royal blue
Virgo	Deep blue, sky blue, pink, gold, yellow
Libra	Green, violet, orange
Scorpio	Yellow, red, rose-red
Sagittarius	Yellow, orange, sky-blue, green and deep blue
Capricorn	Red, purple, green (double dose), violet
Aquarius	Orange, deep blue, violet
Pisces	Deep blue, sky-blue, pink, red

These colours are related to the Rays and can be used in relationship to the right type of flowers, crystals, and so on, that are used in each festival. The 7th Ray also rules inner ceremony, and this entails the new type of meditation that is required in the New Era. Thinking about and meditating upon the different Rays and their qualities and corresponding activities over each festival is part of this meditation. Organization itself should become more magical and celebratory rather than dull and over-structured, which in no way negates efficient organization and planning. 'Elegant simplicity' is the way the Master Racokzi, Master of the 7th Ray, describes the need of this Ray's activities.

The Findhorn Foundation of Northern Scotland has a 2nd Ray (Jupiter) soul and a 7th Ray (Uranus) personality. It is regarded as the foremost pioneering centre of the New Era and its Ray composition indicates why this is so. The USSR and the USA have 7th and 2nd Ray souls and this is why their co-operation is so important. Their 6th Ray personalities are at present under radical transformation, for this Ray of idealism has been their stumbling block in the past. Vaclav Havel, the President of Czechoslovakia, has Aquarius Rising, and this bodes well for his country.

In the Aquarian cycle (20 January to 20 February) of each year it is time to leave behind personal aspirations, goals and activities and move directly into group consciousness and aspiration. All one's energies need to be given over to the larger whole, be this the group, network, community and humanity overall. The highest degree of personal attainment has been relatively achieved in the Capricorn cycle and in Aquarius these achievements must be used in service of one's fellow humanity. The group need takes precedent over the individual need and each individual endeavours to serve the larger good of the group and its purpose and activities.

Although there are many opinions (many intellectual) as to the beginning of the New Era it is important to understand that this era will be inaugurated by the Aquarian Christ (the 6th Lord Maitreya to the Buddhists). It is only the Christ who has the authority to initiate this era for He is the head of our planet's Hierarchy. In the same way that an individual has authority to inaugurate his/her birthday (no one else can) so the Christ has a similar authority when it comes to the birthday of the Earth. Approximately every 2,100 years the Earth has a birthday celebration and its entrance into Aquarius is its next birthday. Humanity is in a process of preparing for this great celebration (even though it does not realize this) and it is going through the same preparatory trauma that an individual goes through just before a birthday. One month before each solar return (the return of the Sun to the birth position, namely the birthday) one goes through a crisis because this month corresponds symbolically to Pisces, the last sign of the zodiac. This pre-birthday month is a cycle of completion and final integration (symbolical death) of the past year and preparation of the new solar (annual) cycle to come (rebirth).

The last twenty-five years of this century are the transition cycle between the two Ages, for the pioneers of the next century and in this case of the next era always appear over this preparatory cycle. A number of esoteric teachings claim that 1998 to 2011 will be a more direct transition cycle (a vacuum of sorts) in which the spirit of Aquarius will anchor its energies more concretely into humanity (see the final chapter).

The keynote of Aquarius is thus applicable to everyone, although Aquarians will be most directly attuned to it: 'Waters of Life am I, poured forth for thirsty humanity.' In Aquarius we recognize and reidentify, embody, distribute and share who and what we already are, namely 'the waters of life'. These waters symbolize the consciousness of the soul, the true higher self, and the qualities of this self – light, or the higher creative mind of the soul; love, or the unifying beauty and harmony of all souls; wisdom, or the intuitive omniscience of the soul and will, or the sacrificial divine purpose of all souls. These two rivers of 'water' are thus symbols of soul-consciousness or love-wisdom which is higher consciousness, anchored in the area of the pineal gland, and spiritual will, anchored in the centre of the heart.

In the Age gone past we had to go in search of God and the Christ self and retreated into the wilderness to achieve this. In the New Age retreat is no longer necessary for we need to identify with the higher self and share the greatness of this self and its kingdom with friends, family, society and humanity. This does not mean that the path towards this goal is easy but what it does mean is that 'the path is the goal' and it is time to *know* who we are, *know* why we are here and *do* what we are here to do.

©FELICITY KEEFE 1991.

PISCES	The 12th and final sign.
Keynote	I leave the Father's house and turning back I save.
Symbol	The two fish swimming in opposite directions, linked by a silver cord.
Rays	The 2nd and 6th.
Rulers	Pluto and Neptune (inner; Ray 1 and 6) and Jupiter (outer; Ray 2).
Festival	3rd phase of winter; Full Sun–Moon.
House	12th of completion, final integration and selfless service to God and the world.
Elemental	Mutable water.

Pisces completes the zodiacal round. Twelve is the number of completion in our universal system. The last 2,000 years of history have witnessed the light and the shadow of this sign and its Rays and rulers. Self-sacrificial service and unconditional love are its greatest qualities, while belief-orientated fanaticism and bloody intolerance are its worst dark characteristics. Jesus was the great divine–human archetype of this sign and His life was a magnificent demonstration of the spiritual life of Pisces. He came into the world (incarnated) in order to serve and save; He went into retreat to be trained and initiated for His work (thus His excursions into Egypt, India and other centres of wisdom); He returned to the world of men to share His love and wisdom without care for himself; He taught and finally demonstrated through the resurrection that the soul is immortal and thus beyond death; He taught that it is not form (Jesus) but the soul (the Christ self) that is reality and that one should 'worship' (put worth upon) the Christ self and not the form self ('Why do you call me Master? There is only one Master and that is God'; will the guru followers ever learn?); He integrated unconditional love and forgiveness (Ray 2), one-pointed spiritual idealism and devotion to the goal (Ray 6), and will or spiritual power (Ray 1), for this will destroys and transforms old structures and belief systems and brings in new teachings and structures (the replacement of Judaism and the God of fear with Christianity and the God of love).

There is no better way to understand the soul of Pisces than to share the life of Jesus, for He was the great human archetype of this sign, just as the Aquarian Christ will be the great divine archetype of the sign of Aquarius. It should be noted, however, that Jesus and the Christ are two different beings. The Christ is the head of the Earth's Spiritual Hierarchy or spiritual government, the Master of Masters and of Angels alike (of the Earth; within the Cosmos He is but a child for the 7th initiation is the 1st cosmic initiation). Jesus is one of the Christ's senior Master disciples and Master of the 6th Ray of religion. Jesus is 'alive and well' (so to speak) and lives in a Syrian body although He is very well travelled. He is the inspiration behind all great religious happenings and according to the Master DK will take over the Pope's position in the near future as part of the preparation for the Christ's return (the book *Initiation – Human and Solar*, Lucis Trust Pub. is the best book to read on the Masters and their work in the modern era).

The Christ is a 7th degree initiate (see Chapter 3). He is the Master of all the Rays and thus has jurisdiction over all the Masters and the Angelic Hierarchy. He overlighted Jesus 2,000 years ago from the time He began His Work (at the age of 30) to the time of His crucifixion at 33. The crucifixion amounted to a major initiation for Jesus (fourth initiation) and the Christ. The Christ is a far more advanced initiate than Master Jesus (if one might put it this way) and for this reason His direct physical return into human affairs will have an unimaginable influence upon planetary evolution. This return is now imminent. Buddha and Jesus both began their work at the age of 29–30, the time of the Saturn return, which is when every individual is offered the opportunity to begin their true life's work. Buddha is also a seventh degree initiate and the Christ and the Buddha work in direct co-operation with one another, as of course do the Christ and all the Masters.

Pisces is the sign of death and rebirth, for completion and final integration signify this twofold process. There are five stages of evolution in form – birth (into form), childhood–teenagehood, adulthood, mature adulthood (so-called midlife and old age) and death–rebirth. This death can be psychological and/or physical. The death–rebirth process and experience occurs on a daily basis for every time we go to sleep we experience death (movement out of the body) and every time we wake up we experience rebirth (incarnation into form). During this unconscious death state we exist in another dimension of consciousness which in itself is a rebirth. In this 'dimension' we integrate the experiences of the waking day gone past and also experience life in a new and more subtle form. This twofold experience is remembered by us through dreams, and the deciphering of dream symbols allows us to understand (to whatever degree) what we experienced and what we have learnt or can learn from this 'out-of-the-body' (death–rebirth) experience. To fear death is to fear sleep; most people fear waking rather than sleep for waking entails consciousness and facing all the responsibilities of the waking state.

Pisces and the 12th house are related to the whole experience of death and rebirth, including its relationship to the dream state, for this is the great experience and lesson of this sign. What Pisces essentially and ultimately teaches is that all form life is one big dream, 'Maya' or illusion in Hindu and Buddhist terminology. All form life, whether it be mental, emotional and/or physical, personal or collective, is subject to constant change and transformation. To rely upon form for security and stability is the height of ignorance for all form is in itself insecure and unstable. Forms are all subject to death and transformative rebirth and provide an unstable ground for reality. The form or personality ('persona' means 'mask') of Jesus was in itself subject to death and yet Christians still worship His form. The paradox about Pisces is that it is the sign related to the follower of forms/gurus because the lower characteristic of the

6th Ray is 'devotion' to forms, while also being related to the destruction (Pluto), dissolution (Neptune) and death (12th house) of forms.

The Christ and the soul's central lesson is to teach the illusion of forms and the reality of the true immortal self. The so-called 'physical immortalists' failed to comprehend this lesson, persuading themselves (Neptune and the 6th Ray) that the form is immortal, despite evidence to the contrary. This is the fanatical side of 6th Ray idealism in action. All 6th Ray religionists and fundamentalists, be they Christian, Muslim or Jew, have the same mentality. Even physical death fails to change their crystallized emotions and thoughts. One can imagine what a shock it must be for these people when they 'awake' on the next level of consciousness to find their sacred truths are false. The 6th Ray idealism of the USA and the USSR has resulted in equal horrors in Vietnam and Afghanistan. The karmic consequences of this emotional fanaticism and ignorance is obvious in the present turmoil in the Soviet Union and the Gulf. The dark and ignorant side of the old 6th Ray era is still with us and manifests most directly through the old religions and a good number of other 6th Ray groupings. The USA has a 6th Ray ego and this is why these groupings emerge out of this country.

The situation in the Middle East is a 6th Ray battleground, for Muslims, Israelis and Americans are all ruled by this outgoing Ray. The terrible destruction that is befalling the Arabic (Muslim) and Jewish (Israeli) peoples, and to a lesser degree the Christian–capitalist Americans and Communist Soviets, is evidence of Pluto's power at work. The 6th Ray rules the solar plexus centre and the 2nd Ray the heart centre. The Middle East is a focal point for this realignment of planetary energy, since it is the solar plexus centre of the world, with Jerusalem being the central focal point. Jerusalem is not the holy city but the most unholy of cities for it embodies the consciousness of the old era. The new Jerusalem is not England's green and pleasant lands either; it is the new consciousness of Aquarius that is manifesting here, there and everywhere. The old forms of Pisces are being destroyed and they are putting on one hell (literally) of a fight as they go down.

In 1979 when I was networking Israel I asked my higher self to clarify the future situation of this country and the Jewish people to me. The next morning I received a powerful dream in which I was shown this future in three stages. The first stage was political and social turmoil. The second was the turmoil and chaos associated with a major catastrophe related to war. This catastrophe resulted in the people of this country going through a period of extremely painful introspection and rethinking of their identity and purpose

198 Transpersonal Astrology

in life. The symbol of this country was an old man with a long white beard, a sort of wise old Saturnian figure; the 3rd Ray rules the personality of the Jews. The final stage was the descent from 'heaven' of a beautiful golden circle of light (which I feel symbolized the Christ). This circle descended onto the ground and the old man walked towards it and accepted it. The circle then turned into a beautiful white-petalled lotus flower and ascended up to heaven. Intuitively I felt this meant that the Jews (I was born into the Jewish race but have long since become a citizen of the human race) would finally accept the Christ as the so-called Messiah and this would free them into their greater purpose, beauty and spiritual destiny.

In Aquarius there is a definite relationship to form for the 5th and 7th Rays are related to form. The 7th Ray provides the new personal, group, organizational (networks) and collective forms that the soul requires to manifest on Earth. In Pisces one works in form (the fish swimming downwards into matter) in order to experience, learn and teach the illusion of forms and the reality of the immortal Christ self. The Piscean Age was meant to teach humanity the reality of the soul or higher self and the illusion of forms. The crucifixion and resurrection were the agencies for this lesson. The ashrams and monasteries of the past Age were the training grounds for this great lesson. These lessons were unfortunately not learned in the Piscean Age (except by a few great saints). In the New Age these training grounds are no longer needed, for 'life' itself is the training ground, as are the many New Age Centres, large (like Findhorn) and small.

Of all the signs, Pisceans are the most inclined to live in a dream state, for the energy of this sign has no boundaries as we understand boundaries from the personality perspective. The personality symbol is a square or equal-armed cross, the symbol of the spirit and soul imprisoned in matter. The symbol of the soul is the equal-armed triangle and the symbol of the spirit the circle of infinity. Pisces is the soul/Christ crucified on the Cross and this represents the duality and mutability of this sign. The spirit–soul descended into matter in Aries, the first sign. In Pisces it has reached its last cycle through the zodiac. It either becomes free of matter (the wheel of death and rebirth) or completes the cycle and returns again into Aries for another round. Initiation determines this destination. The fish of the soul has descended into matter from the Father's house (the Monad or Cosmos) and in Pisces must return back to the Father, back to Spirit. But – and this is the great but – in order to do this it must first give all that it has gained through its evolution to others – to the 'saving' of others/humanity and the world. 'Saving' in this sense entails the recognition that one is 'saved' when one realizes who one truly is, namely an immortal soul, one with an immortal kingdom of souls or, in Christian terms, the 'invisible Church of Christ'.

The recognition of this reality has a number of repercussions. The first is that the soul is a being of consciousness and not form and therefore the reality lying behind everything is the invisible, purposeful, loving and wise soul. The second is that souls are consciousnesses of unlimited and unconditional love, wisdom and selfless service. A soul has no self-consciousness because it is not a personality; it has a natural group and collective consciousness and it serves this greater whole with no consideration of self-interest. This provides the clues to why all the three planets of intelligent love, wisdom and devotional idealism rule this sign. Jupiter (Ray 2), Neptune (Ray 6, which in its higher nature is connected to Ray 2) and Venus (Ray 5, which is exalted). Venus is the planet directly connected to the soul in its individual-group (Ray) context, and Venus is exalted (in its 'highest' influence) in Pisces and the 12th house. The keynote of Venus is 'intelligent love', for true love is not a simplistic energy but rather a unification of mind and heart, of intelligence and feeling. The highest degree of this love is capable of being contacted, embodied and shared in Pisces.

Another implication is that if all form is subject to change and psycho-physiological death and rebirth then one should not get attached to forms, including one's own form or the forms of one's family, friends, group, culture, religion, race, nation or even planet. This is the main reason why Pisceans (and everyone in their own right) experience so much pain and death in their lives, why Jesus had to go through such suffering and final crucifixion. Attachment to form in Pisces brings in the energies of Pluto, the destroyer and transformer of forms, and Neptune, the dissolver and transmuter of forms, the two transpersonal rulers of this sign. Astrologers often find it difficult to understand how Pluto can rule Pisces, but if Pluto is related to death and rebirth and Pisces is the last sign of the zodiac this interrelationship is obvious. Pluto continues the work in Pisces that it started in Scorpio, for both signs are related to the descent of the soul into matter and the transmutation of matter into spirit.

Pluto purges and burns away one's attachments to the past in a painful, disruptive manner. This results in a freeing of blocks, restrictions, fears and pain (painful memories from the past, including past lives) in the energy field of one's personality. The soul can then bring about its own healing of its personality (ourself) and regenerate and expand its consciousness through us. Jupiter, the outer ruler of this sign, is the soul in form, and the 2nd Ray of love is capable of manifesting through the personality of Pisces. Neptune dissolves and transmutes (raises up) the past and its memories and pains for the same purpose. Unconditional love and forgiveness (Neptune and Jupiter) become the major healing agencies of the soul in Pisces, and this includes loving and forgiving oneself and one's past.

Pisceans (and people with planets in the 12th) must therefore learn the art of true healing and become the channels of the soul and the Christ in healing others. In forgetting themselves and dedicating their lives to the healing and 'saving' of others they are themselves healed, for selfless healing and service of others and humanity has its own rightful reward. It might even be said that intelligent selfless service (for selflessness does not entail stupidity) is the fastest way to transform and free the self, for the healing of others through intelligent (5th Ray), loving (2nd Ray), devotional (6th Ray) and purposeful (1st Ray) selfless service automatically heals and frees oneself. This is the great gift of Pisces; it is also the great gift of the soul and the Christ and His Masters and of all true initiates and disciples.

The fish going out into matter to 'save' (as indicated above) needs to be balanced with the fish going up to the spirit. Meditation in its various relaxing, quietening, realigning, reunifying and recharging phases is vitally necessary for Pisceans to maintain their balance. The work of the Piscean (and for that matter all servers) is often exhausting and debilitating and one's system needs to recharge itself. Meditation, exercising (walking, running, yoga, tai chi, excursions into nature, massage and so on) and a healthy diet (as in Virgo) are therefore essential.

Pisces and the 12th house are normally called the sign and house of karma. What this means is that whatever karma is left over from the past (be it this life and/or other lives) will be found in Pisces and its house. Planets in the 12th house, especially within 5 degrees of the Ascendant, are connected to the past life and its karma – in relationship to the present life. For example Moon in the 12th indicates that the powerful karmic (attached) relationship with the mother is directly related to the past life, and it requires major transformation. Saturn in the 12th is similar but connected more to the father or the 'authoritarian' parent. Saturn and the Moon in the 12th often indicate that the past life was lived in some form of isolation, and the karmic relationship with the father/mother was formed in this closeted environment. Neptune is a wonderful planet to have in the 12th (as is Jupiter or Venus), for one becomes the natural reservoir of unconditional love and natural spontaneous healing, and has a deeply intuitive and clairvoyant–clairaudient connection with the soul and other spiritual agencies. My partner Imogen has this placement (cusp 11th/12th) and her contacts and guidance from genuine spiritual sources are quite spontaneous and egoless.

Pisces Rising will therefore have two inner rulers (like Scorpio Rising), and this entails a rather complex interpretation. Pluto and Neptune's position have to be considered in interpreting the soul's purpose. Jupiter and the 2nd Ray rule the personality of Pisces, although many astrologers give Neptune rulership. Neptune is a transpersonal collective planet and has inner rulership of Pisces and Cancer, two water signs (with Pluto also ruling two water signs). Water is the symbol of the emotional or astral plane, which is the plane of illusion, glamour, fear and attachments. This is the plane of least resistance for the vast majority of human beings and Neptune has the task of raising one's consciousness from this plane (the 'toy department' of our inner department store) to the plane of the soul. Neptune's essential qualities are unconditional love and forgiveness, intuitive understanding and selfless service. Its 6th Ray is what causes its well-known problems and delusions, for this Ray has its lower anchorage point in the astral planes. Formlessness and attachment to form intertwine with Neptune's influence, and the 6th Ray's abstract idealism tends to create 'ideals and dreams' that are of themselves out of alignment with the practical (Saturn) realities and experiences of life. Neptune inspires one towards the greater spiritual ideal and dream of 'one world, one humanity, one life', but without its integration with 'time and finite space' (Saturn's position focuses this side of life) and the practical and often painful experiences of life on Earth (a non-sacred planet) it creates as many problems as solutions. Many 'New Age' individuals and groupings are still strongly influenced by the 6th Ray and are caught up in impractical ideals and dreams and glamorous spiritual pursuits. Painful disillusionment is the result of self-delusion and one learns to mature and grow up as time goes on. Neptune's energy must therefore be integrated with that of Saturn and the Earth, the two 3rd Ray planets.

Pisces channels two Rays, both feminine in nature. The 6th rules the solar plexus centre and the personality of this sign and the 2nd the heart chakra and the soul of this sign. The dark aspects of the 6th Ray have been shared earlier in this chapter. One can well see why these two Rays have such a powerful influence in this sign (and Virgo). Many of the world's greatest artists, musicians, poets, dancers and composers have been born in Pisces, for this combination of Rays, combined with Venus' exaltation, provides a wonderful world of artistic inspiration.

Death and rebirth will become a conscious process as we move into the New Era (which is *now* for those who wish it to be). Pisceans and/or 12th house types have a major role to play in this science and art, for they are most directly attuned to the psychology and experiences of death and the afterlife ('afterdeath' is a more appropriate term). 'The Egyptian Book of the Dead' and 'The Tibetan Book of the Dead' were the old texts related to this science, but it is very necessary to discover and explore new and appropriate ways to deal with the whole death and rebirth experience. 'Near Death Experience' (NDE) groups have already begun the work of exploring this experience, as have a number of well-known individuals such as Elisabeth Kübler-Ross. Death and birth are becoming what they have always been, namely the sacred ascent of consciousness out of form and of consciousness into form. Piscean individuals and groups are well suited for this important work.

In the monthly cycle of Pisces (20 February to 20 March) there is an integration and completion of the annual cycle which began in the previous year in Aries (Spring), and an inner preparation for the new annual cycle about to begin. The seeds of this new cycle first appear in Pisces, although they do not take clear form until the Sun enters Aries. Death and rebirth are the keynotes of the Piscean monthly cycle, and all that has been attained over the past eleven months must be given out freely and selflessly. Unconditional love and guilt-free forgiveness of self and others are necessary as one closes the door to the past and prepares for the new dawn of spring and the new year. There are always aspects of the past that remain appropriate for the future and these obviously have to be brought forward into the new annual cycle.

THE ANNUAL ASTROLOGICAL CYCLE AND THE TWELVE NEW AGE FESTIVALS

I have already explained how the Sun transits through the signs of the zodiac over the twelve-month period of the year. The sign, its Rays, its planetary rulers and their Rays, plus the Rays of the Sun (Ray 2) and the Earth (Ray 3) stream into humanity during each of these monthly cycles. I have included a diagram of these energies in the back of this book, using Aquarius as an example. Readers can make up their own blank for use with the other eleven signs. The energies of each sign and the Earth are directly aligned once a month and that is at the time of the Full Sun–Moon. This monthly alignment occurs at the exact time of the Full Sun–Moon cycle (when the Sun and Moon are in opposite signs in the same degree), although this alignment begins to form about six hours before the actual time and takes about six hours after the exact time to move out of alignment. This is why the Full Sun–Moon is such a powerful time of each monthly cycle, and why so many groups meditate at these times. (The Full Moon of Aquarius means that the Sun is in Aquarius and not the Moon, and this is why I call it the Full *Sun*-Moon.)

In the New Era groups should try to meet at two periods of the month. The first is at the New Sun–Moon, when the Sun and Moon are in the same sign and degree (a conjunction aspect). This is the seeding or conceptional cycle of each month/sign. This is the best time (in terms of actual energy) to meet for personal sharing and for planning and organizing things on a practical level. It takes two weeks for the seeds of these New Sun–Moon cycles to sprout and grow into flowering and maturity, namely the Full Sun–Moon cycles. The Sun and Moon, one representing higher consciousness and the other lower consciousness, have now reached opposition (the 180 degree aspect). Their power and influence are in extreme opposition, one pulling upwards (the Sun) and the other pulling downwards (the Moon). One stimulates the higher octave chakras, throat, heart and head, and the other the lower octave centres, base, sacral and solar plexus. Light and darkness are thus activated at the time of these cycles, which is the reason why criminal activity increases at the Full Moons (the symbolical werewolves come out of their lairs). Hospitals are well aware of the increase of blood-flow during these cycles too, for the Moon influences the ebb and flow of tides, and our blood is 75 per cent water.

What is less known is that at each Full Sun–Moon the energies of the sign and its planets and Rays are streaming directly into the Earth, for the Earth and its etheric body are directly aligned and open to these energies. This of course means that the etheric bodies of all life-forms on the Earth are also open to these living, intelligent and dynamic streams of energy, for these life-forms are integrally part of the Earth's system. This alignment automatically entails an alignment of the personality (Moon) of all life on the Earth and the soul (Sun) of this personality. At the Full Sun–Moons the Earth is of course in between the Sun and Moon, just as our individual earth-self (human consciousness) is in between our soul and personality.

The personality or lower self of humanity forms the collective lower centres (mind, emotions and body) of the Earth, while the higher self is represented by the 5th kingdom of souls and the Christ and the Spiritual Hierarchy. The Full Sun–Moon cycles are therefore the best and most powerful times to meditate in group and collective formation, for the soul and personality are potentially aligned and the etheric body is 'open' to fully receive the incoming energies of the solar system. Comprehensive information on these meditations and leaflets containing the exact times of the Full Sun–Moon cycles are available from the Lucis Trust (see Bibliography).

Many groups meditate at the Full Sun–Moon but very few understand how to use the energies of these cycles intelligently and constructively. This is one of the most important if not the most important aspect of New Age astrology and psychology. The finest book in this regard is *The Symphony of the Zodiac* by Torkom Saraydarian (Aquarian Educational Group). All of Torkom's books are well worth acquiring. This New Age science requires an understanding of the signs and their ruling planets and Rays in terms of their purpose, qualities and creative activities, plus the practice of New Age meditation. I stress 'New Age' because the dynamic use of the mind is required if these meditations are to be successful. The negation of the mind in meditation technique is an old form of meditation, for we should remember that the 5th Ray of knowledge rules Aquarius. Knowledge, love, intuitive understanding and organizational ceremonial action are the keynotes of Aquarius, and these all require application in the manifestation of this new science.

Slowly but surely this new astrology and psychology must be put into practice on a daily, weekly, monthly, yearly and seven-year basis, as follows:

1. Study all the information related to the signs, the Rays and the planets and learn to apply this knowledge to appropriate monthly cycles and to the New and Full Sun–Moon cycles, the two focal points of each month/sign.
2. Place the basic information (related to the above) in diagrams based on the one provided for Aquarius.
3. Learn to meditate in a new and dynamic fashion. The best books in this regard are those by Sundial House (see Bibliography).
4. Learn to study, meditate and work in regular group formation and of course do the same as individuals.
5. Be aware of the experiences of each monthly cycle and each year and share these experiences with the group (and write them down in a book if you so wish).
6. See each year as a twelvefold cycle and learn to live and work in attunement to this cycle. For example the initiating 'seeds' of each annual cycle will be seeded in the cycle of Aries; 'individualization' of consciousness for individuals, groups and nations will occur during the 5th Leonian cycle of each year; balance and potential equilibrium will occur in the 7th Libran cycle; expan-

sion into a larger vision, understanding and activity will occur during the 9th Sagittarian cycle; the highest personal achievements will occur over the 10th Capricorn cycle and so on.

7. Use the New Moon cycles (the day itself or one day before or after) to meet as a group to share, discuss and organize your individual and group/network life.

8. Use the Full Sun–Moon cycles (the exact time or the evening before the actual time) to meditate as a group and link up with the kingdom of souls and the planetary Network of Light and to transmit light and love into the world. 'When two or three are gathered in My Name there I Am.'

THE DECANATE RULERS

Every sign of the zodiac encompasses a 30-degree arc of the 360-degree zodiacal circle. Each sign has three subdivisions of 10 degrees each. These are called decanates. The overall sign or archetype is ruled by two planets as has already been explained. The three decanates of each sign are also ruled by a planet and these planets compose the sub-rulerships. The sub-rulers have an important sub-influence and therefore provide an extra understanding and interpretation of each sign. What is the essential meaning of a sub-ruler? The answer is that the spirit of the particular planetary system and its ruling Ray become the secondary governing agencies of the sign's energy distribution into the Earth, just as the spirits of the overall ruling planets are the central governing agents for the same distribution. From a transpersonal or spiritual perspective we are always dealing with the invisible 'Life' that governs a planet (or sign, or nation, or human persona) and not the visible physical body.

In the majority of cases these sub-rulers are the personal planetary rulers of the other two signs ruled by the same element – earth, water, fire or air. For example Scorpio is ruled by Mars and this planet also rules its first 10-degree decanate. Jupiter, the ruler of Pisces, the next water sign after Scorpio, rules the second 10-degree decanate and the Moon, ruler of Cancer, the water sign following Pisces, rules the third 10-degree decanate of Scorpio. This is also the case for Taurus, Leo, Virgo, Sagittarius and Pisces (see Table 7.2). It is not the case for the other signs, for the sub-rulers of the other signs do not follow the same rule. These sub-rulers should be used in the case of chart interpretation and in interpreting the sub-influences of each sign in their monthly cycle over the year. For example in the month of Scorpio Mars and Pluto rule the month overall, but Mars also sub-rules the first ten days of Scorpio, Jupiter the next ten days and the Moon the final ten days.

The decanate rulers are shown in Table 7.2.

Table 7.2: Decanate rulers

Sign	1st decan	2nd decan	3rd decan
Aries	Jupiter	Sun	Mars
Taurus	Moon/Venus	Mercury	Saturn
Gemini	Jupiter	Mars	Sun
Cancer	Venus	Mercury	Moon
Leo	Sun	Jupiter	Mars
Virgo	Mercury	Saturn	Venus
Libra	Jupiter	Saturn	Mercury
Scorpio	Mars	Jupiter	Moon
Sagittarius	Jupiter	Mars	Sun
Capricorn	Saturn	Venus	Sun
Aquarius	Saturn	Mercury	Venus
Pisces	Jupiter	Moon	Mars

For the Ray rulerships of the above planets, refer to the section on the signs. The sub-ruling planets are the rulers given by the Master DK in his transmissions through Alice Bailey (*Esoteric Astrology,* Lucis Trust Pub.). In some cases they are not the traditional rulers. As the Master DK is the Master astrologer of our planetary system I prefer to study and explore his teachings. The rule that the sub-rulers should follow the traditional astrological method is by no means valid, for traditional astrology often followed certain belief systems set up in the past without questioning the validity of these beliefs. The new astrologer must think, question and explore for himself, and many changes will need to be made as this new science emerges into the foreground.

CHAPTER EIGHT

Collective Astrology: Planetary Transformation into the Twenty-First Century

Bush's dream of a new world order hangs on the edge of a volcano, with burning lava already rumbling below. Nothing will be as it was: not the Middle East, North Africa, East or West; not Christianity or Islam, the United States or the rest of the world. (*Ma ariv* – Israeli newspaper, February 1991.)

You will hear of destruction, of disaster and of the cleansings that man has invoked, but I tell you that all who are of me have passed the veil and dwell now in another realm entirely. You share this planet with others, others who hold me within them but know me not. What they invoke is not of your concern . . . heed not nor be concerned for the safety of the world, for I tell you it is contained within me . . . An adult does not become distressed when a child cannot do the same as he. He releases the child to its own level of learning. Do you likewise with the world. You cannot heal a corpse, nor have we any wish for you to do so. The old must pass away. It has served its purpose in the cycles of evolution and must now make way for a new, more expanded and fruitful manifestation. (*'Revelations – Birth of a New Age'* David Spangler, Findhorn Pub.)

I am writing this chapter thirteen days into the Gulf War. As I wrote in Chapter 3, the Middle East is the solar plexus energy centre of the world, with Jerusalem as its centre. The astral energy of humanity focuses through the Middle East, which is why it is such an emotionally chaotic and conflict-ridden area of the planet. The Ray which governs the emotional body is the 6th ('devotional idealism'), and this Ray also governs orthodox religion. The soul Ray of the New Era is the 2nd, the higher octave (the heart centre) of the 6th. The 2nd rules inclusive spirituality, which is the underlying reality of all the religions. It is obvious that as the old 6th Ray moves out of manifestation and the 2nd and 7th Rays move into manifestation that the Middle East will have to undergo an extremely painful transformation. The *Ma ariv* quotation at the head of this chapter indicates that the public at large are also becoming aware (be it through their instincts and/or intuition) that the phoenix of the new world order is being born out of the ashes of the old. This death and rebirth process and the subsequent birth of a New Era and new World Order has been forecast by astrologers for many years, but it is only since the East European revolutions and the Gulf War that politicians and the public alike have admitted to this obvious reality.

The Gulf Crisis began during the Cancer 'total eclipse' New Moon (22 July 1990). Iraq invaded Kuwait at this time in early August 1990. Six months later during the Capricorn annular eclipse New Moon cycle (15 January 1990) the UN Security Council deadline ran out and a few days later the war began. Many ancient cultures considered New Moon eclipses as harbingers of evil. There is a reality behind these myths because a New Moon eclipse blocks out the rays of the Sun, and the Sun is representative of light and consciousness, whereas the Moon symbolizes darkness, the past and unconsciousness. The Sun is hot and it gives heat, light and life whereas the Moon is dead, cold and bereft of life. The Middle East is the major focal point of the planet for the dead forces of the past empowered by the Moon.

There is a great deal in Judaism, Islam and even Christianity that is moribund, for these religions are grounded in the past and not in the present and future. They sow separation and not unification, they are exclusive rather than inclusive, they breed hate rather than love, they worship their own gods and not the one God, they wait for their own Messiah and not for the one World Teacher, the Messiah of all humanity. They each claim their 'chosenness', forgetting that humanity itself is God's chosen race (on Earth). They manipulate, fight and kill to preserve all the above, forgetting that by doing so they serve the forces of darkness (separation and fear) and not the forces of light (unification and love). War was thus an inevitable cleansing, and all these 6th Ray religious forces are intertwined in this conflict. This includes the USA with its 6th Ray personality; we should not forget that the USA used chemical weapons in Vietnam and that the agents of this and other so-called civilized countries have subverted legal governments throughout the world.

The superpowers are responsible for the explosion of nuclear and chemical weapons throughout the world and they are now having to pay the price for this 'crime against humanity'. The Gulf War was not simply a war against Iraq but rather a war in which the seeds of past crimes are being reaped in the present.

The chart for the start of this war (plotted for Baghdad, the centre of this war) has Scorpio Rising with Pluto, Lord of the underworld, just above the Ascendant. The war is therefore a major battle-ground of intensive and painful transformation for all the countries involved. It is a karmic or destined battle because Scorpio and Pluto are concerned with the purging of the dark past into the light of the present in order for transformation and healing to ensue. Scorpio is the sign of forced reorientation towards the future.

There is an interesting connection between the Middle East con-flict and the internal conflict in the USSR. In the book *The Destiny of the Nations* (first printing 1949) the Master DK has the following to say about the destiny of Russia/Soviet Union:

> Behind the closed borders of that mysterious and magnificent country a great and spiritual conflict is proceeding, and the rare mystical spirit and the truly religious orientation of the people is the eternal guarantee that a true and living religion and culture will finally emerge. Out of Russia – a symbol of the world Arjuna in a very special sense will emerge that new and magical religion about which I have so often told you. [Arjuna was the disciple of Krishna in the *Bhagavadgita*; in the symbolical battle of Kushetra Arjuna had to go to war and many of his blood relatives were on the other side. Arjuna did not want to fight because of this but Krishna, symbolizing his soul, stated he must fight because it was his dharma. Arjuna's blood relations symbolize his attachment to matter and his dead past and it was necessary for Arjuna to go to war with his past if he wanted to be free.] I am not here referring (in connection with Russia) to the imposition of any political ideology, but to the appearance of a great and spiritual religion which will justify the crucifixion of that great nation and which will demon-strate itself and be focused in a great and spiritual Light which will be held aloft by a vital Russian exponent of true religion – that man for whom many Russians have been looking and who will be the justifica-tion of a most ancient prophecy. (Page 61).

Since the old world religions are focused in the Middle East and Jerusalem and the new world religion will emerge out of Russia (and also out of the USA, Canada, the new Europe, South Africa and Australia/New Zealand) and in the 'new' Jerusalem (= the inner city of consciousness rather than the outer city of form) the conflicts in the Middle East, the USA and Europe and the Soviet Union are all intrinsically connected. This interconnected conflict and its resolu-tion is part of the preparation for the new world order and the dawn of the New Era of Aquarius. The resolution of the internal conflict in the USSR will come about when the USA has withdrawn from its old imperialistic pursuits, retreated into its own backyard and begun the painful transformation of its own internal dark self (drug and alcohol and sexual disease epidemics, huge housing shortages, ·

avarice, commercial exploitation and economic recession, to name but a few of its internal problems). The conflicts in the USSR, USA and the Middle East are all astrologically interconnected; Scorpio governs the Gulf War, Scorpio is the Sun sign of the Soviet Union and the Sun sign of the USA is in the 8th house of Scorpio.

THE URANUS–NEPTUNE CONJUNCTION

> The peoples of the world are entering the wilderness experience, and will find in the wilderness how little is required for full living, true experience and real happiness . . . Freedom from material things carries its own beauty and reward, its own joy and glory. Thus will humanity be liberated to live the life of the mind.
> *Glamour – A World Problem*, Arcane Teachings, pages 75–6, The Master DK and Alice Bailey

As the old world order continues to collapse with Neptune's transit through Capricorn (until 1998) and Pluto's transit through Scorpio (until 1995) the new order will continue to expand and reveal itself. In this regard, 1993 will be a profound year because Uranus and Neptune conjunct three times in Capricorn (2 February, 19 August and 25 October). Uranus and its Ray (7th) rule the New Era and Neptune and its Ray (6th) rule the old outgoing Era. This conjunction will therefore see a fusion (conjunction) between these two energy systems.

By studying past Uranus–Neptune conjunctions we can get a deeper understanding of their implications for human evolution. The last three were in 1479, 1650 and 1821:

1. The 1479 conjunction in Sagittarius resulted in the fifteenth-century Renaissance and the discovery of North America.
2. The 1650 conjunction was also in Sagittarius. In 1648 the British took control of India and the Treaty of Westphalia was signed which guaranteed the principle of national sovereignty for Europe. The Japanese closed their doors to the world. This was also the seventeenth-century period of Enlightenment, which ended the Medieval Period.

    Uranus and Neptune had not yet been discovered at the time of these conjunctions.
3. The 1821 conjunction was in Capricorn (as is the 1993 conjunction). Uranus had been discovered but not Neptune. This was the time of the fall of Napoleon's France. Many Latin American countries became liberated from Spanish and Portuguese rule. Technologically Faraday's electromagnetism began and the Babbage calculating engine, the world's first computer, was also

Radix			MC	22 15 Aqu	Sun	13 42 Aqu	9
			ASC	27 50 Gem	Moon	13 59 Gem	12
URA-NEP CON				Plac	Mercury	20 50 Aqu	9
			11.	22 50 Pis	Venus	0 0 Ari	11
Date:	2 Feb 1993 Tue		12.	9 58 Tau	Mars	9 43 Can R	1
Time:	12 48 0		2.	14 29 Can	Jupiter	14 39 Lib R	5
Zone:	0 0 E		3.	1 23 Leo	Saturn	20 4 Aqu	9
Latitude:	51 31 N				Uranus	19 34 Cap	8
Longitude:	0 6 W		Node	18 42 Sag R 6	Neptune	19 34 Cap	8
			Point	28 7 Lib 5	Pluto	25 22 Sco	6

URA-NEP CON

Gemini Rising Keynote-
I recognize the other self and in the
waning of that self I grow and glow.

Chart Ruler- Venus (Ray 5) in Pisces (11th House).

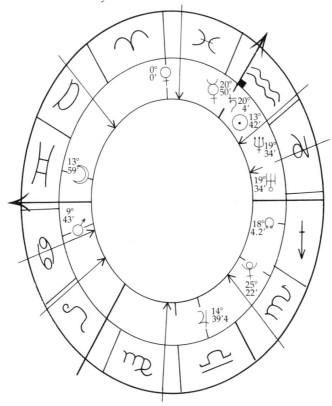

invented (it can be seen at the British Science Museum). Mary Baker Eddy and Walt Whitman were born.

The 1993 conjunction will be in Capricorn (8th house). Ruler: Saturn in the 9th house (in Aquarius) with Mercury conjunct the Aquarian Midheaven. Rising sign: Gemini (decanate of Aquarius). Ruler: Venus (11th house). This conjunction will have a far more powerful influence upon humanity because it is the first conjunction in which both planets have been discovered. The 8th house hides the shadow of humanity and the shadow in Capricorn is political and economic dictatorship, secrecy and manipulation. The financial institutions that hide this economic corruption (banks, stock exchanges, insurance companies, building societies and so on) and their political and social counterparts will be radically disrupted, broken down and revolutionized (Uranus) and dissolved, transmuted and collapsed (Neptune). The effects and results will be (to say the least) of an earthshaking (Uranus) nature and the dark secrets that these institutions (and their heads) have been hiding (8th house) will be purged into the light of human awareness (8th and 9th house Saturn).

With Venus the ruler of the chart on the cusp of Pisces (death) and Aries (rebirth) the purpose of this conjunction is to bring a rapid disintegration and completion (Pisces) to the old order and a rebirth of a new world order based upon sharing, right distribution of resources, justice and right human relationships (Venus). This will have a direct effect upon the whole field of politics, international relations, national and world economics, career and vocational patterns, power and its correct usages and the right use of the mind (11th house). Any remaining dictatorial governments will collapse and be replaced by democratic humanitarian systems of government.

With Gemini Rising in its Aquarian decanate and Uranus the ruler of Aquarius forming one point of the conjunction, plus Saturn the ruler of Capricorn in Aquarius conjunct Mercury and the Midheaven in Aquarius and the Sun itself in Aquarius it is obvious that this conjunction will initiate the 'seeds' of the new 'Aquarian' political and economic order. Gemini Rising is the sign of the Christ communicating to humanity for Gemini rules humanity and its inner ruler Venus is the planet related to the 5th kingdom of souls. Mercury, planet of communications, is exalted in Aquarius and its conjunction to the Midheaven (highest active goals) indicates that the communication of this new and just order will be extremely powerful and effective.

Neptune and Uranus are both transpersonal (spiritually focused) planets. They are connected to the Spiritual Hierarchy of our planet, and to the Master's Jesus (6th Ray), Koot Humi (2nd Ray) and Racoczi (7th Ray) plus to the Christ Himself. This conjunction is thus a focal point for the 'Second Coming' – the re-emergence of Christ-consciousness into human affairs and the direct preparation for the reappearance of the Christ as the world teacher. One or other of the above Masters will begin to play a much more physically 'active' role in human affairs at this time. The Master DK describes the 'Second Coming' in the following way (*The Rays and the Initiations* – Lucis Trust Pub., pages 615–16). It will occur in three stages:

1. The Christ will overshadow all initiates and disciples who are today active in the outer world. He will influence their minds telepathically. This is His 'mental' return.
2. The Christ will pour out His Christ life or consciousness upon the masses everywhere and in every nation. This spiritual inflow will bring about the reorientation of human desire, and will evoke the emotional reaction to His Presence. This involves the release of the energy of goodwill into the hearts of humanity, predisposing them towards right human relations. This is His 'astral' or emotional return.
3. The Christ will appear physically among humanity. Everyone will know where He can be found. The locale of this physical appearance cannot be disclosed for in a sense it depends upon the results of the first two return processes.

This physical return will occur before the end of this century. He also states that 'very definitely the assurance can be given that prior to the return of the Christ adjustments will be made so that at the head of all great organizations will be found either a Master or an initiate who has taken the third initiation' (*Initiation – Human and Solar*; pages 61–2). The three major Masters who will 'prepare the way' for the return of the Christ, the Master of Masters, will be Master Morya (Ray 1; politics), Master Koot Humi (Ray 2; education) and Master Jesus (Ray 6; religion). It is necessary to put astrological prediction into the context of the above return, a fact which most astrologers have completely failed to do. Master Jesus's preparatory work is twofold: He will reappear to the Jewish race in Israel in order that they might take the Piscean initiation and play their rightful part in the New Era, and He will take over the throne of the Pope in Rome in order to raise the religious consciousness of the Church and the masses onto the appropriate higher level of the spiral.

NEPTUNE AND RECESSION

At the time of writing (1991) a major world recession has begun. (Recession and depression are keynotes of Neptune's refining process.) The Gulf War has greatly accelerated this recession. Past economic depressions occurred when Neptune was in earth signs too; Neptune was in Virgo during the 1929 collapse and in Taurus during the nineteenth-century depression.

THE PLUTO TRANSIT

Pluto (Ray 1) is associated with Master Morya and it is obvious that Mikhail Gorbachev is the 'Russian' referred to in Master DK's prediction. After all, he is responsible for setting the course for a new world order, and for communicating the need for new thinking and a new politics. Many people in the esoteric field feel that Master M has overlighted Gorbachev in his work, for no one man has ever changed human history as has Gorbachev. He deserves the full respect and love of humanity.

Pluto's transit through its own sign Scorpio (1984–95) is responsible for 'purging' the hidden and unconscious darkness of humanity. This transit has already produced 'purging' through Chernobyl, massive oil, air, water and land pollution, the Gulf War, AIDS, the sexual abuse of children, drug epidemics and much more. It still has five years to go, and this five-year cycle will be an even more intense transformative experience than before. This is because Pluto has entered its final decanate (20–30 degrees) of Scorpio (1991–5) and this decanate is sub-ruled by the Moon, ruler of Cancer. Cancer rules mass consciousness and the Moon rules the past; Pluto and Mars, the planets of 'going to war with the past', are Scorpio's co-rulers, and they will now enter into a final battle with the Moon (the powers of the past) over this cycle. This battle will directly influence the masses by disrupting their attachments to the old order (personal and collective) and force them to reorientate towards the future. The Gulf War, with its Scorpio Ascendant, is directly related to this Plutonic influence, and we can expect a continuing series of Plutonic eruptions from now on. Pluto is the other transpersonal ruler of Pisces, and its work is to disrupt, purge ('push to the surface') and 'burn away' the old forms (mental, emotional, sexual and physical) that hinder the consciousness of the new world and the new humanity. Gorbachev is a true initiate in this regard for he is consciously and constructively co-operating in this 1st Ray work in a Vulcanian fashion. Whether we realize it or not, so is

MIKHAIL GORBACHEV

MAR 2 1931   10:59:24 PM GMT
Privalnoye
47N29   32E17
MAR 2 1931   22:59:24 GMT

Tropical Placidus True Node

Sagittarius Rising Keynote-
I see a goal, I reach that goal, and
then I see the next goal.

Chart Ruler - the Earth (Ray 3) in Virgo (9th House).

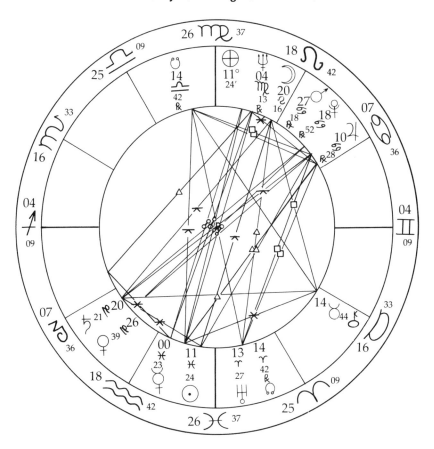

GEORGE BUSH

JUN 12 1924   11:12:52 AM EDT
Milton   MA USA
42N16   71W05
JUN 12 1924   15:12:52 GMT

Tropical Placidus True Node

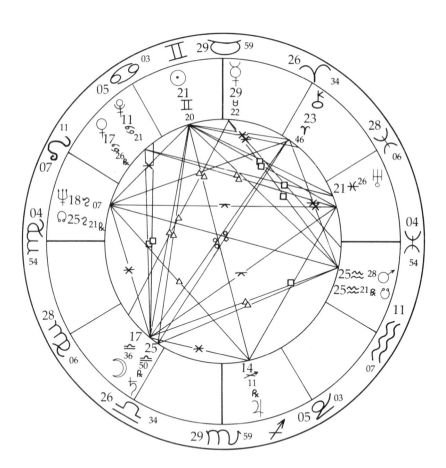

Saddam Hussain, although he is more of an unconscious and dark agent (Pluto) of the 1st Ray of destruction. Someone had to be 'chosen' to act as a catalyst for the purging of the Middle East and Saddam was most fitting.

Pluto's transit through Sagittarius from 1995 onwards will begin the final purging of the old and separative religions and simultaneously regenerate a new collective spiritual awareness. This will be the true collective beginnings of the new world religion, for Sagittarius governs religion, spirituality and the laws that govern the spiritual path. Master Jesus will obviously play a direct role in this religious transformation.

Sagittarius also rules higher education, and New Age or transpersonal astrology, psychology and philosophy will be reintroduced into university curriculae. 'Universe-cities' were originally centres of universal learning, but with the introduction of the age of 'logic' they became 'earthbound cities'. The intuition and the language of symbols will once again play a major role in higher education and in right living, and dream interpretation, meditation and other spiritual realities will become an integral part of life. New types of universities will be opened with 'holistic' curricula and peoples of every nation, culture and race will link resources in developing a completely new education system. A 'planetary' civilization and culture will emerge out of the ashes of the old religious and educational order. The USA and the Findhorn Foundation with Sagittarius Rising will play pioneering roles in this regard. Master Racoczi (7th Ray) and Master KH (Ray 2; education) will play direct inspirational roles in the above. This Pluto transit and the Uranus transit through Aquarius begin in the same year and Sagittarius and Aquarius are in sextile (60 degree aspect) to one another. Both transits are directly interlinked and have to do with the death and rebirth of outdated religion and education and their corresponding philosophies and psychologies. The new religion and education will be a living spirituality with its corresponding 'holistic' psychology that recognizes all things as part of one interconnected whole.

THE URANUS TRANSIT THROUGH AQUARIUS

Uranus will enter Aquarius in April 1995 and remain there for seven years. This will vastly accelerate the vision and unfoldment of Aquarian consciousness and its corresponding structures, because Uranus is the outer ruler of this sign, and the 7th Ray is concerned with vision, ideas and their organization into objective manifestation. Humanity can expect many 'futuristic' scientific discoveries during this seven-year cycle because the 5th and 7th Rays will be operational and scientific discoveries are governed strongly by such a Ray combination. A number of discoveries will be in the field of 'light' and of 'energy' and will open the door into the twenty-first century. Uranus and Neptune will both be in Aquarius from 1998 onwards and this combination will expand the effects of their Capricornian conjunction in 1993. The year 1998 will see the true beginnings of a planetary order based upon 'the brotherhood/ sisterhood of humanity', and can therefore be viewed as direct entrance into the New Era.

Between 1995 and 2002 (the seven-year transit) we can expect the organizational patterns of the New Era to seed themselves into large sectors of humanity. New forms of electronic 'New Age' music will strongly influence humanity's consciousness and new musical instruments will be invented which facilitate this musical revolution. Those people who await the new 'Beatles' (so to speak) can expect this around 1995.

SATURN IN AQUARIUS

Saturn enters Aquarius in February 1991 and remains there until January 1994. This three-year transit will prepare the way for the Uranus transit (above). It will be a time of major opportunity, trial and testing, effort, struggle, experimentation and hard down-to-earth 'group' work. This activity will be focused around Aquarian 'group' consciousness, evolution and organization.

This transit will provide a major opportunity (Saturn offers opportunity) for the Network of Light to become far more inclusive and effective in its planetary work. During the Saturn in Capricorn cycle the Network became far better organized and structured, but personal ambition and power struggles (the shadow of Capricorn) caused a number of problems in its greater work. Ironing out these problems will be necessary as Saturn transits through Aquarius. The years 1991 to 1993 will see hundreds of these new Networks co-operating on a global scale and this will be vastly accelerated and expanded when Uranus moves into Aquarius in 1995.

Individuals will be drawn towards 'groups and networks' of a New Age nature, and people will have to learn 'how' to work in group, network and community formation. This will require a transformation and expansion of consciousness and activity from the 'personal' (not only personal identity in the 'individual' sense of the word but also identifying with one's personal group, organization and nation) to the 'larger' group, network and collective that one is drawn to work in and serve.

The years 1991 and 1992 should be seen as preparation for the Uranus–Neptune conjunctions of 1993. Saturn is the great teacher and trainer; it prepares one for the oncoming initiation (1993). It puts one into situations of training, testing, tension and learning. The three-year Saturn cycle will therefore provide the training ground for group and network activity (in every human field) that is necessary as a practical preparation for the future. For example the East Meets West Network (see end of book) hosted a gathering in the UK in May 1991 which brought together groups and networks from the USSR, East and West Europe and the USA in order to foster the above Saturn in Aquarius vision. Many other similar initiatives are being 'seeded' in 1991 and will consolidate and expand themselves through 1992–3.

Saturn enters Pisces, the last sign of the zodiac, on 21 May 1993, retrogrades back into Aquarius in June and enters Pisces again in January 1994. It remains in this sign until April 1996. This will complete Saturn's twenty-nine-year cycle which began in March 1967. Saturn in Pisces offers the opportunity to give and serve selflessly and to love and forgive unconditionally in order to complete its karmic round through the zodiac. Karma, or actions and reactions, emanating from the past twenty-nine years of its cycle can be accepted, integrated and neutralized through the power of selfless love and service, thus preparing the way for its new cycle beginning in April 1996 when Saturn enters Aries, the first sign of the zodiac. Saturn remains in Aries until March 1999, and this three-year Saturn cycle will plant the seeds for the next twenty-nine years of evolution.

THE SATURN–JUPITER CONJUNCTIONS

Saturn and Jupiter conjunct in Taurus on 28 May, 2000. This conjunction sets the pace for the evolution of consciousness for the next twenty years. Saturn (3rd Ray) and Jupiter (2nd Ray) conjunct every twenty years. Taurus is a fixed earth sign and this conjunction will signal the time for the building of those structures and forms required to 'house' the consciousness of the New Era and the new world order. The initial stages of this reconstruction will occur from 1992 to 1998 (see 'The Planetary Seven-Year Cycles' at the end of this chapter). The years 2000 to 2020 will therefore be a time in which the spirit of Taurus will inspire humanity in the reconstruction of a new economical and financial order. A balance of fusion (conjunction aspect) between expansive Western (Jupiter) and restrictive Eastern (Saturn) economics will occur and a new, balanced and just global economic system will emerge. The consciousness of this order will manifest during the 1990s but the forms, structures and institutions required to house this consciousness will be built during these twenty years.

The Saturn–Jupiter conjunction of 1981 (to 2000) occurred in Libra, the sign of equilibrium and the balancing of karma. The purpose of this twenty-year cycle was to balance the karma of the twentieth century and the past Era. The spirit of Libra is the guarantee that real catastrophe will not hit the planet, for it ensures that 'the scales of justice' are balanced; yin balances yang and vice versa and there is no catastrophic swing to either side of life. Once again we are reminded that the signs of the zodiac and the planets are cosmic lives and not simply abstract energy fields or physical bodies.

THE TRANSFORMATION OF THE USA

The USA is at present undergoing a huge and extremely painful political, economic, social and spiritual transformation. Without going too deeply into the chart for the USA, this transformation can be understood by studying the effects of transiting Neptune as it moves through Capricorn in the chart's 2nd house. Neptune refines, dissolves and transmutes material energy in order that a far more real, humane and spiritual system can unfold itself, and this will be the effect upon the nation and peoples of the USA.

Neptune's transit (2nd house) opposed the USA's Sun sign in Cancer (8th house) throughout 1990. The 2nd and 8th houses are both connected to material values, possessions and attachments, the acquisition and use of finances, financial institutions such as banks, stock exchanges, insurance companies and so on, emotional, sexual and material desires and activities and 'power' and its usages. The Sun in a nation's chart governs its leadership and its policies, and the general 'personality' characteristics of its peoples. The Rising sign indicates the greater spiritual purpose of the nation.

There is an extremely interesting relationship between the Sun and Rising sign in the chart of the USA, as in any chart with Sagittarius Rising. This is because the transpersonal ruler of Sagittarius Rising is the Earth, and the Earth is always placed exactly opposite the Sun – in this case in 13 degrees Capricorn. In other words the purpose of the higher self of this nation is exactly in opposition to the hidden character of its leadership. The Earth is the area in a chart that requires refining and transmuting for it represents the gross side of human nature. Once it is transformed it can focas the soul of the nation. Sex, money, gross materialism, economic and sexual manipulation (and all that this entails) are the deep inbuilt shadow of the USA and Neptune's transit over the Earth in 1990 has brought this dark self to the surface through the agency of the Gulf War, the housing shortage, recession and many other factors. The USA is a great country with a great destiny but it cannot fulfil this destiny (the 'real' American dream) until its lower self has been radically transmuted.

When Neptune opposed the Sun in Cancer in 1990 and conjuncted the Earth in Capricorn this double effect brought to a head (one might say it brought to the 'heart', because Neptune sensitizes the feeling nature) the USA's huge budget and trade deficit, its catastrophic housing problem, the continuing collapse of hundreds of its banks and other financial institutions (a follow-on of the 1987 Wall Street Stock Exchange collapse which occurred when Neptune opposed Jupiter in the USA chart), the massive increase and discovery of the sexual abuse of children, its huge drug addiction crisis, and its continual waste of billions of dollars on military hardware. This objective manifestation of the USA's dark self is a mirror (8th house) of its dark hidden self which continually uses financial and political manipulation (2nd/8th houses) to secure its political ends. When a nation's Sun sign is in the 8th house of Scorpio its dark self is kept secret from its peoples and is projected upon other nations. This is why the USA always finds a scapegoat (Russia and Communism, Nicaragua and Communism, Iraq and so on) behind which to hide its shadow. Neptune's influence illuminates this shadow and through circumstances of an uncontrollable nature (such as the Wall Street collapse, the Irangate scandal and the Gulf War) begins to dissolve and eradicate this secretive evil nature of the nation.

One of the major repercussions of a Neptune transit is that the old ideals and dreams of the nation begin to die for it becomes obvious that they are indeed dead (Neptune rules Pisces, the sign of crucifixion). A deep depression settles over the people and they lose faith in their leaders and their nation's hopes and dreams. The Irangate scandal initiated this process of soul-searching. Neptune's influence has a paradoxical effect because it tends to create an upsurge of self-delusion and escapism (for a period of time), which is an unconscious attempt to cover up or hide from the confusion and pain that its transit brings to the surface of consciousness.

Neptune will oppose the USA Mercury in 1992 and this transit will dissolve the limited, enclosed, exclusive and fear-ridden mental barriers (Mercury rules the mind) of the nation's leaders and people. The thinking, idealizing, emoting, communicating and commercial patterns of the USA will undergo a massive change. The illusion of American superiority will fall away (a superiority complex which hides a deepfelt and hidden inferiority complex) and the nation will retreat into itself, just as the USSR has had to do over the past seven years. It will be a very painful time of self-examination with a great deal of guilt thrown in to boot (8th house), but it will force this great nation into a rapid and transformative recognition of its dark self and it will allow a new and deepfelt sensitivity and spirituality to emerge into the nation's psyche. Communism and capitalism (in their corrupt forms) must fall together in order for a new and more humanitarian political, economic and social system to emerge into the world.

Cancer is well known for its patterns of enclosed isolation and the Sun and Mercury in this sign create these patterns in the American psyche. The American people have never had to face war or terrorism in their own country (outside of the Civil War) and the Cancerian tendency towards self-protected isolation and emotional patriotism must be dissolved. This Cancerian shell will crack when Neptune begins its transit to Mercury in 1992. It was the final transit of Neptune to the Sun in Cancer (December 1990) that resulted in the start of the Gulf War (Neptune by the way rules gases, oil, petrol and all 'liquid' energy), a war whose underlying cause was the control of the oil and petrol reserves of the Gulf. The war will also force the USA and the world to seek more refined and less ecologically damaging forms of energy (Neptune in the 2nd).

One of the major reasons for the USA's shadow is that the ruler of Cancer is the Moon, the planet which symbolizes the bygone past. The Moon is in Aquarius in the USA chart and this creates (at an unconscious level) an emotional attachment to the old and dead 'dream' – the dream of America being 'the land of the 'free' and the nation which has the capacity to teach the rest of the world what is right and wrong. This illusionary dream is long dead but the USA administration and the majority of this country's citizens do not want to recognize this. The Gulf War and all the other factors mentioned above will force the USA to recognize the fallacy of this dream and to begin to live up to its higher dream, a dream associated with its spiritual and humanitarian destiny rather than its political and economic ambitions, which are out of touch with the new world order. Swords will have to be turned into ploughshares.

The new socio-political order and the new world religion are inclusive to one another for both will recognize the reality of 'one humanity, one planet and one destiny', and every human being, nation, race and culture will be seen as an integral and vital part of this new planetary civilization and culture. Religion will not be seen as the following of a particular figurehead, teaching, dogma or ritual but rather as the application of spiritual principles to one's daily living. This application will be personal and collective, for people will recognize that they and their nations are part of one human family and one planetary home. They will recognize that there is only one God, one head of the Spiritual Hierarchy of our planet and one divine plan. This new spirituality will have to enter the political, economic and social infrastructures of the world, and the transits of Uranus and Neptune through Capricorn, the sign governing these infrastructures, is meant to bring about these changes. The Christ and His Masters and initiates, plus the new group of world servers have the central role of reintroducing spiritual government into the new world order, for Uranus and Neptune represent these spiritual forces. The 1993 Uranus–Neptune conjunctions will be a focal point for this massive transformation. The Saturn transit through Capricorn (1988–91), and the Uranus–Saturn conjunction (1988) and Neptune–Saturn conjunction (1989), prepared the way for this planetary turning-point. I include a chart of the 1989 conjunction (see page 224) because it was such an amazing year; not only did it free Eastern Europe from its forty-year yoke but it also resulted in the global ecological revolution. Cancer was Rising and this sign governs the 'heart' of the masses (when it is Rising); the transpersonal ruler Neptune is found in the 6th house of Virgo, the sign/house of purification, health, healing and ordered activity. 'Ecology' is the purification and healing of the planet and the revolutions of East Europe were miraculously peaceful and ordered (outside of Romania; Romania has the Sun in Aries and Leo Rising, and Mars, exoteric ruler of Aries, is the god of war). The year 1988 disrupted and revolutionized (Uranus) the past (Saturn) and 1989 dissolved and collapsed (Neptune) the past (Saturn), thus 'seeding' in the new consciousness and experimental structures of the New World Order.

THE TRANSFORMATION OF THE SOVIET UNION

Pluto is associated with death and rebirth and Pluto has just completed its transit conjunction to the Soviet Union's Sun and Mercury (in Scorpio; see the birth chart of the USSR). Pluto actually transited the Sun sign five times as it retrograded twice over 1989 and 1990. It

SATURN NEPTUNE CONJUNCTION
MAR 3 1989   12:06 PM GMT
London   England
51N31   0W06
MAR 3 1989   12:06:00 GMT

Tropical Placidus True Node

Cancer Rising Keynote-
I build myself a lighted house and therein I dwell.

Chart Ruler- Venus (Ray 5) in Pisces (11th House).

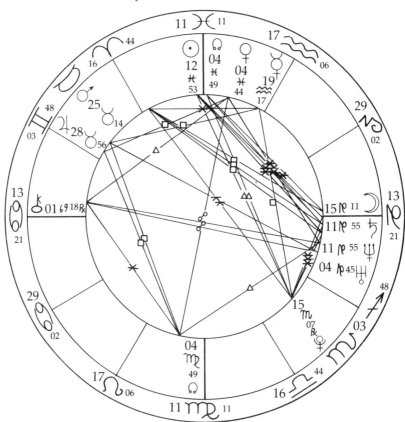

only completed its transit over Mercury at the end of 1990 and it takes a good year for 'things to settle down' after such a powerful and purging transit. Pluto's aim is to bring the darkness of the 'nine-headed hydra' to the surface of consciousness, and the darkness of the leaders and the peoples of the Soviet Union has indeed been purged into the open over 1989/90.

People might associate this darkness solely with the political, economic and military leaders of this great country, with Gorbachev being the obvious focal point of this leadership. This is a simplistic viewpoint; this darkness includes the self-centredness, selfishness and intolerance of the various nationalities of this country (including Christian Armenians, Islamic Azaris, the Russians themselves and the Baltic States), each vying for their own independence and demanding their own exclusive rights without considering the consequences of these decisions on the whole country. The peoples of this country are also having to face their own fears, confusion, anger and projections as they pillory the very man who brought *perestroika* to their country, who pioneered the new East–West agenda, who freed East Europe from the clutches of the old Communist order and who initiated the beginnings of a new USSR and World Order.

The shadow of the peoples of this great and diverse nation is their tendency to only wish to see their own narrow and dark point of view and to project their own self-destructive nature onto other individuals, groups, races and cultures and in the process destroy themselves. This is typical of the lower self of Scorpio, and no sign has a darker self than Scorpio, with its two non-sacred planets Pluto and Mars. The Russian people and the other nations of the USSR tend to have an instinctive and thus unconscious desire to destroy what they create, a typical negative trait of Scorpio. They also have a warrior-like courage and a capacity to accept and handle suffering like no other nation. The paradox of this nation is that there is no other country in the world that has the capacity and guts to handle the highly intensive energy of Scorpio. The purpose of this sign is the transformation of matter, and this requires the destruction of attachment to form.

Communism in one sense is a system of anti-matter (Scorpio) just as capitalism is a system of pro-matter (Taurus). Capitalism is attachment and imprisonment to material desires and forms and Communism is the opposite, for its underlying (and unconscious) purpose is to destroy attachment to material forms. This is the deeper psychological reason lying behind the material inefficiency of the USSR, for if one is at depth 'at war' with the illusion of materialism, one cannot be concerned and efficient at what one does materially. The military machine is the exception because the fear of suffering and defeat by the capitalist enemy is so strong that it enables this inefficiency to be overcome: 20 million dead during the Second World War is a powerful incentive.

This deep-seated Communistic (anti-matter) ethos is buried deep in the Russian psyche for it has a profound spiritual reality to it. The problem is that the above factor is unconscious and therefore manifests itself in a typical Scorpionic self (matter) destructive manner, for the lower self of the individual and the nation is its material self. The unbelievable courage, tenacity, self-sufficiency, passion and endurance of Scorpio is part of this equation, but so is the arrogance, pride, stubbornness and crystallization of the fixed water (emotional) element of Scorpio.

The great and necessary challenge for the USSR is to bring this unconscious side of their nature and purpose to the surface of consciousness and to learn to use matter for the good of the whole (rather than be used by matter as is the case of the USA). In order for this to come about, matter must be used as an instrument by which to manifest spirit or the consciousness of the soul. The 4th Ray rules Scorpio and the keynote of this Ray is 'harmony, beauty and the art of living – through conflict' (see Chapter 5). The Scorpionic chart (October Revolution) of the USSR has Virgo Rising, and this is one major reason why mundane 'order and purity' plays so important a role in its daily make-up. Order (Virgo) and chaos (Scorpio) dance together in the psyche of this nation, and the integration of these two valid principles of life is the key to true understanding, wisdom and freedom. It should be remembered that these two signs are in sextile aspect and the Mother Mary principle (Virgo) and Mary Magdalena principle (Scorpio) are therefore interrelated. Gorbachev is in fact an archetype of the above for he often calls for *perestroika* and order simultaneously. The Right only want order and the Left desire revolution and both are needed. To reject Communism and become possessed by capitalism is not the purpose of the USSR and this problem lies at the root of its present conflict. The USSR has passed through its seventy-year crucifixion (see the quotation from Master DK, page 209) and its resurrection is thus guaranteed.

The old guard in every country is putting up its last fight and this is no less so in the USSR. The old world is finished and a new type of humane socialistic system needs to emerge through the USSR. It is just a matter of time before this begins to materialize. The swing to the left from 1985 onwards was followed by a swing to the right in 1989/90 and this in turn will be followed by a swing to the centre from 1991. The Soviet Union and the East European nations have the destiny of exploring and finding a path in between Communism and capitalism. This is a difficult path to tread but the leaders and peoples of the USSR are qualified as pathfinders in this regard. They need the spiritual, psychological and material support of the world. The 1990s will see the USSR come into the light and demonstrate to the world a new living spirituality.

It might be of interest to note that the Sun and Mercury sign of the USA (Cancer) and the USSR (Scorpio) are in trine (harmony) to one another. These placements are part of the modern-day charts used for these countries. It is also interesting to note that Gorbachev's Sagittarius Rising ('I see a goal, I reach that goal and then I see the next goal') is the same Rising Sign as the USA, and Bush's Virgo Rising is the same Rising Sign as the USSR (October Revolution chart). These two leaders therefore have the capacity to understand the soul of one another's countries and to work and co-operate together.

According to the Master DK the original charts of these two nations both have Aquarius Rising. The USA has Gemini Sun, a 2nd Ray soul, and a 6th Ray personality. The USSR has Leo Sun, a 7th Ray soul, and a 6th Ray personality.

It is obvious why these two nations are so connected – both have Aquarius Rising ('Waters of life am I poured forth for thirsty humanity') and this is their interlinked spiritual purpose. The 2nd and 7th Rays are the ruling Rays of Aquarius and the New Era, and the USA holds the key to the 'consciousness' (love and intuitive wisdom, group-consciousness and service, Christ-consciousness), whereas the USSR has the key to the objective actualization of this consciousness (the socio-political infrastructures). The USSR is in the process of experimenting with this 7th Ray organization, and the decentralized design of the new USSR will gradually emerge as we proceed into the 1990s. A new type of kibbutz-style social community might form part of this system. In many senses the partly centralized, partly decentralized community system developed by the Findhorn Foundation with its 2nd Ray soul and 7th Ray personality holds a microcosmic clue to what will need to unfold in the Soviet Union.

Both nations have 6th Ray (devotional idealism) personalities and this is why 'idealism' in both its higher spiritual and lower emotional form plays such a powerful part in their make-up and expression. Communism and capitalism and the collective and the individual are the opposite and complementary 'ideals' that govern these nations. They have much to learn and to give to one another; the problem is that Gorbachev and many Soviet people understand this but the American leaders and most Americans do not. The USA tends to see the Soviet system as downright wrong and fails to realize that it holds many pro-socialistic clues to the balance that American society requires. One can only hope that as the USA economy collapses it will seek to learn from its sister nation, for simple living will be one of the major factors of the new economic order.

THE NEW LEADERSHIP

The old type of nationalistic, separative, ambitious, deceptive and corrupt leadership is coming to a close. Capricorn governs leadership and the Uranian Neptunian transits guarantee the emergence of new leaders (in every field) and new leadership. Havel, Mandela and de Klerk and Gorbachev are four examples but Masters and 3rd degree initiates (Capricorn rules the 3rd initiation) will assume leadership of all the major organizations of the world, and this includes political and economic organizations. It was Gorbachev who stated that 'new thinking' was required for politicians; it was Gorbachev who turned the old world order into the seeds of the new world order; it was Gorbachev who ordered the troops out of East Europe and who thus seeded the way for a new East European and whole European order; he did the same for the South African continent when he withdrew his support for the Cubans in Angola, thus paving the way for South-West Africa's independence and the new South Africa. Gorbachev opened *perestroika* to the USSR and allowed the dark Plutonic cat out of the bag. He is the first political leader in human history to have undertaken such a visionary task and only an initiate of a high order could have accomplished it. Fortunately, we can expect leaders of his calibre to emerge into the light in the years to come. The 1993 conjunctions will be focal points in this regard.

There are a number of spiritual texts which claim that by the year 2,000 (plus-minus) there will be 144,000 third degree initiates in the world. Each will be the 'head' of a group of 2nd and 1st degree disciples. These groups will obviously be manifesting one of the seven Ray energies and will therefore be focusing through politics (Ray 1), education (Ray 2), economics (Ray 3), the arts (Ray 4), science (Ray 5), religion (Ray 6) and a synthesis of all the above (Ray 7). In other words there will be 144,000 leaders and groups that will help guide humanity into the New Era under the overall guiding leadership of the Christ, the head of the Spiritual Hierarchy, and a number of His Masters (see the final chapter for more on this subject).

THE PLANETARY SEVEN-YEAR CYCLES

The planetary seven-year cycles are extremely important indicators of collective changes. These cycles were first revealed by the Master DK in the Arcane Teachings which he transmitted through Alice Bailey (Lucis Trust Pub.). Each of these seven-year cycles begins on the winter solstice day of 21 December (for example 21 December 1977, 1984 and 1991). The seeding time of the cycle lasts seven days, that is from 21 to 28 December. During these seven days the Spiritual Hierarchy of the Earth transmits certain needed energies into our planetary system which are appropriate for the oncoming seven-year cycle.

A good example of these seven-year cycles is the present one which started on 21 December 1984. The following year, 1985, was therefore the first year of this new global seven-year cycle Gorbachev came to power in April (the Aries cycle) of that year, and immediately initiated a new revolution in his country and in East–West relations. The first USA–USSR Peace Summit took place in Geneva in October (Libra, the sign of co-operative partnership), and the six ongoing summits have since occurred in each succeeding year since then. Since 1985 much has come to pass: the Cold War has come to a timely end; East Europe has become free of its Communist yoke; the USSR has entered into a new phase of its evolution; Nato and the Warsaw Pact have become radically transformed; South Africa has entered a new and positive phase of change, and has pulled out of South-West Africa, allowing it to become independent; Haiti has become a democracy and has a priest for its new leader; South American countries have become largely free from their dictatorships; a new Middle East order is on the way; and a new world order has begun to take shape. There has never been a cycle quite like it. The challenges facing this new order are obviously tremendous but death and rebirth (on such a planetary scale) is a massive transformative experience and birth into a new life is always a traumatic process. Tens of millions of people have undergone a huge shift in *consciousness* and for this reason alone there can be no going back to the past.

What needs to be realized is that the 1984–5 seven-year cycle was also the beginning of a new eighty-four-year cycle (12 times 7 = 84). In other words the beginning of the present seven-year global cycle completed the eighty-four-year cycle of this century (1900 to 1984), and began a new one. Eighty-four is the number of cyclic completion in astrology because 7 and 12 are the two sacred numbers of our universal and planetary system; there are twelve signs of the zodiac, there are twelve planets (including Vulcan) and there are seven major Rays. The present seven-year cycle from 1985 to 1991 is the first 'Arien' (seeding) phase of this new eighty-four-year cycle. This is why the 1985 to end 1991 seven-year cycle has had such a profound transformative effect on planetary evolution.

The final year of this cycle is 1991. The method of interpreting these seven-year cycles is exactly the same as interpreting personal seven-year cycles. In the lifetime of an individual there are twelve seven-year cycles (= 84 years, although a person might live for + − 84 years), and each of these cycles is symbolically ruled by one of the twelve signs of the zodiac: 0–7 – Aries, the first sign, and its rulers; 7–14 – Taurus, the second sign and its rulers; 14–21 – Gemini, the third sign and its rulers; 21–28 by Cancer, the fourth sign; 28–35 by Leo, the fifth sign; 35–42 by Virgo, the sixth sign; 42–49 by Libra, the seventh sign; 49–56 by Scorpio; 56–63 by Sagittarius; 63–70 by Capricorn; 70–77 by Aquarius; and 77–+ − 84 by Pisces, the twelfth and last sign.

This system was first deciphered by Dane Rudhyar, one of the world's foremost astrologers. The book *Cycles of Becoming* by Alexander Ruperti (CRCS Publications) provides a further understanding of how to interpret these cycles. By studying the signs in Chapter 7, and learning how to apply them to each of the seven-year cycles, one can gain a deep understanding of the astrological and psychological purpose, consciousness and activities of each cycle. For example the fifth cycle (Leo) between 28 and 35 years is the cycle of individualization. It is the time to discover one's true inner identity, one's individual dharma or part in the plan and one's unique creative gifts. At 28 one has to 'cut the chains' to the past and leave behind the belief systems of one's blood family, friends and society (the Cancer cycle – 21–28 years) and move ahead into the Leo cycle of individual discovery, identity, creativity and destiny.

Each seven-year cycle can be interpreted in the above fashion and can be applied to individual, group or collective evolution. It provides a great deal of constructive understanding and helps to clarify the underlying purpose, direction, consciousness and creative expression of each cycle. It provides an added dimension to birth chart, transit and progression interpretation.

The seven individual years of each seven-year cycle are deciphered in the same fashion, each year corresponding in meaning to the first seven signs of the zodiac. (See Table 8.1.)

The fourth year of each cycle is the 'crisis' year because it is the 'mediating or bridging' year between the first three years and the last three years. This year is a cycle of 'tension and choice' between the past (three years) – where one has come from – and the future

Table 8.1: Seven-year cycles

Year	Personal cycle	Sign	Planetary cycle
1	28–29 years	Aries	1992–3, seeding
2	29–30 years	Taurus	1993–4, building
3	30–31 years	Gemini	1994–5, clarifying
4	31–32 years	Cancer	1995–6, earthing
5	32–33 years	Leo	1996–7, flowering
6	33–34 years	Virgo	1997–, purifying
7	34–35 years	Libra	1998, completing

(three years) – where one is going to. The sixth-month period between the fourth and fifth years (for example 31½–32) is the most tense period of the cycle. Humanity will experience this collective crisis in 1995, which is the year in which Uranus enters Aquarius. As one enters the fifth year cycle (for example 32 years of age; 1996 in planetary terms) there is a 'breakthrough' into the future and a release from the tension of the past. The fourth year of these cycles is ruled by Cancer, the 'doorway into matter' (physical form), and the fifth year is ruled by Leo, the 'doorway into the light' of individuality.

The seed energy of the seven-year cycle is generated and manifested in the first years (Aries), and the cycle closes down and balances itself in the last years (Libra). The year 1985 was therefore the seeding year of the present seven-year global cycle. The fourth 'crisis' year was 1988. The USSR Congress met in July (Cancer month) of that year to decide upon the future of its country. The Congress was a great success. The fifth 'Leo' year was 1989, a time of great expansion for the Soviet Union and its new co-operative relationship with the USA. It was also the year of the East European revolutions. The fifth (Leo) successful USA–USSR Summit took place in this year too.

In 1990, the sixth 'Virgo' year, there was a sudden swing back to the Right in the USSR which took everyone by surprise. Virgo is the sign which harvests the results of the past five years (Aries to Leo). Its task is to integrate and 'conserve' what has already been accomplished. There is a puritanical note to Virgoan energy for it tends to eliminate that which is unnecessary to the health of its system. It tends to veer towards the feminine (introversion) and the 'conservative' in this regard as a balancing factor (6th year cycle) to the over-expansion masculine (extroversion) cycle of Leo (5th year cycle). This is exactly what occurred in the USSR in 1990, the sixth year of the global seven-year cycle, when Gorbachev swung towards the Right and gave more power to the military and KGB (this sixth year corresponded with Pluto's transit to Mercury in the chart of the USSR). At this stage pornography, crime, black marketing and nationalism were on the upsurge and the forces of 'law and order' (Virgo is concerned with ordered living) attempted to bring order (as they saw it) back to the nation. One of the better-known characteristics of Virgo is the tendency to see only what is wrong with a situation and to get trapped by the small things in life. Nevertheless the small things need to be put right if the larger things are to proceed accordingly. Virgo Rising in the USSR chart creates the above Virgoan situation in the psyche and behaviour of this country.

The final 'Libran' year of the seven-year cycle is 1991. A balancing of all the extremes occurs in these seventh years – a balance between Left and Right, conservative and liberal, masculine and feminine, spirit and matter, soul and personality and past and future. This year will therefore see a swing back to the centre in the Soviet Union (and other nations) and a cyclic completion and resolution of the past seven years.

From the point of view of the annual cycle (see Chapter 7) the new year starts in Aries (21 March to 20 April) and this 'balancing' cycle will emerge from this time onwards in 1991. By the end of 1991 this balancing and harmonizing process will have taken place in the Soviet Union, between the Soviet Union and the USA, in South Africa, in Eastern Europe, in South America and all over the globe. The seven-year cycles, applied on a personal, group, national and/or collective basis, provide some wonderful clues to the yang–yin principle of life and how it works. Where there is yang (masculine) this will be followed by yin (feminine) and vice versa, and always these polarities will be followed by a swing to the centre (the Tao) in order to achieve equilibrium.

From 21 to 28 December 1991 a new seven-year global cycle will begin. The seeds of this cycle will be planted in human consciousness during these seven days. These seeds will be the ideas, visions and inspirations (Aries energy) that will guide human evolution till 1998. In 1992, the first year of this new cycle, the EEC will begin to play a new and expanded role in European affairs. Similar seed energies will unfold themselves in all the nations of the world and through collective humanity itself. Groups, networks, organizations and individuals ('attuned' to global cycles) will also be stimulated and inspired by this new seven-year cycle energy. The cycle will unfold itself over the seven years from 1992 to 1998 (see Table 8.1).

The new seven-year cycle (1992–8) corresponds overall to the second sign Taurus, because the cycle between 1985 and 1991 was the beginning of a new eighty-four-year cycle and was governed by Aries, the first sign. Aries is essentially concerned with abstract spiritual ideas, visions and inspirations (see Aries in Chapter 7) and their basic manifestation into matter. Taurus is more concerned with the actual physical forms that are required to 'consolidate, house and build upon' these ideas. The inspirations and the effects of the new seven-year cycle will therefore be related to all that is concerned with Taurus. All Taurian-ruled values, structures, forms and activities will be affected and this includes:

• material values as a whole;
• money and its correct acquisition, use and distribution;
• financial institutions that house money, such as banks, insurance companies, building societies and stock exchanges;
• property and the property market, including estate agencies;
• agriculture, farming and food (and thus ecology and the environment);
• employment and the work forms required to make money;
• emotional and sexual relationships and therefore sexuality as a whole;
• material desires and therefore the 'desire' nature; and
• the spiritual aspirations of humanity, for this is related to the soul of Taurus.

This seven year Taurian cycle falls within the scope of the Uranus–Neptune conjunction in 18/19 degrees Capricorn, the decanate of Taurus (see end of Chapter 7 for decanates). It only goes to confirm that 1992–8 is the major cycle in which the material/economic values, institutions and activities of humanity are going to be radically transformed.

The 'seed' energies of this Taurian cycle will manifest in 1992, especially from 21 March (Aries) onwards, and these seeds will provide the clue to the unfolding patterns of evolution until 1998, just as the Gorbachev era in 1985 provided the seed for the 1985–91 cycle. The collapse of the old economic order has already begun (1991) with severe recession hitting the USA, UK, Western Europe and Australia. 1992–3 will continue this collapse but the 1993 conjunction will reveal the new values, activities, work patterns and economic system that will revolutionize (Uranus) the new world order.

An entire book could be written on the global seven-year cycles; it plays such a vital role in astrological psychological interpretation. When we combine the normal predictive side of astrology, namely the transits of the planets, with these seven-year cycles we have a system of wisdom which is of immense importance to the individual, the group and humanity itself. There are many other transits during the 1990s which are of great importance, but I am limited by space. The final quotation of this book puts the final years of the twentieth century and the 2,000-year Piscean Era into a real and profound context. It is the Christ's return that humanity, consciously and unconsciously, is preparing for, and all events in the 1990s should be seen within its planetary scope. The quote is once again related to the return of the Christ or Lord Maitreya, and therefore also to the return of spiritual government to our planet. We are but a few years away from this return and it guarantees the inauguration of a new and joyful Era for humanity. There will be much darkness before the light as is always the case in the life of an individual or a collective. Death and rebirth are the twins that dance together to produce true love, wisdom, purpose, knowledge, maturity, revelation, regeneration and resurrection. Speaking of Christ's return, Alice Bailey writes, in *The Reappearance of the Christ* (Lucis Trust Pub.):

> His reappearance and His consequent work cannot be confined to one small locality or domain, unheard of by the great majority, as was the case when He was here before. The radio, the press, and the dissemination of news will make His coming different to that of any previous Messenger; the swift modes of transportation will make Him available to countless millions, and by boat, rail and plane they will reach Him; through television His face can be made familiar to all, and verily 'every eye shall see Him'.

May we all play our small but vital part in the preparation for this return and in the inauguration of the New Era and the New World Order now upon us. May the light, love and will of the Christ and of the soul, the Christ within us all, manifest through us, and may it bring healing to humanity and to the world. Let light and love and purpose and laughter restore the plan on Earth.

Soul-Alignment Meditation

The following meditation is aimed at helping the alignment of the personality and soul. This alignment or 'building of the Rainbow Bridge' helps to establish a 'line of communication' between the higher self and the lower self.

PREPARATION – STAGE 1

- Sit in a comfortable position with the spine straight but relaxed, the chin slightly bowed and the hands relaxed in the lap. Close the eyes. Relax the muscles of the body, especially the shoulders, back and thighs.
- Breath in and out deeply a few times to relax the breath. Let the breath settle into a natural, even rhythm.
- If you feel so drawn, sound the OM three times (mentally or verbally). Feel the vibration of the OM cleansing your physical, emotional and mental body.

ALIGNMENT AND IDENTIFICATION – STAGE 2

- Feel and visualize a bright liquid golden light at the base of the spine; feel and visualize this light ascending up the spinal cord (like a thin beam of light) to the area where the spine and head merge – the medulla at the back of the skull.
- Feel and visualize this beam ascend from the medulla through the skull to the area in between the eyebrows – the brow centre – and from here feel it ascend to the crown of the skull and then six inches above the skull to 'link' with the eighth transpersonal centre (the 'Soul Star'). This can be visualized as a glowing sunball about 6 inches in diameter or a five-pointed star with its apex

pointed upwards. Feel that you are linking up with your higher self from this point.

- Affirm the following: 'I am a point of divine light; I am a point of divine love; I am a point of divine power (or purpose); I am fixed design.' Say these affirmations with awareness, focus and will. You can use this simple but powerful affirmation or use 'The Affirmation of the Disciple' (see end of meditation).

- Visualize the beam extending upwards into the heavens (as far up as you can go – with practice this extension finally reaches into the 'heavens'). Visualize a 'link up' with a great triangle of fiery light; feel your link with the collective soul of humanity and the Christ.

- Bring the beam back to the soul star, back into the head and back to the centre in between the eyebrows. Focus the 'light' at this centre – on the surface of the skin. Do this without tension.

When you wish to link up with family, friends and/or co-workers you can link up from your soul star to their soul star. This can be done when you first link to the soul star or when you return to the soul star after the triangle link.

CONTEMPLATION – STAGE 3

- Contemplate or 'think deeply about' any particular subject, question, query, vision and/or activity that is of importance to you. This can be related to your daily personal life and/or to your larger group/societal life. Over the new and Full Sun–Moon cycles this 'pondering' can be focused around the energies of the Rays and signs entering the planet (during the Aries cycle one can 'think about' Aries and its Rays and planets and how best to attune to and manifest them in one's daily life). This contemplation can last a few minutes to ten to fifteen minutes.

MEDITATION – STAGE 4

- Release all that you have been thinking about and enter a period of 'aware' silence. Feel as if you are 'holding' your consciousness in the light of your higher self. If thoughts enter your mind (they will), watch them enter and feel them disappear. Keep bringing back and maintaining your awareness in the light of the soul. Try to feel as if your consciousness is focused 'on top of your own inner mountain' (the centre in between the eyebrows). This meditation can last from five to forty-five minutes, depending upon the time available.

TRANSMISSION – STAGE 5

- Sound the Great Invocation, the Mantra of the New Era. Say it slowly and with focus.
- Sound the OM three times and visualize and transmit the light of the OM into your local area/city/town, into the network of your country and lastly into the greater network of the world. See these networks lit up and feel them being healed and regenerated.
- Last but not least, feel your home, family (immediate, plus parents and so on), close friends and co-workers being infused with this healing light.

COMPLETION – STAGE 6

- Relax and let the light of the meditation settle into your mind, heart and whole system. Slowly come out of meditation – take at least 30 seconds to do this. Remain relaxed.
- Do not take a bath/shower or eat (a proper meal) for at least 10 minutes after meditation. Bathing before meditation is of course recommended. Do not eat before meditation.
- Learn to use the alignment system at all times of the day and night. One should eventually be able to align to the soul star and back to the head or heart centre at will.

THE AFFIRMATION OF THE DISCIPLE

I am a point of light within a greater Light.
I am a strand of loving energy within the stream of Love divine.
I am a point of sacrificial Fire, focused within the fiery Will of God.
　　　　　　　And thus I stand.

I am a way by which men may achieve.
I am a source of strength, enabling them to stand.
I am a beam of light, shining upon their way.
　　　　　　　And thus I stand.

And standing thus, revolve
And tread this way the ways of men,
And know the ways of God.
　　　　　　　And thus I stand.

The Lucis Trust

THE GREAT INVOCATION

From the point of Light within the Mind of God
    Let light stream forth into the minds of men.
        Let Light descend on Earth.

From the point of Love within the Heart of God
    Let love stream forth into the hearts of men.
        May *Christ return to Earth.

From the centre where the Will of God is known
    Let purpose guide the little wills of men –
        The purpose which the Masters know and serve.

From the centre which we call the race of men
    Let the Plan of Love and Light work out
        And may it seal the door where evil dwells.

Let Light and Love and Power restore the Plan on Earth.

---

* Many religions believe in a World Teacher, knowing him under such names as The Lord Maitreya, the Imam Mahdi and the Messiah, and these terms are used in some of the Hindu, Muslim, Buddhist and Jewish versions of the Great Invocation.

Ray Energy Flow Diagram

THE FULL SUN-MOON IN

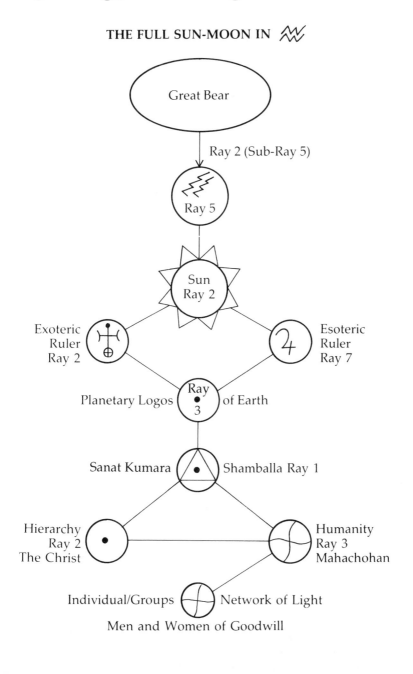

BIBLIOGRAPHY

Alder, Vera Stanley *From the Mundane to the Magnificent*, Rider &
  Shambhala, 1979
—— *The Finding of the Third Eye*, Rider & Shambhala, 1987
Arroyo, Stephen *Astrology, Karma and Transformation* CRCS Pub.,
  1978
Bailey, Alice *Esoteric Astrology*, Lucis Press, 1972
—— *Esoteric Psychology 1*, Lucis Press, 1972
—— *Esoteric Psychology 2*, Lucis Press, 1972
—— *Initiation, Human and Solar*, Lucis Press, 1922
—— *From Bethlehem to Calvary*, Lucis Press, 1937
—— *The Destiny of the Nations*, Lucis Press, 1949
—— *The Reappearance of the Christ*, Lucis Press, 1948
Bailey, Alice and Khul, Djurhal *Ponder on This*, Lucis Press, 1979
Burmester, Helen *The Seven Rays Made Visual*, DeVorss, 1986
Caddy, Eileen *God Spoke to Me*, Element Books, 1981
—— *Flight into Freedom*, Element Books, 1988
—— *Opening Doors Within*, Element Books, 1987
Capra, Fritjof *The Turning Point*, Fontana, 1983
Eastcott, Michal J. *Meditation and the Rhythm of the Year*, Sundial
  House Pub.
—— *The Plan and the Path*, Sundial House Pub., 1976
—— *Entering Aquarius*, Sundial House Pub.
—— *The Spiritual Hierarchy of the World*, Sundial House Pub., 1973
Gorbachev, Mikhail *Perestroika*, Collins, 1987
Greene, Liz *Saturn*, Arkana, 1990
—— *Relating*, Aquarian Press, 1986
Hilarion *Astrology Plus*, Marcus Books, 1980
—— *A New Heaven, a New Earth*, Marcus Books
—— *Nations*, Marcus Books
Joseph, Joan *Jan Smuts, South African Statesman*, Julian Messner, 1969
Jung, Carl *Man and His Symbols*, Pan, 1978
—— *Memories, Dreams and Reflections*, Fontana, 1983
—— *Modern Man in Search of a Soul*, Routledge & Kegan Paul, 1984
—— *Symbols of Transformation*, Penguin Books, 1967

Maclaine, Shirley *Dancing in the Light*, Bantam Books, 1987
—— *Out on a Limb*, Bantam Books, 1987
Mayo, Jeff *Astrology*, Hodder & Stoughton, 1979
McLaughlin, Corrine and Davidson, Gordon *Builders of the Dawn*, Sirius
  Pub., 1986
Oken, Alan *Alan Oken's Complete Astrology*, Bantam, 1988
—— *Soul Centred Astrology*, Bantam, 1990
Rudhyar, Dane *The Lunation Cycle*, CRCS Pub., 1986
—— *New Mansions for New Men*, CRCS Pub., 1978
—— *From Humanistic to Transpersonal Astrology*, CRCS Pub.
—— *Astrology and the Modern Psyche*, CRCS Pub.
Ruperti, Alexander *Cycles of Becoming*, CRCS Pub., 1978
Sabri, Mousa *Sadat: The Truth and the Legend*, Collins
Sadat, Anwar *In Search of Identity*, Collins
Sadat, Jehan *A Woman of Egypt*, Coronet Books, 1989
Sakoian, Francis and Acker, Louis S. *Predictive Astrology*, Harper &
  Row, 1977
—— *The Astrologer's Handbook*, Penguin Books, 1981
Saraydarian, Torkom *The Symphony of the Zodiac*, Aquarian Ed Group,
  1980
—— *The Triangles of Fire*, Aquarian Ed Group, 1977
—— *The Hierarchy and the Plan*, Aquarian Ed Group
Sasportas, Howard *The Twelve Houses*, Aquarian Press, 1985
Schulman, Martin *The Moon's Nodes and Reincarnation*, Aquarian
  Press, 1984
Smith, A.C.H. *The Dark Crystal*, Futura, 1987
Smuts, Jan, *Holism and Evolution*, Greenwood, 1973
Spangler, David *Revelation – The Birth of a New Age*, Findhorn Publica-
  tions, 1978
—— *Towards a Planetary Vision*, Findhorn Publications, 1981
—— *The Laws of Manifestation*
Tansley, David V. *Ray Paths and Chakra Gateways*, C.W. Daniel, 1986
—— *Subtle Body*, Thames & Hudson, 1987
—— *Chakras – Rays and Radionics*, C.W. Daniel, 1982
Van der Post, Laurens *Jung and the Story of our Time*, Penguin Books,
  1978

Index

For further information on talks, workshops and courses on transpersonal astrology and psychology, and the East Meets West Network contact:

> The East Meets West Network
> 2 Eaton Place
> Kemp Town
> Sussex BN2 1EH
> UK